Why Irrational Politics Appeals

Why Irrational Politics Appeals

Understanding the Allure of Trump

Mari Fitzduff, Editor

 PRAEGER™

An Imprint of ABC-CLIO, LLC

Santa Barbara, California • Denver, Colorado

Library of Congress Cataloging-in-Publication Data

Names: Fitzduff, Mari, editor.
Title: Why irrational politics appeals : understanding the allure of Trump /
    Mari Fitzduff, editor.
Description: Santa Barbara, California : ABC-CLIO, LLC, 2017. | Includes
    bibliographical references and index.
Identifiers: LCCN 2016042449| ISBN 9781440855146 (alk. paper) | ISBN
    9781440855153 (EISBN)
Subjects: LCSH: Trump, Donald, 1946—Public opinion. | Presidents--United
    States—Election—2016. | Political culture—United States. | Personality
    and politics—United States. | United States--Politics and
    government—2009-
Classification: LCC E901.1.T78 W54 2017 | DDC 973.932092—dc23
    LC record available at https://lccn.loc.gov/2016042449

ISBN: 978-1-4408-5514-6
EISBN: 978-1-4408-5515-3

21 20 19 18 17   1 2 3 4 5

This book is also available as an eBook.

Praeger
An Imprint of ABC-CLIO, LLC

ABC-CLIO, LLC
130 Cremona Drive, P.O. Box 1911
Santa Barbara, California 93116-1911
www.abc-clio.com

This book is printed on acid-free paper ∞
Manufactured in the United States of America

Contents

CHAPTER ONE

Introduction: All Too Human: The Allure of Donald Trump

Mari Fitzduff

It's a thing to behold, almost as if he'd grabbed the slender wrists of the crowd with those big hands of his, felt for the pulse of their darkest hearts and then whispered the words they so long to hear. (Malone, 2016)

The idea for this book came about when it became apparent in the summer of 2016 that Donald Trump's campaign for the presidency had, against all odds, gained traction. The idea that such an apparently outrageous personality, without any governance experience or visible moral consistency, could become the Republican candidate was hard to believe. There was however reassurance from the polls and the pundits that this was as far as it could go: Trump could never become president. But, since the results poured in on the night of November 8, the commentators who had been so unanimous in their prediction of a Trump defeat began to rethink many of the assumptions that guided their beliefs—not just about presidential elections but also about the very fabric of democratic life in the United States.

The authors of the chapters in this book began that process a little earlier. In this collection we have brought together the finest minds in their respective fields to reflect on people who took the Trump phenomenon seriously from the outset, and who, as his campaign took off, used a variety of disciplines such as social and political psychology, neuroscience, and evolutionary and leadership/followership studies to analyze the processes by which apparent irrationality came to be viewed by a large slice of the American population as the rational choice.

We understand that there are many people who dismiss Trump's followers as irrational and ignorant and who will condemn them for their support of someone whom they see as fickle, ill-informed, vulgar, divisive, and with worrying autocratic tendencies. As noted by Reicher and Haslam (chapter 2), "It is far too easy and too common to dismiss those whose political positions we disagree with as fools or knaves—or, more precisely, as fools led by knaves." However, by just reproaching and condemning such followership, we may miss, or avoid, understanding why their support for Trump makes sense for them, given the contexts in which they live, and our human predispositions that make their desire for a leader such as Trump explicable. If we fail to take the time to hear and understand them, we may fail to note the very serious questions that their support for Trump raises for our society and democracy in the years ahead.

Who Were Trump's Initial Followers?

Is Trump's success a product of his own creation? Or is it a product of the particular social context at this moment of time in U.S. and global history? The Trump phenomenon appears to have risen from an unusual convergence of an economic and social context that is unsettling for many people, political systems that seem to be permanently unproductive, and a desire for a different style of leadership and politics.

By the summer of 2016, a consensus had built among media commentators. Drawing upon polling evidence, they characterized Trump's core supporters as being male, white, and nominally Christian (Thompson, 2016). Trump entered the political leadership arena at a time when many of them were feeling economically and psychologically excluded from the promise of the American dream, that is, the opportunity for prosperity, success, and upward social mobility for their families and children. Their wages were an average of $72,000 per annum, which is just above the median wage of $56,000. For two decades, they have seen their wages stagnate or even decline in real terms (Stone et al., 2015). Relatively speaking, they are increasingly worse off, as most financial gains are now accruing to the top 1 percent of society (Boxer, 2016). They are progressively finding themselves unemployed because manufacturing has been outsourced as part of globalization, and because migrants are more willing to take up the poorly paid jobs that are available (Comen & Stebbins, 2016).

The coal industry, previously a major employer, is particularly in decline because of new energy policies. In June 2016, estimates showed that coal production was down across the country by 29 percent in the first 10 weeks of 2016 compared with the same period in 2015 (Goldenberg, 2016). The decline has not only resulted in growing and sustained poverty, but it has also significantly affected the mortality rate for middle-aged white people in the United States. A 2016 analysis notes that between 1999 and 2014, mortality rates in the United States rose for white Americans aged 22 and 56, while before that death rates had been falling by nearly 2 percent each year since 1968 (Case & Deaton, 2015). This decline has been attributed to "less-educated workers' increasing disengagement from the mainstream economy; declining levels of social connectedness; weakened communal institutions; and the splintering of society along class, geographic, and cultural lines" (Khazan, 2016).

Trump's initial followers were 89 percent white. He appealed most strongly to those whites that hold negative views of African Americans. Thirty-three percent of Trump early voters agree with the statement "blacks are less intelligent than whites," as opposed to 22 percent of other parties, and 40 percent of Trump supporters believe "blacks are more lazy than whites," versus 26 percent of other parties (Reuters/Ipsos, 2016). Many of them also feel that too many current policies favor the rights of black and LGBT citizens more than they support the rights of poor whites, and these showed a disproportionately greater support for Trump during the primary elections (Tesler & Sides, 2016).

They fear immigrants: a 2016 survey of likely Republican voters showed that over 60 percent of respondents who strongly agreed that "immigrants threaten American customs and values" supported Trump in the primaries (Pollard Mendelsohn, 2016) They are also increasingly worried about the advancement of terrorism, such as recent attacks in Boston (2013), San Bernardino (2016), and Orlando (2016), which many of them associate with immigrants already living in their neighborhoods. They feel that American supremacy is diminishing, as is the capacity of their government to protect them from such violence, and they also see European governments as unable to control terrorism because of attacks in Paris, Belgium, Madrid, and Nice.

While 66 percent of people in the United States overall say that life has become worse for people like them as compared to 50 years ago, early Trump voters are the most pessimistic. Seventy-five percent of them say that things are worse for people like themselves (Doherty & Kiley, 2016).

What have also been lost today are many of the social institutions that were the glue that held communities together. Although most of them are nominally evangelical Christians, actual church attendance has fallen significantly (Vance, 2016).

They also feel disrespected. In chapter 7, Henriques addresses what he calls the divide between the cultural traditionalists and the cultural cosmopolitans. Cultural cosmopolitans have the (apparent) capacity to step outside their local knowledge and background to explore and embrace diversity. They also emphasize multiculturalism, globalization, and an intellectual analysis of issues. Cultural traditionalists, in contrast, take pride in their local perspectives and hometown values, American exceptionalism, and Christianity. The U.S. traditionalists of today feel disrespected. According to Henriques, "a central dynamic between the two groups is that traditionalists resent being looked down upon or perceived as ignorant or racist or hyper-religious by the cultural cosmopolitan elites." They also "feel unheard, unfairly treated, left behind, and betrayed by the dysfunctional establishment."

Distrust of the federal government is evident in their choice of voting. Republican primary voters who said that they were angry with the federal government supported Trump 47 percent, compared to 27 percent for Ted Cruz and 8 percent for John Kasich (CNN, 2016). Voters who indicated that they felt betrayed by Republican politicians also overwhelmingly preferred Trump, and in many of the primaries, most Republicans, including those with college degrees, voted for him (Thompson, 2016). Many of his supporters also feel left out of local and national decision-making processes. According to a survey from RAND Corporation (2016), voters who agreed with the statement "people like me don't have any say about what the government does" were 86 percent more likely to prefer Trump. This feeling of powerlessness was a much better predictor of Trump support than age, race, college attainment, income, or attitudes toward Muslims, illegal immigrants, or Hispanic identity.

More men than women have backed Trump. In April 2016, a Gallup poll found that 7 in 10 women had an unfavorable opinion of him (Newport & Saad, 2016). He was also mainly supported by men who would prefer to see women in their traditional gender roles: more than half of Trump's supporters believe that society would benefit if "women adhere to traditional gender roles" (Public Religion Research Institute/Atlantic, 2016). However, such adherence is rapidly declining and is thought to be assisting the erosion of the traditional male self-image as provider and protector of the family. About a third of women now make more money than their husbands, and for many white men, this is a further blow to their increasing sense of what has been called "precarious masculinity" (Bosson & Vandello, 2013). Trump represents what many men want—power, wealth, and attractive women—and many feel they can live vicariously through him. According to Henriques, Trump "embodies a narcissistic fantasy and defense against anxiety that is present in traditional Christian white males (TCWM), especially those who have lower than average socioeconomic status." About half of his supporters support Trump primarily because they intensely dislike Clinton (Reuters, 2016).

Despite his three marriages, and his flip-flopping on such issues as abortion and gay marriage, many evangelical Christians also support Trump. This is only understandable when you hear Jerry Falwell Jr., one of the foremost U.S. evangelicals, say that "all the social issues—traditional family values, abortion—are moot if ISIS blows up some of our cities or if the borders are not fortified" (Trip, 2016).

Trump's initial supporters do not necessarily agree with traditional Republican fiscal or social conservatism, as noted by Prims et al. in chapter 11. Trump has gained support from trade unions that are fighting to claw back lost jobs. In many cases, Trump tends to take a more flexible and pragmatic approach to social issues than mainstream Republicans. What Prims et al.'s data analysis shows is that while both Ted Cruz and Bernie Sanders remained ideologically driven for the duration of their political careers, both Trump and Clinton, not being ideologues, are likely to prove themselves to be more pragmatic than either Sanders or Cruz in their actual policy making.

Strangers to Ourselves

According to many of our authors, it appears that we are often strangers, even to ourselves, in terms of our leadership choices. Contrary to what most of us believe, our capacity for rational judgment is much shallower than we think. As Popper and Reina show in their chapters (4 and 13, respectively), our capacity to make thoughtful leadership choices is often limited by our nature as human beings whose very existence throughout history was often dependent on instincts and emotions to survive. Despite such frequent reminders as loss of temper, road rage, overeating, falling in love, and so on, we often find it hard to accept this. Being instinctual is often our default, particularly when we are together as part of a group—for example, football matches, social and political rallies, riots, wars, etc.

As Plato said, "In our heads we have a rational charioteer who has to rein in an unruly horse that barely yields to horsewhip and goad combined." Mostly, it is the emotional horse that drives us, in this case the amygdala, the part of our brain that deals with our emotions. Its processes are automatic, and we have little choice about the feelings it produces. According to Popper, millennia of evolution have imprinted in us "software" in our brains that dictates many of our feelings. Research using functional MRI (fMRI) shows that feelings usually precede cognitive functions, particularly in times of stress, and they often impact our abilities to carry out complex and rational thinking. The cortex—the part of our brain that contributes to more analytic and logical reasoning—provides such thinking. These differing parts of our brains, the "emotional" and "reasoning" minds, or "fast versus slow thinking," as it has been termed recently (Kahneman, 2012), coexist uneasily, and more so for some of us than others. Genetically, the power of the amygdala can differ from person to person. It can enable some of us to tolerate uncertainty more easily and to be more open or closed toward others, particularly to strangers (Hatemi, 2012).

As Reina notes in chapter 13, such factors influence our choices of leaders, which are often instinctual, dictated not only by our genetics and our brain structures but also by hormones such as adrenaline, norepinephrine, and cortisol, which inform our response to fear messages. Thus, when Trump tells us that we are being threatened from all sides by law and disorder, terror attacks, and influxes of immigrants, many of whom are taking our jobs, he taps into our amygdala fears, which often overwhelm the cortex thinking that is needed to rationally respond to complex and changing situations. As Popper suggests in chapter 4, this supremacy of emotions in choosing our leaders is particularly relevant in situations termed "weak psychological situations," such as crises or situations characterized by uncertainty.

We are also at the mercy of what scientists call "mirror neurons" in our affective brain circuits (Reina). These neurons are linked to our capacity for empathy—the emotion that enables us to better understand other people's intentions and feelings and allows us to see the world from another's point of view. They are part of the neural circuitry that provides our emotional response to the distress or excitement of other people. Unfortunately, when we encounter people from groups we perceive as strangers to us, the brain often appears to switch off the empathetic neuron almost completely and actively resists any emotional connection with the perceived "other" group (Bruneau & Saxe, 2010). Mirror neurons also have the effect of increasing emotional contagion so that, as Reina notes, during election years, and especially in a political landscape where fear is high and emotions are strong, there is quite a bit of emotional contagion occurring between individuals. The effect of such "emotional contagion" was obvious in the growing numbers attending Trump rallies, where the prevailing emotional atmosphere was often one of excitement, bonding, and hero worship.

Truth Is What We Believe

In addition to being vulnerable to our biopsychological tendencies in terms of our emotions, many of us are also woefully ignorant about our systems of politics. A study by the McCormick Tribune Freedom Museum found that although 22 percent of Americans could name all five family members on *The Simpsons* (an American TV show), this compared with just 0.1 percent (1 in 1,000) of people who could name all five First Amendment freedoms—speech, assembly, religion, press, and redress of grievance. In addition, 55 percent of Americans and 75 percent of Republicans and evangelicals believe that Christianity was written into the Constitution and that the Founding Fathers wanted "One Nation under Jesus" (Stone 2007). It helps us to understand many of today's attitudes toward Muslims, and toward President Obama, whom many people still believe is Muslim, when we realize that such confusion prevails about the Constitution. Given that immigrants must pass a naturalization test to become U.S. citizens, which includes an examination of their knowledge about U.S. history, the Constitution, and U.S. laws and political systems, it is likely that most legal immigrants in the United States actually know more about the workings of the United States than many U.S.-born citizens do.

An added problem is that not only are many of our beliefs based on ignorance, but also that what we see as "truth" is often determined by our innate needs for beliefs and values and the cultural context in which we live. Many of our beliefs are what Haidt (2012) terms "groupish" rather than necessarily true. In other words, beliefs often come from our social context and from our capacity to tolerate uncertainty and fear. As Grillo has noted, these will determine what predispositions we have that are related to prejudice and to what Popper and Leary call "implicit beliefs." Once we form our beliefs, we have a tendency to see and find evidence in support of them and ignore evidence that challenges them. What fMRI studies show is that, when faced with logical contradictions to their deeply held beliefs, people may feel negative emotions, but there is no actual increase in their reasoning cortex (Westen et al., 2006). However, it is important to note, as Reicher and Haslam do in chapter 2, that while people may seem obdurate to constantly dismiss official evidence, such as

Obama being an American-born Christian, it may be more helpful to see such a dismissal as a lack of trust in the sources and the filters through which we learn about facts rather than a lack of intelligence. Thus, the "truths" espoused at Trump rallies will matter far more to many Trump supporters than those expounded in newspapers, by other politicians, or by academics.

Our Savannah Leader?

My president needs bravado … somebody who is big and loud, strong and powerful. (BBC, 2016)

When it comes to choosing our leaders, our instincts are often unconscious to us, but unequivocal. As noted by many of our authors, our human instincts particularly come into play in our choice of leaders. In most cases, these instincts operate below the level of our conscious awareness, and as implicit, rather than explicit, assumptions. According to Leary, in chapter 3, people's judgments of leadership are heavily based on nonconscious processing: "In listening to a political candidate, we often quickly conclude that the person is or is not fit for office without a great deal of deliberative thought. If asked, we can justify our conclusion, but our initial reaction was often not based on conscious deliberation of the person's qualifications." When asked to identify the reasons why they prefer one candidate over another, people often offer unclear or apparently illogical answers and are usually unaware of the part their all-too-human instincts play in their choices.

What are these implicit theories, and what instincts are they based on? As noted by Popper and Reina, such choices are often based on assumptions about leadership that belong to our distant history and not necessarily our current needs as a globalizing, interconnected world. They are the instincts that made people choose leaders to help the group survive in the caves or on the savannah and are often based on surface cues that signal strength. As noted by Popper, in chapter 4, it takes people just a 10th of a second when looking at a photograph to draw an inference about the subject's possible leadership capacities and other traits. Mostly, we prefer leaders who are taller and have features such as square jaws and pronounced brows, which are associated with aggression and strength. This is particularly true when we feel threatened. In chapter 9, on terror management theory (TMT), Cohen et al. note that when participants were asked to write about their own deaths, they evinced significantly more favorable impressions of, greater admiration for, increased confidence in, and a higher likelihood of voting for Trump than people who had not written about their mortality. In addition, and as noted by Popper, in times of crisis, people may vote for candidates that they clearly do not even like only because they appear to have an adaptive value to our survival.

Cohen et al., quoting Hoffer, note that such charismatic leaders need not be exceptionally intelligent, noble, or original. Rather, a leader's primary qualifications seem to be "audacity and a joy in defiance; an iron will; a fanatical conviction that he is in possession of the one and only truth; faith in his destiny and luck; a capacity for passionate hatred; the complete disregard of the opinion of others, the singlehanded defiance of the world … [and] some deliberate misrepresentation of facts" (Hoffer, 1951). Note that such a description would seem to correlate with much of what is said by Trump's many detractors today.

We often prefer our leaders to speak with certainty about issues we are concerned about, irrespective of the substance of their arguments. Leaders who express uncertainty and espouse consultation often make us feel uneasy, hence the many objections to President Obama as "weak" because of the time and care he took to consult with others on major decisions (Kessler & Wong-Ming, 2009). According to a 2013 poll, only 36 percent of Republicans and about 50 percent of Democrats indicated that they liked elected officials who "make compromises with people they disagree with" (Pew Research Center, 2013). In addition, people who find it hard to tolerate uncertainty often feel so profoundly uncomfortable with the idea of uncertainty that they prefer a slightly negative yet certain outcome to a potentially more positive yet uncertain one. Nuances worry them and make them anxious.

In addition to certainty, voters also prefer simple messages. They like their leaders to help them understand complex information, and Trump has this particular talent in abundance. Traveling around America's South, Paul Theroux (2016) noted, "Virtually everything Donald Trump says, you can find on a gun show bumper sticker. Anti-Obama stuff, anti-Muslim stuff, anti-Mexican stuff, anti-immigrant stuff." As we know from many nationalist and regional movements, such simple phrases and viewpoints, which often offer little in the way of substance but are evocative in terms of feelings, are often used in abundance and are very successful in building up a following. In chapter 6, Grillo (who sees Trumpism as having many of the characteristics of American nationalism) notes that political scientists are theoretically divided between rationalist and symbolic political approaches to nationalism. For some scholars, "realist" assumptions that imply that individuals rationally pursue innate material interests, such as power, prosperity, and safety, are the most important in explaining nationalism. Others see nationalism as driven by predispositions (e.g., prejudice, ideology, values, biases) that prompt people to respond emotionally to stimuli, and those responses in turn become the basis of their decision making. Grillo's study shows that symbolic political approaches are predominant among Trump supporters. His results suggest that if an individual has the predispositions and negative feelings addressed in the model, that is, resentment and fear of terrorism, he or she is more likely to support Trump.

Grillo also notes how Trump is assisted by "referent power," which is the followers' willingness to devote themselves to a particular leader because of a person's celebrity status. A related concept is the "attribution error" noted by both Popper and Korostelina that suggests that when we see the actions of another person, we believe that it reflects the person's personality rather than the situation the person might be in. Allied to this is a cognitive bias called the "halo-effect" in which an observer's overall impression of the success of a person in one sphere will be taken to mean that he or she will be successful in another. The fact that Trump is a successful businessman makes him a cultural hero in today's world and signals competence to many who believe that what he has done for his business he will do for the United States.

It also seems that our desire for a strong leader who will provide us with security can significantly outrank our desire for democracy. The World Values Survey of 2011 found that 34 percent of Americans approved of "having a strong leader who doesn't have to bother with Congress or elections," and the figure rose to 42 percent among those with no education beyond high school. This takes us dangerously close to a position where one in three voters would prefer a dictator to democracy. This rise in authoritarian tendencies among the populace has become a major concern: 44 percent of white Americans are now presenting as authoritarian, with 19 percent registering "very high" on the authoritarian scale (Taub, 2016).

As MacWilliams notes in chapter 8, individuals with a disposition to authoritarianism often demonstrate a fear of "the other" and a readiness to follow and obey strong leaders. They tend to see the world in black-and-white terms and are by definition attitudinally inflexible and rigid. They demonstrate little concern for U.S. constitutional freedoms and favor limiting many of them, and they rank proportionately high among Trump supporters: "Trump voters are statistically more likely to favor requiring all U.S. citizens to carry a national identification card and show it to police upon request. They favor limiting free speech by prohibiting the media from reporting on secret methods the government is using to fight terrorism." Even more worrying is their significant support for ending the constitutionally guaranteed writ of habeas corpus: "Trump voters, especially those who are the most authoritarian and fearful, are more likely than the supporters of other Republican candidates to favor allowing police and other law enforcement agencies to *arrest and detain indefinitely* anyone in the United States who is *suspected* of belonging to a terrorist organization." Such authoritarian tendencies are not a stable personality trait, but they can easily be activated when people's social or economic context becomes threatening to the individual.

We Prefer People Like Us

At a Trump rally in Greensboro, North Carolina, in July 2016, a Trump supporter looked at a reporter who was there to comment on the rally and said in a hostile tone, "You don't look right" (Sexton, 2016a). Without a word being said between them, the supporter instinctively understood that this person was someone different than his own people and therefore to be viewed suspiciously. People who are "different" pose a real problem to Trump supporters. Despite the economic hardships experienced by many Trump voters, the data presented by Grillo suggests that fear and racial resentment and not economic factors are the primary driving forces of Trump's support. Many of Trump's voters see racial equality as a zero-sum game, in which gains for one group mean losses for the other.

Part of the reason for today's racism in America toward immigrants may be the fact that while immigrants from previous generations were mainly white Europeans, by the 1990s, Europeans had fallen to 16 percent of the total and South American, Asian, African, and Middle Eastern immigrants were taking their place. (Pew, 2015). The United States (like most other countries) has always struggled with diversity and resentment toward out-groups, and the categorization and treatment of African Americans, Latinos, and Native Americans and African and Asian immigrants as societal "others" continues apace today in much of the United States. The histories of our modern wars teach us that even seemingly small differences, such as those between Sunni or Shia, or Catholic or Protestant, or French or English speakers, can provide a framework for tensions and violence, particularly in contexts of uneven power and resources. These differences serve as ever-ready fodder for use by leaders and would-be leaders, who are unfortunately assisted in this by our network of interacting neural circuitry and hormone processes that make such categorization so easy.

As Riggio (chapter 5) notes, gathering out-group bias is perhaps the most common strategy that leaders use to persuade followers to work together. Today's world and its increasingly diverse contexts supplies us with an ever-increasing number of out-groups both within and from outside of our borders, and there is little doubt these can be psychologically unsettling. Such numbers are at an unprecedented high. The number of foreign-born people in the United States as a whole is now 40 million out of a total U.S. population of almost 309 million—an increase of about 9 million since the 2000 census (U.S. Census Bureau, 2010).

This increasing number of perceived out-groups provide a perfect target for politicians wishing to appeal to voters by signaling to their supporters where they can direct their anger. Both Riggio and Cohen et al. note how easily leaders can elicit external enemies to become the object of the in-groups. Trump's suggestions of groups to fend off as enemies, such as Muslims, Mexicans, all illegal immigrants, and the Chinese, have been eagerly taken up by his supporters. While the use of out-groups to increase cohesion is not new to politicians, he uses this tactic in a way that is unprecedented. By June 2016, the *New York Times* had complied a list of 239 targets who had been insulted by Trump (Lee & Quealy, 2016). In chapter 10, Korostelina notes how such insults are useful for Trump and his followers. She suggests that through Trump's insults and his harassment of others, Trump helps his supporters to "achieve high self-esteem and increase their perception of power, to create distance with people they detest, to stress their advantages in comparison with others, to blame others for their own inappropriate actions, and to increase legitimacy of their views and positions." They love the fact that, on their behalf, Trump blames and insults those they feel (or are told) are responsible for their economic and social bad luck.

Many of Trumps voters are harking back to a past in which their people won the wars and their communities were made up of white Europeans. A Public Policy Polling survey in 2016 of 897 likely South Carolina primary voters indicated that 80 percent support banning Muslims from entering the United States, 62 percent want a national database of Muslims living in the United States, and 40 percent would support shutting down all mosques. Of Trump's South Carolina supporters, 31 percent would also like to bar homosexuals from entering the country. In fostering such attitudes, Trump also appeals to an ancient fear of contagion, which analogizes out-groups to parasites, poisons, and other impurities and seeks to ensure the security, purity, and virtues of the in-group—to keep the good stuff in and the bad stuff out. In this regard, it is perhaps no psychological accident that Trump displays a phobia of germs, seems repulsed by bodily fluids, and often uses the word "disgust" in his campaign. He promises to build borders for his followers to save them from the contagion of immigrants who are dirty, criminal, and rapists. Who knows where they might have been? "People want to see borders," Trump has said "They don't necessarily want people pouring into their country that they don't know who they are and where they come from" (Lemire, 2016).

We Like Beer Buddies

It is important to recognize that it is not Trump who has created the views of his voters. Anger at perceived antiwhite bias, free trade agreements that seem to leave behind many white male men, and minority and immigrant bias have long been present in American politics. Trump has not created such biases, but his candidacy for presidency and his biased language have provided the context for such ideas to come to the surface. As George Saunders (2016) has asked, "What fantasy is Trump giving his supporters the liberty to consider? What secret have they been hiding from themselves?" It turns out that what they have been hiding—or at least not previously expressing too openly—are racist views about many of their newly arrived neighbors, and those yet to come. What they love about Trump is that he is not afraid of being politically incorrect or of offending minority and other groups. He enables them to feel comfortable with themselves and their views, which hitherto they have only felt comfortable expressing within their families or to their beer buddies. They don't like to feel they have to walk on eggshells, being careful about what they say lest they be termed racist or prejudiced. They like being associated with someone who says what they actually think about having to share their neighborhoods with people who are of a different color or religion to them and about being forced to accept state and federal laws about not discriminating against groups whom many of them see as alien to a white Christian nation. They like being associated with someone who does not denigrate the love many of them still have for the Confederate flag, their feelings of disgust at the sight of two men openly kissing, and their horror about a president who is black and whom many of them still see as probably a Muslim.

Many of Trump's voters are probably suffering from what is termed psychological "reactance," that is, an aversive affective reaction in response to regulations or impositions that impinge on one's freedom and autonomy (Moss, 2016). Some people will reject a policy or action that is to their advantage when they feel pushed or forced into making the "correct" decision. When people feel they are denied the right to say what they think, feelings of hostility will often simmer until given a chance to express them safely. Trump's campaigns, and his rallies, provide such an arena for people who are relieved to be free from the burden and discomfort of political correctness. Trump permits them to say what many actually feel and not what they are supposed to feel. This newly found comfort with their fellow supporters makes them feel warm and grateful toward Trump: "Trump comes along and punches political correctness in the face. Anyone feeling some degree of anti-PC reactance is going to feel a thrill in their heart, and will want to stand up and applaud. And because feelings drive reasoning, these feelings of gratitude will make it hard for anyone to present arguments to them about the downsides of a Trump presidency" (Haidt, 2016). Trumps supporters feel validated, and it has been noted by Sexton (2016b) that it may be his supporters who are using him, rather than him using them. They like their new identities as Trump supporters, which not only permits them to voice their negative opinions about other groups without fear of being ostracized but also actually encourages it. As noted by Reicher and Haslam in chapter 2, Trump's political success derives much from his skills as an "entrepreneur of identity," giving his followers newfound personas for themselves and fellowship with each other.

However, it is important to note, yet again, that Trump did not create the prejudices evident in his followers. As Grillo notes, a leader's success is dependent upon whether his or her rhetoric aligns with the predispositions of his or her potential followers. An experimental study that presented respondents with a speech from a fabricated congressional candidate proposing anti-Muslim policies similar to Trump's (e.g., religious markers on IDs, a Muslim ban) found that individuals with an existing dislike for Muslims were emotionally moved by the speech, which prompted support for the policies. Conversely, individuals not having anti-Muslim attitudes were turned off by the speech and rejected the policies (Grillo, 2014).

Outside the Norms

Perhaps the most potent attraction that Trump has for his followers is that he is different. He feels no compunction about not abiding by the established rules of normal politics, and this adds significantly to the thrill he generates in the room and in the audience watching on TV when he dares to reject the rules of whatever game he is playing. "For those voters who feel the game is rigged—who feel that the game has turned them into perennial losers—the sight of someone prepared to defy its conventions is exhilarating. It signals the arrival of an outsider, a maverick unbound to the old order and ready to destroy it in favor of something entirely new" (Freedland, 2016). His supporters believe his story that he is an outsider to the political game and that he has no political handlers. For many of his voters—and for many who have never voted before—Donald Trump is a new kind of politician. Against a context of ever-increasing distrust for politicians, for many voters, this is an attractive trait. In 2015, just 19 percent of people said they could trust the government always or most of the time, and elected officials are held in such low regard that 55 percent of the public say "ordinary Americans" would do a better job of solving national problems (Pew, 2015). Trump is generally seen as saying exactly what is on his mind without concern for perceptions or politics. In a poll conducted in December 2015, more than three-quarters of GOP voters believed that Trump "says what he believes" rather than saying "what people want to hear." Despite the fact that he changes his mind on many issues, or consistently distorts facts, his many supporters respond to this by saying that they feel that he is honest. They may find him to be disagreeable, abrasive, or downright unlikeable. "But because of his reputation for 'telling it like it is' and 'being honest to a fault,' they also feel certain that they can believe Trump means it, at least at the time he says it, when he says he's telling the truth" (Tannebaum, 2016).

In contrast to their usual political representatives, they find him unique and refreshing. "He's a breath of fresh air amid the staleness of modern politics. It's as if he's thrown open a window to let a cool breeze rush through the stagnant smoke-filled room of politics as usual. Many people who've felt trapped in the room—frustrated, disenfranchised—are rushing to the open window. The view out the window is immaterial" (The Independent Whig, 2016). His supporters also feel that Trump actually enjoys being with them. He brings great energy to his campaigning, which is infectious for his audience. They find his new kind of politics exciting and entertaining, which is not surprising given that much of what he has learned about how to entertain his audience was learned from the entertainment industry itself.

Bread and Circuses

By May of the election year 2016, it was estimated that Donald Trump had received the equivalent of nearly $3 billion in free advertising in 2015. For her part, Hillary Clinton had earned the equivalent of $1.1 billion in free advertising, based on media coverage and the equivalent advertising rates (MediaQuant, 2016). While this could not have happened in much of Europe, where state media are required to act as a kind of referee for inclusive political discussion, the bottom line for the commercial channels in the United States is their shareholders' profit. This was not always the case. In 1949, the U.S. Federal Communications Commission had rules called the Fairness Doctrine and the Equal Time Doctrine to guarantee the nonpartisan nature of the TV and radio stations. However, after the advent of cable television in the 1970s, this was all changed in the period of the Reagan administration, when it was said that the emergence of hundreds of channels would ensure pluralism. What it did not take into account was the fact that people tend to seek out the channel that fits their predisposed beliefs, and they stay there.

Prior to his political career, Trump had helped NBC's commercial ratings and profits by starring in the reality TV series *The Apprentice*. The show ran for 14 seasons from 2004 to 2015. Much of the popularity of this series lay in the shock value of Trump himself. His aggression, his bullying, his respect only for winners, and his alpha male persona were the very aspects of the show that appealed to many viewers. Thus, the series had created a public persona for him that was to serve him well as he began to campaign for the presidency. What is presented on television very quickly becomes the norm. What would have previously been seen as undesirable behavior on the part of any real-life CEO became riveting. It also accustomed his millions of viewers to see him in a setting that could have been deemed presidential. As Setoodeh (2016) noted, even Trump's boardroom was

> a dramatic setting clearly designed to accentuate his power. The mahogany oak table, the superior lighting, the American flag in the background and the informed advisers (who double as Secret Service agents offering him protection) conjure an image of Trump as pseudo-president. Maybe the reason so many voters are comfortable backing him is because he's appeared in their living rooms for so long, playing a fictional commander.

Trump excels in theater both on television and at his rallies. He knows how to appeal to people's emotions, which is a far more powerful skill than getting people to think. He creates excitement for them, and with them, wherever he goes. People were prepared to wait for many hours to attend his rallies. They were often on tenterhooks, waiting for his next transgression—which rule will he break next? And he takes care to keep their excitement in play. Trump is captivating as a speaker.

There was nothing like the usual litany of careful gratitude towards the local political machinery. Instead, he went straight to the red meat, to vivid, hard-punching words: six million dollars. Veterans. Press. Killing. . . . Any given portion of his speech contained a lively mix of boasts, jokes, grievances, name-calling, threats, exaggerations and non sequiturs—all of it delivered theatrically, without notes and with great comic timing, aided by his guttural accent and his gift for crude but memorable language. (Eggers, 2016)

Politics as entertainment is nothing new. As noted by Lane (2015), the Lincoln-Douglas debates were like a traveling circus: "Thousands of spectators, playing hooky from their monotonous farms flock to each small-town venue from the surrounding countryside. Bands played. Cannons boomed. The candidates literally led parades to the stage. Cheers, applause and heckling repeatedly interrupted the candidate speeches, which were abundantly seasoned with humor and theatrical gesticulating." However, as Chou and Ondaatje note in chapter 12, because of the now ubiquitous nature of the media, political reality has become almost inseparable from political illusion, and Trump has taken this a step further not just by using entertaining politics but by establishing entertainment itself as politics.

Given his success as a TV star, it was not surprising that Trump approached the campaign trail as if it were a stage for his ideas and the language he used that had previously been so successful. As has been noted by Chou and Ondaatje, melodrama is Trump's forte, and he brought all of this to his campaigning. This was most evidenced by his nomination speech in July 2016, when he offered a vision of a black-and-white universe in which there were good and bad people, and the policies he suggested for security and comfort were those that would fit perfectly within a melodramatic paradigm.

Trump's previous campaign manager, Corey Lewandowski, when asked whether Trump should change his campaigning style, famously said, "Let Trump be Trump." However, as Chou and Ondaatje note, presidential elections that rely mainly on being a spectacle and on engaging and humoring audiences and voters have their very serious downsides. In April 2016, a top Trump aide disclosed to a group of leading Republican officials that his candidate was just "projecting an image" during the early phases of the election campaign. He reassured them that the part he portrayed was not Donald Trump's real self and that come the general election, Americans should expect to see a more "presidential" act. It is difficult to imagine any other political candidates who could retain their reputations by blithely noting that what they say or do at different times is just them displaying their acting abilities. And of course, it raised very serious concerns about the persona that such a person will adopt in the confines of the White House, away from the adoring crowds. The next four years will tell. Against all of the polls and the pundits, against the advice of many major businesses, social and media institutions, and many distinguished military and political figures, some of whom were Republicans, on November 8, 2016, Donald Trump was selected by the people of the United States to be their president.

Who Supported Trump in the Presidential Elections?

While it was true that the vote of the white middle class left behind by technology and the outsourcing of manufacturing jobs was important in securing the momentum for Trump's victory, it became apparent following the election that Trump's support had broadened between his nomination and the elections (Edison, 2016). In the end, white voters voted 58 percent for Trump and 37 percent for Clinton. While men voted 53 percent for Trump and only 41 percent for Clinton, survey data collected during the campaign showed an antipathy toward Trump among female voters, but the actual voting patterns revealed a more complex relationship between gender and race than had been expected. Overall, 54 percent of women did vote for Clinton, and 42 percent for Trump. However, a surprising 53 percent of white women voted for him, while women of color, in contrast, voted overwhelmingly for Clinton: 94 percent of black women and 68 percent of Latino women. As expected, Trump got little overall support from black voters, 88 percent of whom supported Clinton, or from Hispanic voters, who also voted for Clinton by 65 percent to 29 percent for Trump.

While 45 percent of college graduates voted for Trump, he did best among white voters without a college degree, 67 percent of whom voted for him as opposed to the 28 percent who voted for Clinton. Clinton however won more significantly among postgraduates, 58 percent of whom voted for her as opposed to the 37 percent who voted for Trump. He also won the vote of Evangelical Christians, 81 percent of whom voted for him as opposed to the 16 percent who voted for Clinton.

Among the slightly odd findings of the postelection poll (Edison, 2016) was the fact that almost a quarter of Trump voters gave him their support despite saying he was not qualified to be president, and one in four Trump voters backed him while saying he did not have the temperament to be president. So what was behind the nomination and subsequent election of a candidate who appeared to break so many of the ethical and cultural norms that had previously been established as the necessary criteria for a candidate aspiring to be president of the United States? And one whose victory appeared to be assured by a large percentage of people who believed he was neither qualified nor had the right temperament to be president?

In the end, it was the support and momentum of his initial followers, along with the desire for a change on the path of many other voters that appeared to matter most to the voters in the final election. After eight years of Democratic rule, four in ten voters said they wanted the next president to bring "needed change" (Edison, 2016). Trump, as the candidate who had continually harked upon the positive changes he would bring about in the United States, won overwhelmingly according to the rules of the electoral system, and to the astonishment of millions of people in the United States and many throughout the world. So what had been missed by the polls and the commentators in their reassurances that Trump could never win?

A Politics of Hope?

In chapter 2, Reicher and Haslam debunk the idea that "Trump crowds are mindless mobs led by primitive urges and stirred up by a narcissistic demagogue," as they say that this perspective can obscure our ability to appreciate what events are telling us about the way Trumps supporters see the world. "In simple terms, a Trump rally is a dramatic enactment of a particular vision of America. Or, rather, it enacts how Trump and his followers would like America to be. In a phrase, it is an identity festival that embodies a politics of hope." Trump gives his supporters this hope by expressing for them a view of their lives that helps them to "make sense of their lived experience, to understand their problems, and to entertain the hope of being able to deal with them. In doing so he tapped into a yearning for change, and for a difference among not only his initial supporters but a significant swath of the American public, which desire in the end became the most powerful factor in his winning the election.

The fact that many of his supporters, particularly those who supported him during the primaries, appear to be largely driven by intuitive factors, as much of this book will suggest, does not in any way mean that many of their social, economic, and cultural fears are baseless. Those who do not understand their apparent irrational appreciation for Trump fail to understand the logic of his supporters' feelings. Such feelings make a great deal of sense in the face of a rapidly changing society in which the ever-widening gap between rich and poor leaves them little hope that their children will fare any better than they have. And for many who voted for him in the final election, normal politics as they know it has failed to deliver: they have noted the almost complete shutdown of its deliverables in terms of their world. Trump, on the other hand, has offered them hope, a new vision, and solutions. Those solutions may not be the ones many of us feel we can condone, understand, or believe to be workable or effective. But they are on the table, and, like it or not, they bring his supporters more hope than that which is being offered by most of the existing political, economic, and social institutions of today. In that sense, Trump's success may actually be our collective failure, and one that we need to acknowledge and urgently address if more Trumps are not to become the norm for leaders in all of our futures.

References

BBC. (2016). US election: 50 Trump supporters explain why. Retrieved from http://www.bbc.co.uk/news/election-us-2016-36253275

Becker, Ernest. (1971). *The birth and death of meaning* (p. 161). New York: The Free Press.

Bosson, J. K., Vandello, J. A., & Caswell, T. (2013). Precarious manhood. In M. K. Ryan & N. R. Branscombe (Eds.), *The Sage handbook of gender and psychology* (pp. 115–130). Thousand Oaks, CA: Sage.

Boxer, Benjy. (2016). Confused why Donald Trump's message is resonating? Relative comparison theory and income inequality explain a lot. Retrieved from https://medium.com/@boxerbk/confused-why-donald-trumps-message -is-resonating-1154c977697b#.41wf143ke

Bruneau, Emile, & Saxe, Rebecca. (2010). Attitudes towards the out group are predicted by activity in the precuneus in Arabs and Israelis. *NeuroImage, 52*. Retrieved from http://saxelab.mit.edu/resources/papers/Attitudes _towards_the_outgroup.pdf

Case, A., & Deaton, A. (2015, December 8). Rising morbidity and mortality in midlife among white non-Hispanic Americans in the 21st century. *Proceedings of the National Academy of Sciences of the United States of America, 112*(49):15078–15083. doi:10.1073/pnas.1518393112. Epub 2015 Nov 2.

CNN. (2016). Exit poll taken during the first 13 primaries through March 15, 2016. Retrieved from http://edition.cnn.com/TRANSCRIPTS/1603/15 /sitroom.02.html

Comen, Evan, & Stebbins, Samuel. (2016). America's 25 dying industries. *24/7 Wall St.* Retrieved from http://247wallst.com/special-report/2015/12/16/25 -dying-industries

Dizikes, Peter. (2016). New study shows rich, poor have huge mortality gap in U.S.: In unprecedented detail, lifespan gap shown to be large and growing rapidly. MIT News. Retrieved from http://news.mit.edu/2016/study -rich-poor-huge-mortality-gap-us-0411

Doherty, Caroll, & Kiley, Jocelyn. (2016). Campaign exposes fissures over issues, values and how life has changed in the U.S. Pew Research Center. Retrieved from http://www.pewresearch.org/fact-tank/2016/06/22/key -facts-partisanship

Edison Polling. (2016, November 10). Behind the numbers: The 2016 national election exit poll. Retrieved from http://www.edisonresearch.com /behind-numbers-2016-national-election-exit-poll

Eggers, D. (2016). "Could he actually win?": Dave Eggers at a Donald Trump rally. Retrieved from https://www.theguardian.com/books/2016/jun/17/could-he -actually-win-dave-eggers-donald-trump-rally-presidential-campaign

Goldenberg, Suzanne. (2016, April 8). The death of US coal: Industry on a steep decline as cheap natural gas rises. *The Guardian.* Retrieved from https:// www.theguardian.com/environment/2016/apr/08/us-coal-industry -decline-natural-gas

Haidt, Jonathan. (2012). *The righteous mind: Why good people are divided by politics and religion.* New York: Pantheon.

Haidt, Jonathan. (2016). When and why nationalism beats globalism scientific interest. *The American Interest, 12*(1). Retrieved from http://www.the -american-interest.com/2016/07/10/when-and-why-nationalism -beats-globalism

Hatemi, Peter. (2012). *The intersection of behavioral genetics and political science.* London: ICON Books.

Hedlin, Simon, & Sunstein, Cass R. (2015). Does active choosing promote green energy use? Experimental evidence. Social Science Research Network. Retrieved from http://papers.ssrn.com/sol3/papers.cfm?abstract_id=2624359

Hoffer, Eric. (2009). *The true believer: Thoughts on the nature of mass movements.* New York: Harper and Row.

Independent Whig. (2016, January 6). Understanding Trump's appeal. *The Independent Whig.* Retrieved from https://theindependentwhig.com/2016/01/06 /understanding-trumps-appeal

Kahn, Chris. (2016, May 9). Exclusive: Top reason Americans will vote for Trump: "To stop Clinton"—poll. Reuters. Retrieved from http://www.reuters .com/article/us-usa-election-anti-vote-idUSKCN0XX06E

Kahneman, Daniel. (2012). *Thinking fast and slow.* London: Penguin.

Kessler, E. H., & Wong-Ming, D. J. (2009). *Cultural mythology and global leadership.* Northampton, MA: Edward Elgar.

Khazan, Olga. (2016, January 29). Why are so many middle-aged white Americans dying? *The Atlantic.* Retrieved from http://www.theatlantic.com /health/archive/2016/01/middle-aged-white-americans-left-behind -and-dying-early/433863

Lane, Charles. (2015, August 5). It's not just Donald Trump—politics has always been about entertainment. *The Washington Post.* Retrieved from https:// www.washingtonpost.com/opinions/politics-as-spectacle/2015/08/05 /97bc3e86-3b88-11e5-b3ac-8a79bc44e5e2_story.html

Lee, Jasmine, & Quealy, Kevin. (2016, January 28). The 239 people, places and things Donald Trump has insulted on Twitter. *The New York Times.*

Retrieved from http://www.nytimes.com/interactive/2016/01/28/upshot
/donald-trump-twitter-insults.html

Lemire, Johnson. (2016, June 24) Trump, in Scotland, links Brexit vote to his
campaign. AP, June 24 2016. Retrieved from http://bigstory.ap.org/article
/69835cb3eaf8484586bfa2247080da74/trump-arrives-scotland
-visit-his-golf-resort

Malone, Claire. (2016, March 23). Why Donald Trump? A quest to figure out
what's happening in America. *FiveThirtyEight*. Retrieved from http://
fivethirtyeight.com/features/why-donald-trump

McCann, S. J. H. (1992). Alternative formulas to predict the greatness of U.S.
presidents: Personological, situational, and zeitgeist factors. *Journal of
Personality and Social Psychology, 62*, 469–479.

MediaQuant. (2016). Retrieved from http://mediaquant.net

Moss, Simon. (2016). Psychological reactance theory. Sicotests. Retrieved from
http://www.sicotests.com/psyarticle.asp?id=65

Newport, Frank, & Saad, Lydia. (2016, April 1). Seven in 10 women have unfavorable opinion of Trump. Gallup Poll. Retrieved from http://www.gallup
.com/poll/190403/seven-women-unfavorable-opinion-trump.aspx

Pew Research Center. (2015, September 28). U.S. foreign-born population
trends. Pew Research Center. Retrieved from http://www.pewhispanic
.org/2015/09/28/chapter-5-u-s-foreign-born-population-trends

Public Policy Polling. (2016). Retrieved from http://www.publicpolicypolling
.com/main/2016/02/trump-clinton-still-have-big-sc-leads.html

Public Religion Research Institute/Atlantic Survey. (2016). Two-thirds of Trump
supporters say nation needs a leader willing to break the rules. Retrieved
from   http://www.prri.org/research/prrithe-atlantic-survey-two-thirds
-trump-supporters-say-nation-needs-leader-willing-break-rules

Putnam, Robert D. (2000). *Bowling Alone*. New York: The Free Press.

Putnam, Robert D. (Ed.). (2002). *The dynamics of social capital*. Oxford: Oxford
University Press.

RAND. (2016). 2016 RAND presidential election panel survey. Retrieved from
https://www.rand.org/labor/alp/2016-election-panel-survey.html

Reuters/Ipsos. (2016, June 28). Racial attitudes of presidential candidates' supporters. Reuters. Retrieved from http://fingfx.thomsonreuters.com/gfx
/rngs/USA-ELECTION-RACE/010020H7174/USA-ELECTION-RACE.jpg

Romano, Andrew. (2011, March 20). "How ignorant are Americans?" *Newsweek*.
Retrieved from http://europe.newsweek.com/how-ignorant-are-americans
-66053

Saunders, George. (2016). "Who are all these Trump supporters?" *The New Yorker*
(July 11 & 18). Retrieved from http://www.newyorker.com/magazine
/2016/07/11/george-saunders-goes-to-trump-rallies

Schroeder, Robert. (2016, May 6). Trump has gotten nearly $3 billion in "free"
advertising. *MarketWatch*. Retrieved from http://www.marketwatch.com
/story/trump-has-gotten-nearly-3-billion-in-free-advertising-2016-05-06

Setoodeh, R. (2016). "The Apprentice": 9 lessons about Donald Trump from binge-watching the first season. Retrieved from http://variety.com/2016/tv/news/donald-trump-republican-president-the-apprentice-fired-nbc-1201819990

Sexton, Jared. (2016a, June 15). A journalist went to a Donald Trump rally yesterday and came back shocked. Political Scrapbook. Retrieved from https://politicalscrapbook.net/2016/06/a-journalist-went-to-a-donald-trump-rally-yesterday-and-came-back-shocked-here-are-his-tweets

Sexton, Jared. (2016b, July 1). Is the Trump campaign just a giant safe space for the right? *The New York Times*. Retrieved from http://www.nytimes.com/2016/07/01/opinion/is-the-trump-campaign-just-a-giant-safe-space-for-the-right.html

Stenner, Karen. (2010). *The authoritarian dynamic: Cambridge studies in public opinion and political psychology.* New York: Cambridge University Press.

Stone, Andrea. (2007, September 11). Most think founders wanted Christian USA. *USA Today*. Retrieved from http://usatoday30.usatoday.com/news/nation/2007-09-11-amendment_N.htm?loc=interstitialskip%22

Stone, Chad, Trisi, Danilo, Sherman, Arloc, & Debot, Brandon. (2015). A guide to statistics on historical trends in income inequality. Center on Budget and Policy Priorities. Retrieved from http://www.cbpp.org/research/poverty-and-inequality/a-guide-to-statistics-on-historical-trends-in-income-inequality

Tannenbaum, Melanie. (2015, August 14). Decoding Trump-mania: The psychological allure of hating political correctness, part 1. *Scientific American*. Retrieved from http://blogs.scientificamerican.com/psysociety/decoding-trump-mania-the-psychological-allure-of-hating-political-correctness-part-1

Taub, Amanda. (2016, March 1). The rise of American authoritarianism. *Vox*. Retrieved from http://www.vox.com/2016/3/1/11127424/trump-authoritarianism#discovery

Tesler, Michael, & Sides, John. (2016, March 3). How political science helps explain the rise of Trump. *The Washington Post*. Retrieved from http://pscourses.ucsd.edu/ps108/May%2026%20Rise%20of%20Donald%20Trump/Tesler%20and%20Sides%202016-%20How%20polisci%20explains%20Trump.pdf

Theroux, Paul. (2016, March 24). Why is Trump so popular? Visiting the South gave one writer some clues." *The Guardian*. Retrieved from https://www.theguardian.com/books/2016/mar/24/donald-trump-popularity-deep-south-paul-theroux-book

Thompson, Derek. (2016, March 1). Who are Donald Trump's supporters, really? *The Atlantic*. Retrieved from http://www.theatlantic.com/politics/archive/2016/03/who-are-donald-trumps-supporters-really/471714

Trip, Gabriel. (2016, February 27). Donald Trump, despite impieties, wins hearts of evangelical voters. *The New York Times*. Retrieved from http://www

.nytimes.com/2016/02/28/us/politics/donald-trump-despite-impieties
-wins-hearts-of-evangelical-voters.html

Trump Has Insulted on Twitter: A Complete List. (2016, July 25). *The New York Times*—The Upshot. Retrieved from http://www.nytimes.com/interactive /2016/01/28/upshot/donald-trump-twitter-insults.html

U.S. Census Bureau. (2010). United States Census. Retrieved from http://www .census.gov/2010census

Vance, J. D. (2016). *Hillbilly elegy: A memoir of a family and culture in crisis.* New York: HarperCollins.

Westen, Drew, Blagov, Pavel S., Harenski, Keith, Kilts, Clint, & Hamann, Stephan. (2006). Neural bases of motivated reasoning: An fMRI study of emotional constraints on partisan political judgment in the 2004 U.S. presidential election. *Journal of Cognitive Neuroscience, 18*(11), 1947–1958.

World Values Survey. (2011). Retrieved from http://www.worldvaluessurvey.org /wvs.jsp

CHAPTER TWO

The Politics of Hope: Donald Trump as an Entrepreneur of Identity

Stephen Reicher and S. Alexander Haslam

Introduction: Making Sense of Those Who Don't Make Sense to Us

At the risk of appearing like cuckoos in the nest, we need to start by raising a concern about the title of this book—*Why Irrational Politics Appeals: Understanding the Allure of Trump*—lest the title be seen to imply that the notion of irrationality is transferred from a political to a psychological level. It is far too easy and far too common to dismiss those whose political positions we disagree with as fools or knaves—or, more precisely, as fools led by knaves. If those on the right of the political spectrum have long had a general mistrust of the masses (which has been translated into a classic psychology according to which the individual descends several rungs on the ladder of civilization by virtue of joining the mass; Le Bon, 1895, 1947), those on the left tend to reserve their contempt for the masses when they fail to act in ways that left-wing politics suggests they should. If the poor and oppressed vote against larger government and higher taxes or for policies that pathologize and target other poor and oppressed groups, they are seen to suffer from false consciousness, to be incapable of identifying their own interests, to substitute emotion for reason, and to be afflicted by bias (see Cramer, 2016).

All these tendencies are abundantly displayed in the reaction to Donald Trump's remarkable rise through the 2016 primary campaign. The inability of even the most successful pundits to grasp the reality of Trump's victory has been paralleled by an unprecedented assault on Trump and his supporters, the core of which questions their grasp on reality. For instance, in a debate in the British Parliament (responding to a petition calling for Trump to be banned from the country), the then Republican candidate was various described as a "buffoon," a "demagogue," and (more colorfully still) a "wazzock."[1] Such assessments are paralleled by both politicians and by the general public in the United States itself. A Suffolk University/*USA Today* poll asked 1,000 people to describe Trump in their own terms. The most popular response was "idiot/jerk/stupid/dumb," followed by "arrogant." and then "buffoon/clown /comical/joke."[2]

Similar epithets are used to characterize those who vote for Trump. A report carried by the Web site PoliticsUSA on October 5, 2016, was headlined "American Idiots: Poll Proves Trump Supporters Are the Stupidest People in the US."[3] The report was based on the finding that 65 percent of Trump supporters believe that Obama is a Muslim, 59 percent think he was not born in the United States, and only 13 percent think he is a Christian. It suggests that they have been duped by the fear, bigotry, and bias of the conservative media. It repeatedly sums up their position as "bigoted stupidity."

The linkage of stupidity with bigotry and racism is important, for racism is generally taken as evidence of judgment without evidence, of sentiment trumping reason, of the triumph of bias. Thus, the label of racism implies lack of reason, even if stupidity is not explicitly mentioned. And the notion that people support Trump because of racism is very widespread. For instance, a piece by Jason McDaniel and Sean McElwee on the Official Blog of the Western Political Science Association argues that Trumps supporters are primarily characterized by racial resentment.[4] An analysis on the *Salon* Web site is more trenchant, as indicated by the headline "Hideous, Disgusting Racists: Let's Call Donald Trump and His Supporters Exactly What They Are."[5]

We are reminded here of Theodore Abel's fascinating text *Why Hitler Came into Power* (Abel, 1938/1986), though we need to preface our observations with a comment. There has been much discussion recently of Godwin's law—the tendency, as discussion continues, to compare one's opponent or their argument to Hitler and Nazism. While invoking some amusement, this tendency is a means of seeking to silence and obliterate the other. It makes consensus impossible and thereby destroys the common ground of reasoned discussion. As such, it should be taken very seriously and indeed reflects the very tendencies we are addressing in this book. As a consequence, let us be absolutely explicit. We are not comparing Trump, his supporters, or their arguments to the Nazis in any way. What we are doing is addressing some problems in the ways that we analyze and explain behaviors of which we disapprove.

In 1934, Abel ran an essay competition based on autobiographies of Nazi Party members. He received around 600 responses, and from these, he was able to glean the reasons why so many Germans supported Hitler. Certainly, there was a fair degree of anti-Semitism involved. There were also some expressions of virulent hatred of Jews. And no one was unaware of the party's anti-Semitism and so had to be prepared, at the very least, not to object to such racism to support the party. In this sense, they were indeed racists. But this is very different from saying that they joined and remained in the party primarily or even partially *because* they were racists. Many other motives were involved, such as a sense of the decline of Germany, a desire to rediscover past greatness, a fear of social disorder, and the desire for a strong leader.

We would argue that the same is true of Trump supporters. Some, undoubtedly, are white supremacists. All are prepared to live with his statements about Muslims, Mexicans, and others. But are racism, bigotry, and bias the most important explanations for why people support Trump? Or, rather, are we seeing a double case of projection? First, there is a danger that our own inability to understand why people act in certain ways is transformed into the assertion that the behavior is based on their own lack of understanding. Take, for instance, attitudes to nuclear power. Lay respondents tend to be more negative and rate it as far riskier than experts. A classic study by Slovic and colleagues (1981) shows that women voters and students rate nuclear power as first out of a list of 30 risks, whereas experts rate it as 20th. One response is to say that this reflects biases in the way that people process information, laying far too much emphasis on "dread-related" risks over which we have no control and which have the potential to be catastrophic.

But the notion of overestimation relies on accepting as "objective" the official figures about the harm done by nuclear radiation. The problem is that people don't always accept official evidence. When, years ago, we did research with environmentalist activists, they would list examples to demonstrate why official figures are not to be trusted: nuclear accidents that were covered up and so on. Their conclusions were not based on an inability to calculate probabilities from the figures but on a rejection of those figures. By the same token, are people stupid to dismiss official evidence that Obama is an American-born Christian? To do so definitely indicates a problem, but is it a problem of intelligence or of trust? Our response parallels that of Katherine Cramer when she deals with the argument that those who vote against (what analysts consider to be) their interests are ignorant: "I would like to suggest the possibility that the issue is not about the facts they know. Instead, the issue has to do with the perspectives through which they encounter facts and conceive of possible solutions" (p. 145). In the Trump case, then, we would do well to ask what, for those who support him, these perspectives are.

The second act of projection has to do with assuming that the things that most concern us about Trump are the same things as most concern those who back his campaign. Because we so abhor racism, we assume that racism lies at the center of their motivations. To risk another extreme comparison, what concerns the West about ISIS is the appalling brutality of its supporters' actions. So we focus on the obscene images of beheadings that they post online and ask why anyone is attracted to such images. Yet, a systematic analysis of ISIS propaganda shows that only about 5 percent of images show such brutal scenes. These may dominate the Western media, but most of the images in ISIS propaganda show scenes of group cohesion, of group triumph, and of members fixing sewage systems and providing health care and education. They are portrayals of an ideal caliphate (see Lewis, 2015; see also Reicher & Haslam, 2016). So if we want to understand the ISIS phenomenon, we need to start from the experience of insiders, not that of outsiders. In the case of ISIS, we need to ask why they might be attracted to an idealized caliphate more than why they are attracted to the pornography of violence. In the case of Donald Trump, we likewise need to analyze the way he appeals to people and why this elicits their support.

In this chapter, we plan precisely such an analysis. That is, we aim to try and get inside the Trump campaign and take seriously what we find there. We need to respect those we study if we want to understand their worldview, their preferences, and their decisions. The more distant these are from our own, the harder this becomes, but also the more important it becomes. Yet, rather than dismiss them as senseless, we want to see how they make sense of things. That way, we may better understand how to challenge and even change their perspectives.

In the next section, we go inside a Trump event to look in detail at what actually goes on. That is, we address *how* Trump appeals to his audience. For this, we are indebted to a particularly insightful analysis by the journalist Gwynn Guilford, who, acting as an ethnographer, participated in Trump rallies across the state of Ohio in March 2016. Following that, we analyze *why* Trump appeals to his audience. To answer this question, we draw upon what we have referred to as the *new psychology of leadership* (Haslam, Reicher, & Platow, 2011). This conceptualizes effective leadership as being rooted in a relationship between leaders and followers in a social group. It therefore leads us to ask (a) how people conceptualize their group memberships (that is, how do they segment the world into "we" and "they"?); (b) how the leader is positioned in relation to these groups (are they "one of us" or "one of them"?); and (c) how the leader's proposals are related to group interests (do they advance or retard what we want?). It is Trump's skill in these matters, we suggest—his ability to shape and respond to the collective perspective of his audience, and hence to make good sense to them—that is the secret of his success.

Inside the Trump Machine

A Trump rally is about more than a Trump speech. Important though his words may be (and we shall be looking at them in some detail), it is even more important to look at the event as a whole as the performance of a particular worldview. Once again, the charge of irrationalism can serve to obscure this. The powerful idea that Trump crowds are mindless mobs led by primitive urges and stirred up by a narcissistic demagogue can obscure our ability to appreciate what events are telling us about the way those who are present see the world. In simple terms, a Trump rally is a dramatic enactment of a particular vision of America. Or, rather, it enacts how Trump and his followers would like America to be. In a phrase, it is an *identity festival* that embodies a *politics of hope*.

The rally starts long before Trump arrives. Indeed, the long wait for the leader is part and parcel of the performance. It affects the self-perception of audience members ("if I am prepared to wait this long, this event and this leader must be important to me"). It affects the ways audience members see each-other ("if others are prepared to wait this long, this event and the leader must be important to them"). It thereby sets up a norm of devotion in the crowd and a sense of shared identity among crowd members ("we are joined together in our devotion to this cause").

The wait also provides time for other ritualized acts that help shape the worldview of the audience. Guilford describes the security process in the events. Trump's procedures are more rigorous than those of any other candidate. At every venue, the audience members pass through a metal detector gate. Inside, highly visible security agents abound. They fan out, their backs to the stage, and make eye contact with audience members to check for intruders. Audience members join in the exercise. One doesn't have to express overt opposition to be suspect; so woe betide anyone who doesn't show sufficient enthusiasm.

About an hour before Trump speaks, crowd members are instructed over the PA system not to touch any protestors they spot. Rather, they should alert security by chanting "Trump! Trump! Trump!" This happens repeatedly, often a false alarm. But when it does happen, the entire audience is alerted to possible enemies in their midst. In these various ways, crowd members are induced to act *as if* they were under threat, and observing both themselves and others acting in this way serves to validate the presumption that they are under threat both from enemies without and enemies within.

In this way, as identity festivals, the success of Trump rallies owes much to an audience who perform their devotion to Trump and to an audience and security apparatus who perform as a community under threat. Yet, there is one more set of actors who—perhaps unwittingly, certainly unwillingly—play a key part in the drama. These are the media who are generally kept together behind Trump. They are positioned as a visible presence to be derided when maligned by Trump as the voice of a hostile establishment. Guilford describes one such incident: "Trump scowls at the media cattle pen in the back of the room and calls the press the 'most disgusting' and 'most dishonest' people he's ever seen, pantomiming his disdain with an elaborate sneer before goading his supporters to turn and glare too. On cue, the crowd turns and boos." In this moment, the tables are turned. The media and establishment are no longer big and powerful. They are small and cowed by Trump's legions.

All in all, even before we consider the content of Trump's speeches, his rallies bring to life a powerful representation of social relations. But the speech itself confirms and fleshes out this representation. Trump's rhetoric is largely consistent from rally to rally and can be seen as a particular example of a general form called the American Jeremiad (Bercovitch, 1980). This is the notion that America has an exceptional mission in the world, but it is falling short and therefore needs to change to fulfill its original vision. What marks out Trump's version from the original Puritan version is, first, that the failings are a matter of power and wealth rather than of moral purpose and, second, that they are due to the depredations of others rather than our own weaknesses.

More specifically, Trump's argument has three elements. The first asserts that America, once great, is now weak and repeatedly humiliated by others. So, in his presidential announcement speech, given at Trump Tower in New York City, Trump asserted,

> Our country is in serious trouble. We don't have victories any more. We used to have victories, but we don't have them. When was the last time anyone saw us beating, let's say China in a trade deal? They kill us.

Or again:

> When did we beat Japan at anything? They send their cars over by the millions, and what do we do? When was the last time you saw a Chevrolet in Tokyo? It doesn't exist, folks. They beat us all the time.

Or yet again:

> When do we beat Mexico at the border? They're laughing at us, at our stupidity. And now they are beating us economically. They are not our friend, believe me. But they're killing us economically.

It is worth noting too that, as examples of American decline, Trump focuses on trade. Here America's decline is primarily measured in the loss of jobs—something that he made particularly explicit in a speech at a metal-recycling plant in Monessen, Pennsylvania:

> We tax and regulate and restrict our companies to death and then we allow foreign companies that cheat to export their goods to us tax-free. How stupid is this? How could it happen? How stupid is this? As a result, we have become more dependent on foreign countries than ever before. Ladies and gentlemen, it is time to declare our economic independence once again.

The second element in Trump's argument is already implied in this last quotation. The reason for America's decline has to do with the actions of its enemies. These enemies are in part external: China and Mexico and other countries who cheat and who are corrupt and who take the jobs and wealth of ordinary Americans. To cite again from Trump's presidential announcement speech, "Our real unemployment is from 18 to 20 percent. Don't believe the 5.6. Don't believe it. That's right. A lot of people up there can't get jobs, because there are no jobs, because China has our jobs and Mexico has our jobs. They all have jobs."

But these external enemies only thrive because of the actions of many enemies within. Sometimes, these are enemies due to their incompetence, their inability to do deals that favor America. Sometimes Trump targets

particular individuals (Obama, Clinton, his Republican rivals), and sometimes he targets the political class as a whole. Hence, this passage from
his presidential announcement speech:

> I've watched politicians. I've dealt with them all my life. If you can't make
> a good deal with a politician, then there's something wrong with you. You
> are certainly not very good. And that's what we have representing us. They
> will never make America great again. They don't even have a chance.
> They're controlled fully—they're controlled fully by the lobbyists, by the
> donors, and by the special interests, fully.

This extract points to another reason why other politicians act as enemies: they are controlled by others who are enemies to the American people. This is made even more explicit in Trump's Monessen speech when
he pillories his chief Democratic rival:

> The people who rigged the system are supporting Hilary Clinton because
> they know as long as she is in charge nothing is going to change. The inner
> cities will remain poor. The factories will remain closed. The borders will
> remain open. The special interests will remain firmly in control. Hilary
> Clinton and her friends in global finance want to scare America into think-
> ing small.

In short, America is losing out because the enemy within colludes with
the enemy beyond.

But as well as identifying a problem and a cause to that problem, in the
third part of his argument, Trump also identifies a solution—himself.
Throughout his speeches, Trump insists on the fact that he isn't like other
politicians. He knows how to make a deal (as exemplified by his book *The
Art of the Deal*). He insists that he has been so successful and become so
rich that he cannot be bought. For instance, in one of many anecdotes,
Trump recalls, "One of the big banks came to me and said, 'Donald, you
don't have enough borrowings. Could we loan you $4 billion?' I said, 'I
don't need it. I don't want it.' And I've been there. I don't want it."

As a consequence of these nonpolitical attributes, Trump positions
himself as being able to restore what America has lost. To illustrate that,
let us return to Trump's presidential announcement speech and his assertion that "Our country is in serious trouble. We don't have victories any
more. We used to have victories, but we don't have them. When was the
last time anyone saw us beating, let's say China in a trade deal? They kill
us." The next line is "I beat China all the time. All the time." To this, the
audience applaud and chant, "We want Trump! We want Trump!"

Then let us also look at the words with which Trump closes the speech: "If I get elected president, I will bring it back bigger and better and stronger than ever before, and we will make America great again." This significantly extends the argument through the use of the term "we." Trump brings in his audience and insists that it is not just Trump but the Trump movement that will restore greatness. And this invocation of the crowd bookends the speech.

Let us conclude our analysis by rewinding from the closing words to the opening words:

> Wow. Whoa. That is some group of people. Thousands. . . . This is beyond anybody's expectations. There's been no crowd like this. And I can tell you, some of the candidates, they went in. They didn't know the air-conditioner didn't work. They sweated like dogs. They didn't know the room was too big, because they didn't have anyone there. How are they going to beat ISIS? I don't think it's gonna happen.

Here, our analysis comes back full circle. We see the rhetorical and the performative come together: the crowd is reflected back to itself as a demonstration of its power to achieve change. The relationship between the crowd, Trump, and threatening enemies within the event is translated into a vision of the world in general: ordinary Americans who have fallen from their rightful place in the world due to attacks from without and betrayals from the political class within, but who have the power, united behind Trump, and the will to employ it, to restore this place. Everything coheres. Everything that is used as evidence of pathology—from the rough language and baying at foes to the devotion and reverence for one who violates all the rules of politics—makes sense within the terms and scope of this vision. It is a vision realized in its very telling. It is an enactment of Trump's new America. It is not only a politics of hope, but the lived experience of all that is hoped for.

The Entrepreneur of Identity

As we have seen, Donald Trump makes much of his economic entrepreneurial abilities and his ability to make deals—although this has come under some critical scrutiny. The ghostwriter of *The Art of the Deal*, Tony Schwartz, has described it as a work of fiction and said, "I feel a deep sense of remorse that I contributed to presenting Trump in a way that brought him wider attention and made him more appealing than he is."[6] And a report in *Fortune* on August 20, 2015, notes that Trump would have made over four times as much money if he had simply invested his money in an index fund.[7] But whatever the truth of the matter, our argument is that Trump's political success derives from his skills as an *entrepreneur of identity*.

By this, we mean the ability of the would-be leader to represent himself and his platform in ways that make them articulate with the ways in which his would-be followers experience their world and hence render himself representative of this world. There is much controversy over exactly who this followership is. For instance, it is often asserted that they are uneducated, white, and poor. In terms of education, it is certainly true that the percentage of Trump supporters with college degrees (around 20%) is much lower than the percentage of Americans with college degrees (roughly 40%), but at the same time, in many of the primaries, most Republicans with college degrees voted for Trump.[8] Equally, it is true that, on average, Trump supporters earn less than supporters of his main rivals ($72,000 vs. $91,000 for Kasich), but at the same time, they earn considerably more than the median wage ($56,000) and supporters of both Clinton and Sanders ($61,000 apiece).[9] What does seem to hold, however, is that Trump supporters are primarily white, and they live in areas of "long-simmering economic dysfunctions" (Irwin & Katz, 2016), even if they themselves are not poor. To quote further from Irwin and Katz, "one element common to a significant share of his supporters is that they have largely missed the generation-long transition of the United States away from manufacturing and into a diverse, information-driven economy deeply intertwined with the rest of the world." That is, Trump's constituency consists largely of people who are part of a declining sector of an economy that is, at best, stagnating (see Smith, 2016) and who have been hit particularly hard by trade deals that open the United States to competition from low-cost manufacturing elsewhere in the world.

The second major factor about this constituency is their lack of trust in politics, politicians, and political institutions. They are not alone in this. A Pew Research Center report shows that overall trust in government has fallen from 74 percent in 1958 (rising to a peak of 77% under Johnson in 1964) to a mere 19 percent in 2015. Only 20 percent of people think government programs are well run.[10] When one takes party identification into account, the figures are even more stark. Less than 10 percent of Republicans currently have trust in government. Even for Democrats, the figure is only a little over 30 percent.[11] What is more, if people feel distanced from government and that government does not represent them, there is good reason to conclude that this is rooted in their actual experience. A recent analysis (Gilens & Page, 2014) shows that, whereas economic elites and business groups have considerable influence on U.S. government policy, average citizens and mass interest groups have none.

Trump's accomplishment is to take these inchoate feelings of decline and marginalization and to provide a perspective that not only makes sense of them but also, as we saw in the previous section, provides a solution to them. In so doing, he acknowledges the real problems of his audience (where others ignore them or even contribute to them), he understands them, and he empowers them to participate in the process of resolving those problems. But he does one more thing. For as we also saw previously, Trump's narrative is not only about the world and the place of his audience within it. It is also himself, about his own place, and hence about his relationship to his audience.

Trump's argument is a classic populist confection in which the world is divided into the common people and a privileged elite. The people are defined in national terms—as Americans—and the elite primarily in political terms. Trump's claim to leadership is primarily rooted in the work he does to position himself firmly among the former (and to position his rivals firmly among the latter). This has a number of key elements that we see as key to successful identity entrepreneurship (Haslam et al., 2011).

To start with, Trump construes himself as prototypical of the "ordinary American" in-group. Not typical. Trump is far from typical. How many ordinary Americans are worth something in the region of $4 billion and have their own tower, university, and jet? No, he is *proto*typical, which means that Trump represents the key values and attributes that distinguish the group from others. This is how Andrew Sullivan puts it:

> He did not hide his wealth in the late 20th century—he flaunted it in a way that connected with the masses. He lived the rich man's life most working men dreamed of—endless glamour and women, for example—without sacrificing a way of talking about the world that would not be out of place on the construction sites he regularly toured. His was a cult of democratic aspiration.

This is how Trump is described on his own Web site: "Donald J. Trump is the very definition of the American success story, continually setting the standards of excellence while expanding his interests in real estate, sports and entertainment." And, perhaps most eloquently, this is how Trump's son described his father in his speech to the Republican Convention:

> We didn't learn from MBAs. We learned from people who had doctorates in common sense.... It's why we're the only children of billionaires as comfortable in a D10 Caterpillar as we are in our own cars. My father knew

that those were the guys and gals who would teach us the dignity of hard work from a very young age. He knows that at the heart of the American dream is the idea that whoever we are, wherever we're from, we can get ahead, where everyone can prosper again.[12]

So, the way Trump dresses (always immaculate in a tie and expensive suit, never dressing down in jeans to pretend to be the "ordinary guy," being American by signifying his success); the way he talks (the crude, undiplomatic, violent forms of expression); and what he says are not incidental. They are part of his performance as an exemplary American. What is more, they separate him equally clearly from being a typical (or prototypical) politician. What is thought to be a weakness (lack of political experience) is touted as a strength. The constant violations of the political rules, so often seen as presaging Trump's decline, actually consolidate his ascendancy. The attacks by heavyweights of the Republican establishment—Mitt Romney, George Bush—only served to increase his poll ratings. This has caused some bemusement, but the reason is simple. To fail by the rules of politics and to be rejected by the political class only serves to consolidate a candidate's in-group status in the eyes of an anti-political audience. Most critically, in Trump's case, it confirms that he is "one of us" not "one of them." All this helps to explain what *The Guardian* calls "the paradox that has been at the heart of the Trump phenomenon," that is, "how can a billionaire businessman from New York be the one who 'gets' the struggling working class?"[13]

But it is not enough to be "one of us." As we note in *The New Psychology of Leadership*, success also depends on being seen to "do it for us" by acting for the in-group interest. As we have already seen, this is one of Trump's constant refrains. Once again, his wealth acts for him as opposed to against him in this regard. He is not acting to enrich himself; we have heard Trump boasting that he has money. He has been there. He doesn't need anymore. Equally, he cannot be bought to serve the interests of others—the international (i.e., non-American) elite. Whereas Hilary Clinton is in thrall to Wall Street and gets paid to speak for Wall Street, Trump is free to "tell it like it is." This is something that is constantly cited as a source of Trump's strength (for instance, former Arizona governor Jan Brewer praised Trump for "kind of telling it like it really truly is" when he linked immigration to violent crime) and that constantly comes out as one of the major reasons why people vote for him.[14]

And finally, even "doing it for us" isn't enough if a leader lacks the support or ability to be successful in advancing the group interest. The effective leader has, above all, to "make it real" in the sense of turning group values into lived experience. One major challenge here is that it is clearly difficult for an aspirant to power to actually achieve anything before they have been elected. As we have seen, Trump rises to this challenge by making much of his previous successes and his credentials as an inspired business leader and deal maker. The other part of the answer lies in creating a simulacrum of reality within the very movement designed to change reality. And, again, we have also seen how carefully Trump choreographs his rallies to achieve precisely that.

In sum, Trump's campaign was all about creating a particular sense of "us" (to which articulating a sense of "them" is critical but secondary) and then establishing the way in which he is representative of the group in a symbolic and practical way so as to gain the ability to represent the group at the political level. The skill, the complexity, and the subtlety with which he does this (even when it comes to his use of crudity) helps us understand why Trump proves so appealing to his audience.

Conclusion

Our argument in this chapter is simple. It is that while it is easy and tempting to reject those we disagree with as either ignorant or irrational, this is a mistake. The temptation to do so becomes all the greater as the polarization between groups increases and it becomes ever harder to understand—or even want to understand—what others do. Our aim becomes to dismiss, to discredit, and to obliterate rather than to understand. But if we take the effort to look at things from the perspective of the other, we generally find that, from their perspective, what they do makes sense. To do so is not to condone that perspective. It is to understand why positions we may abhor can prove so appealing—and hence to be in a better position to properly contest them.

More concretely, we contend that Trump succeeds by providing a categorical grid—a definition of groups and intergroup relations—that allows many Americans to make sense of their lived experience, to understand their problems, and to entertain the hope of being able to deal with them. In this, he establishes himself as a champion and as a voice for people who otherwise feel unchampioned and voiceless. Ironically too, in a politics controlled by wealth and privilege, his wealth frees him of the charge that he is in hock to the money men. Above all, Trump has an intuitive grasp of how to establish himself as the voice of America in both his words and his actions.

What is more, Trump's successes must be seen in the light of the failure of others. Most particularly, his rivals have not succeeded in providing an alternative grid based on alternative categories to make sense of what many Americans are experiencing. They have not elaborated an alternative politics and an alternative set of solutions. In that context, Trump has had a relatively free run.

This point, though, brings us to the last and strongest reason for avoiding an explanation of Trump's success that lays the blame on his inadequacies and those of his followers. This is that, while it is cozy and reassuring, such an account avoids the deeply uncomfortable but equally essential task of asking whether his success may not ultimately derive from our own failings. Certainly, like those pro-European Britons who woke up to news of Brexit's electoral success in June, should we wake up in November to a Trump election victory, we will need to ask what we and our leaders might—and should—have done to present a more inclusive narrative of "us" that deals with the real problems people face, to embody that "us" in all we say and do, and to develop a politics that provides solutions to those problems.

Notes

1. Reported in the British *Daily Telegraph* on January 18, 2016. See http://www.telegraph.co.uk/news/worldnews/donald-trump/12105940/donald-trump-muslim-ban-uk-debate-live.html.

2. Reported in *Salon* on September 30, 2015. See http://www.salon.com/2015/09/30/jerk_idiot_buffoon_voters_choose_brutal_words_to_describe_donald_trump.

3. See http://www.politicususa.com/2016/05/10/american-idiots-poll-proves-trump-supporters-stupidest-people.html.

4. See https://thewpsa.wordpress.com/2016/03/27/racial-resentment-and-the-rise-of-donald-trump.

5. Reported on March 29, 2016. See http://www.salon.com/2016/03/29/hideous_disgusting_racists_lets_call_donald_trump_and_his_supporters_exactly_what_they_are.

6. Reported in the *New York Times* on July 18, 2016. See http://www.nytimes.com/2016/07/19/us/politics/trump-book-tony-schwartz.html?_r=0.

7. See http://fortune.com/2015/08/20/donald-trump-index-funds.

8. See http://www.politico.com/story/2016/03/5-myths-about-trump-supporters-220158.

9. See http://fivethirtyeight.com/features/the-mythology-of-trumps-working-class-support.

10. See http://www.people-press.org/2015/11/23/beyond-distrust-how-americans-view-their-government.

11. See http://www.brookings.edu/blogs/fixgov/posts/2015/09/16-republican
-debate-hetherington.

12. For the entire speech, see http://edition.cnn.com/videos/politics/2016/07/20
/rnc-convention-donald-trump-jr-entire-speech-sot.cnn.

13. See https://www.theguardian.com/us-news/2016/jul/20/donald-trump-jr
-convention-speech-american-dream.

14. See http://thehill.com/blogs/ballot-box/presidential-races/247376-ex-arizona
-governor-trump-telling-it-like-it-is.

References

Abel, T. (1938/1986). *Why Hitler came into power.* Cambridge, MA: Harvard University Press.

Bercovitch, S. (1980). The American Jeremiad. Madison: University of Wisconsin Press.

Cramer, K. (2016). *The politics of resentment: Rural consciousness in Wisconsin and the rise of Scott Walker.* Chicago: University of Chicago Press.

Gilens, M., & Page, B. I. (2014). Testing theories of American politics: Elites, interest groups and average citizens. *Perspectives on Politics, 12,* 564–581.

Haslam, S. A., Reicher, S. D., & Platow, M. (2011). *The new psychology of leadership.* London: Psychology Press.

Irwin, N., & Katz, J. (2016, March 12). The geography of Trumpism. *The New York Times.* Retrieved from http://www.nytimes.com/2016/03/13/upshot/the-geography-of-trumpism.html?_r=0

Le Bon, G. (1895/1947). *The crowd: A study of the popular mind.* Mineola, NY: Dover.

Lewis, H. (2015, November 20). The utopia of ISIS: Inside Islamic State's propaganda war. *New Statesman.* Retrieved from http://www.newstatesman.com/politics/uk/2015/11/utopia-isis-inside-islamic-state-s-propaganda-war

Reicher, S. D., & Haslam, S. A. (2016). Fueling terror: How extremists are made. *Scientific American Mind, 27*(3), 35–39.

Slovic, P., Fischhoff, B., Lichtenstein, S., & Roe, F. J. C. (1981, April). Perceived risk: Psychological factors and social implications. *Proceedings of the Royal Society of London, Series A: Mathematical, Physical and Engineering Sciences, 376,* 17–34.

Smith, N. (2016, March 3). Trump has a point about American decline. *Blomberg.* Retrieved from https://www.bloomberg.com/view/articles/2016-03-03/donald-trump-has-a-point-about-american-decline

Sullivan, A. (2016, May 1). America has never been so ripe for tyranny. *New York Magazine.* Retrieved from http://nymag.com/daily/intelligencer/2016/04/america-tyranny-donald-trump.html#

CHAPTER THREE

Unexamined Assumptions about Leadership: Why People Follow Trump

Mark R. Leary

The Role of Voters' Implicit Leadership Theories in Support for Donald Trump

Whatever flaws our preferred candidate in an election may have, most of us feel that he or she is an incontrovertibly better choice than the alternative, and we often cannot understand why someone would support the opponent. So, perhaps it is not surprising that Hillary Clinton's supporters cannot fathom why anyone would vote for Donald Trump, and Trump's supporters find support for Clinton equally incomprehensible. Yet, this schism in voters' views of the candidates seems to be more pronounced in 2016 than in previous presidential elections, suggesting that the divide extends beyond ideological and political differences to deep disagreements in people's judgments of the candidates' qualifications for office. Indeed, Republicans themselves are split on Trump's suitability for the presidency.

This chapter examines people's reactions to political candidates, and to Donald Trump specifically, by considering voters' beliefs about the characteristics of an effective leader. The central thesis of the chapter is that the Trump phenomenon arose from an unusual confluence of worldviews, beliefs about leadership, and personal motives that have not coalesced in such a way in recent presidential politics. Furthermore, some of the central factors involve voters' *implicit* beliefs—assumptions that voters do not consciously consider or explicitly articulate but that nonetheless exert a strong effect on their choices. And, because most other voters, including the pundits who struggle to explain political trends, do not share this critical configuration of implicit worldviews, beliefs about leadership, and motives, many people do not understand Trump's appeal.

Predictors of Leadership Emergence

A prevailing question in the study of leadership has involved the topic of leadership emergence: who tends to become a leader and why? During the early part of the 20th century, research on leadership was dominated by the "great leader" perspective, which as first championed by historian Thomas Carlyle (1841/2007) in the 19th century (although Carlyle called it the "great man" theory). This perspective assumes that certain people possess characteristics that predispose them to arise as leaders and to perform well in leadership roles. This assumption led social and behavioral scientists on a search for attributes that predict who does and who does not become a leader.

Although early results of this research were not promising (Mann, 1959), later studies identified several characteristics that are more common among people who become leaders (Derue, Nahrgang, Wellman, & Humphrey, 2011; Judge, Bono, Ilies, & Gerhardt, 2002; Lord, De Vader, & Alliger, 1986). No one will be surprised to learn that leaders tend to score higher in such traits as assertiveness, dominance, and confidence, as well as in characteristics that are associated with getting things done, such as conscientiousness and self-control. They also tend to be more extraverted, interpersonally skilled, and emotionally stable and, depending on the organization, higher in character strengths such as honesty.

Although leaders generally tend to have these personality characteristics, the qualities that characterize an effective leader obviously differ across types of groups, contexts, and tasks. Thus, research on leadership has moved beyond a focus on leaders' traits to an interactionist perspective based on the idea that the characteristics of the person interact with the characteristics of the situation to influence who becomes a leader in a particular situation at a particular time (Seyranian, 2010). Not only will different kinds of people emerge as leaders in different settings, but the desired characteristics of a leader sometimes change as a group's circumstances change. Thus, the leader of a start-up company will likely possess somewhat different characteristics than the CEO of an established organization, and the candidate that voters prefer in peacetime may be quite different than the one they want in times of war. In addition, followers' worldviews and motives play an important role in who emerges as a leader by making certain leader characteristics particularly attractive or unattractive. By and large, there are no all-purpose leaders who rise to positions of power no matter what group, context, or task is involved. Different situations and different follower attributes favor people with different configurations of personal characteristics.

Of course, leaders do not automatically emerge by virtue of the fact that their characteristics mesh with the needs of a group, organization, or country. Rather, the process is mediated by those who formally (through selection) or informally (through deference) give the leader power to manage the collective's activities. Thus, to understand why certain people emerge as leaders—including as leaders of political movements—we must consider the beliefs, perceptions, and motives of potential followers (in our case, voters) that lead them to decide that someone will be an effective leader.

Implicit Leadership Theories

People make some decisions in life consciously and deliberately but make other decisions with little or no conscious thought. When people make choices nonconsciously, their judgments, preferences, decisions, and other reactions arrive in conscious awareness fully formed, having been generated by processes operating outside of conscious awareness. We often know that we like X, want to do Y, or detest Z without having consciously thought through our reactions.

An important and exceptionally illuminating discovery in psychology involves the existence of two distinct modes of thinking or information processing. One mode is nonconscious, automatic, and fast, and the other mode is conscious, deliberate, and slow (e.g., Evans, 2008; Sloman, 1996). These two systems, which Kahneman (2011) popularized as System 1 and System 2, respectively, are mediated by different regions of the brain and serve different functions. There is nothing remotely Freudian or mysterious about the idea that people process a great deal of information nonconsciously. Indeed, we could not possibly function in life if we had to consciously think about every decision we make. Fortunately, the non-conscious system does a reasonably good job of gathering and processing

information without our having to deliberate consciously. Although decisions that arise from System 1 processing are largely nonconscious, they
are nonetheless informed decisions in the sense that they are influenced
by information stored in the brain, including memories, beliefs, assumptions, expectations, and criteria for making judgments. However, because
the processes are not conscious, the person is not privy to all of the factors that contributed to his or her final decision. In contrast, decisions
that arise from System 2 processing involve conscious thought in which
the person contemplates the evidence, considers the pros and cons of various alternatives, and can provide an explanation for why he or she made
a particular choice.

Most relevant to this chapter, people's judgments of leadership are
heavily based on nonconscious processing. Although people sometimes
think deliberately about a person's qualifications for leadership, the identification of a leader is, to some extent, a nonconscious, System 1 decision.
In listening to a political candidate, we often quickly conclude that the
person is or is not fit for office without a great deal of deliberative thought.
If asked, we can justify our conclusion, but our initial reaction was often
not based on conscious deliberation of the person's qualifications. Just as
Supreme Court Justice Potter Stewart said that he could not define hard-
core pornography but knew it when he saw it, people often know (or
think they know) good leaders when they see them. But on what basis are
such decisions made?

Robert Lord and his colleagues (Lord, Foti, & De Vader, 1984; Lord &
Maher, 1991) introduced the concept of "implicit leadership theories" to
explain this process. According to this perspective, people hold implicit
assumptions about the characteristics of good leaders. These assumptions
are "implicit" in the sense that people don't consciously and explicitly
articulate all of their beliefs about leaders and leadership. Rather, they
have a set of nonconscious beliefs ("implicit theories") about what a good
leader is like. When questions of leadership arise, they make automatic
judgments regarding a person's suitability, often without thinking deeply
about them (Shondrick & Lord, 2010).

For example, most people's implicit leadership theories assume that
good leaders are intelligent, energetic, and decisive. Thus, most people
will quickly judge intelligent, energetic, and decisive people as more qualified for leadership positions than people who are stupid, sluggish, or
indecisive (Junker & van Dick, 2014). But they usually don't make this
decision consciously, as if they were checking off items on a mental list.
Rather, their implicit personality theories rapidly handle the decision outside of awareness.

Beyond some basic characteristics (such as intelligence, energy, and decisiveness), people differ in their implicit assumptions about leaders, and they may have different theories about leaders in different groups, contexts, and cultures (Epitropaki & Martin, 2004; Kenney, Schwartz-Kenney, & Blascovich, 1996; Kono, Ehrhart, Ehrhart, & Schultze, 2012). Imagine two voters who have different implicit leadership theories. Voter A implicitly associates leadership with a rational, measured, and unemotional approach to issues. In contrast, Voter B's implicit leadership theory associates effective leadership with an energetic, motivational, and emotional approach. These voters might lean toward different candidates irrespective of the candidates' positions or qualifications. And, because these are not the characteristics that they consciously consider when judging candidates, neither voter might identify them as the reasons that they prefer one candidate over the other. People are often not aware of the factors that influence their judgments and may even deny that they were influenced by factors that, in fact, caused them to react as they did (Nisbett & Wilson, 1977).

To be clear, people are certainly aware of and have thought about a few salient characteristics of the candidates, but they are not aware—and, indeed, cannot be aware—of all of the implicit factors that influence their choice. This fact has two important implications. First, because people generally cannot report on all of the reasons for their preferences and decisions, we cannot fully understand people's voting decisions simply from what they tell us. Although we certainly might learn something useful by asking voters why they prefer Clinton or Trump, they usually cannot tell us the full set of reasons because many of those reasons are implicit and, thus, out of conscious awareness.

The second implication is that people cannot examine or attempt to verify their implicit beliefs. Because the beliefs are implicit, questionable assumptions will not be examined and potentially modified unless they are thought about consciously or explicitly challenged by others. In the meantime, the person's choices may be based on incorrect assumptions or faulty criteria.

Assumptions about Effective Leaders

In the context of American presidential leadership, voters' explicit beliefs about the most important characteristics that are needed in a president seem reasonable and do not differ a great deal across political parties. Democrats, Republicans, and Independents agree that intelligence, honesty, and leadership are the most important of 10 desirable traits for a president to have, although they rank them in different orders (Hankin & Ivanic, 2015).

However, some of the traits that people seek in political candidates are known to be markers of ineffective leadership, suggesting that voters may not have explicitly thought about them. For example, a 2013 poll showed that only 36 percent of Republicans and about half of Democrats and Independents (59% and 53%, respectively) indicated that they liked elected officials who "make compromises with people they disagree with" (Pew Research Center, 2013). In an earlier poll specific to presidential qualifications, only 38 percent of voters indicated that "willingness to compromise" is essential in a president (Pew Research Center, 2003). Voters who believe that willingness to compromise is not necessary seem to have an implicit belief that an effective president need not—or, perhaps, should not—compromise, even though in other contexts most people would probably agree that effective leaders should look for common ground when disagreements exist rather than always trying to impose their personal views on others. Failure to work toward compromise means that either nothing whatsoever gets accomplished or that the desires of large segments of one's constituents are ignored entirely (Gutmann & Thompson, 2012). Ironically, voters indicate that gridlock and the inability to get anything done is the primary reason that they are angry with the federal government (Gallup, 2013), yet many say that the willingness to compromise is not an important characteristic for elected officials!

Along the same lines, about half of respondents in the poll indicated that it is essential for a president to maintain consistent positions, and about a third indicated that it is essential for presidents to show party loyalty. Again, these beliefs fly in the face of the fact that effective, judicious leaders must consider multiple perspectives, be open to alternative ideas, and respond with flexibility (Yukl & Mahsud, 2010). In her book *Team of Rivals: The Political Genius of Abraham Lincoln*, Doris Kearns Goodwin attributed Lincoln's success in managing the Civil War to the fact that he purposefully populated his cabinet with strong-willed men who held a broad range of viewpoints and could be counted on to offer divergent ideas and disagree with him. More broadly, Simonton (2006) found that the degree to which U.S. presidents were high in openness (which includes openness to alternative ideas and courses of action) correlated with ratings of their effectiveness in office as judged by 12 presidential historians. (In fact, openness predicted presidential success about as strongly as intelligence did.) By stressing the importance of consistency and party loyalty, many voters seem to believe, at least implicitly, that they want a president to behave in ways that, according to many leadership experts, do not promote effective leadership (Gutmann & Thompson, 2012; Yukl & Mahsud, 2010).

If voters were explicitly asked, "Would you like a wise and judicious president with sound judgment who considers all of the facts and options before taking action?" the vast majority would likely say yes. It would seem absurd to want a president who is foolish and imprudent, follows the party line even when it's not in the best interests of the country, and doesn't consider all options. Yet, these polls suggest that many voters have implicit beliefs that a president should have traits that are incompatible with making the best, most effective decisions (LePine, Colquitt, & Erez, 2000; Yukl & Mahsud, 2010).

Although most voters consider certain aspects of the candidates' qualifications thoughtfully and can articulate a few salient things about a candidate's positions and style that they particularly like and dislike, their preferences also reflect a host of influences that they do not consciously consider. Most people who say that the willingness to compromise is not necessary in a president or that consistency and party loyalty are essential have probably not thought carefully about the immense implications of those beliefs for making good decisions on behalf of the country. They are simply part of their unexamined assumptions about leadership.

Implicit Beliefs among Committed Trump Supporters

We will now consider the possible role of implicit leadership theories specifically among Trump's supporters. This analysis does not apply to people who primarily support Trump because they intensely dislike Clinton (about half of his supporters as of May 2016; Reuters, 2016) or because their support for Trump is motivated by other personal goals even though they do not regard him as qualified to be president (such as Republican politicians who feel compelled to support him despite their reservations). We are focused here on his committed supporters.

To understand the Trump phenomenon, I will draw a distinction between two sets of beliefs. One set involves the worldviews and personal motives that lead voters to resonate to Trump's ideas regarding the country's problems and their solutions; the other set involves reasons that voters think that Trump can effectively address those problems, reasons that are based on their personal leadership theories, many of which are implicit. These are often quite distinct sets of beliefs: a voter could reasonably believe that Trump understands the country's problems yet lacks the experience or ability to fix them, or, alternatively, that Trump is a potentially effective leader but has wrong-headed ideas about the problems or solutions. Trump's strongest support presumably comes from those who both agree with his worldview and policies and believe that he can successfully implement changes that will benefit the country, if not them personally.

Although implicit worldviews and leadership theories are not available to direct observation—either by the individual or by observers—we can make inferences about what these theories may be by examining the ways in which voters describe their reasons for supporting Trump, as well as their attitudes and demographic characteristics. In a sense, we can reverse engineer the implicit beliefs by asking what assumptions must be operating for a person to respond in a particular way.

Resonating to the Trumpian Worldview

The central thesis of Trump's message—the one that he repeats in rallies and that provides an integrative theme to his rhetoric—is that the United States was once a great and respected country that has lost power, economic strength, and respect due to an assortment of unwelcome influences, including illegal immigrants who steal Americans' jobs and commit crimes, Muslims who hate America and promote terrorism, a political establishment that has pursued policies that have weakened America economically and militarily, the mainline Republican party, the media, and an assortment of other specific individuals (Guilford, 2016; Malone, 2016). Trump promises to fix these problems and "make America great again."

Voters who resonate to this message are those who also believe that America is in decline and blame its problems on any or all of the reputed culprits that Trump identifies. For example, voters who believe that whites have been treated unfairly showed disproportionately greater support for Trump during the primary elections (Tesler & Sides, 2016). In the same vein, a survey of likely Republican voters showed that over 60 percent of respondents who strongly agreed that "immigrants threaten American customs and values" supported Trump in the primaries (Pollard & Mendelsohn, 2016). Distrust of the political establishment is also palpable: Republican primary voters who said that they were angry at the federal government supported Trump 47 percent, compared to 27 percent for Ted Cruz and 8 percent for John Kasich (CNN poll for 20 primaries through March 15, 2016). In the primaries, Trump was also overwhelmingly preferred by voters who indicated that they felt betrayed by Republican politicians (CNN exit poll taken during the first 13 primaries through March 15, 2016).

In brief, Trump's most ardent supporters believe that Trump grasps the social, political, and economic factors that have undermined Americans' greatness and contributed to their personal challenges and disenfranchisement. Trump's central message rings true to people who believe that America is in decline, resent the country's changing racial and ethnic demographics, and feel ignored and disrespected by the powers that be.

Implicit Theories of Trumpian Leadership

In addition to the fact that they believe he has accurately diagnosed the problems, Trump's supporters believe that he has the qualifications to lead the country in new, desired directions. The primary characteristics that his supporters mention as evidence of his viability as a leader are explicit; that is, they have thought about and can articulate the attributes that they believe qualify Trump to be president. However, these explicit beliefs are often based on unexamined, implicit assumptions that may be questionable and with which many people disagree. Five such implicit assumptions seem central.

Trump the Businessman and CEO

Trump's supporters often point to his extensive business experience as evidence that he has the leadership attributes that will allow him to "get things done" as president. Underlying this belief is the implicit leadership theory that the same skills that contribute to success as a businessman and CEO promote effectiveness as president. Although some personal characteristics may predispose people to be successful leaders across politics and business, business leaders and political leaders accomplish goals and get things done in quite different ways. A CEO, particularly one who owns his own businesses, simply gives commands for subordinates to carry out desired actions. He can unilaterally set the direction of the company and institute policies without the agreement of other people, although the wise executive generally tries to bring others on board and may allow subordinates input into the process. Trump can get things done in business simply by willing them to happen. Although a president has certain powers to make executive decisions, most decisions that will actually change the direction of the country or create new laws require working with other people (specifically members of Congress), people over whom the president has no direct power and who, in fact, are often motivated to thwart his or her plans. A president needs a quite different approach toward leadership than a business executive and a somewhat different set of management skills as well.

Given the widespread frustration with the deadlock in Washington, the public is understandably fed up with the status quo, and the appeal of a Washington outsider who is not a politician is easy to understand. But, the implicit assumption that national problems can be solved as if the president of the United States were the CEO of a very large corporation is questionable. This does not necessarily mean that Trump does not have the requisite skills, but it does suggest that many of his supporters have probably not explicitly considered this assumption.

Toughness

Many Trump supporters praise his toughness and strength, and a president certainly needs both. But one may reasonably draw a distinction between being tough and strong in the face of serious problems and being belligerent, blunt, and brash as a matter of course. Supporters seem to implicitly interpret Trump's forceful personality as strength, when a more explicit, nuanced examination might question that interpretation.

Research shows that people's implicit leadership theories change to favor more forceful leaders when they feel anxious and insecure. Conditions that elicit uncertainty and fear lead people toward more conservative views and to prefer more dominant and even authoritarian leaders (Doty, Peterson, & Winter, 1991; Jost, Glaser, Kruglanski, & Sulloway, 2003). For example, one study found that research participants who were led to think about their own deaths began to view effective leaders more in terms of agentic traits such as independence, confidence, determination, and competitiveness (Hoyt, Simon, & Innella, 2011). Interestingly, the effects of external threats on authoritarianism may be greater for people who are not normally authoritarian (Hetherington & Suhay, 2011). In any case, voters who are particularly worried about economic and terrorist threats—as Trump's supporters seem to be—will implicitly prefer tougher leaders.

Authenticity

Trump is also praised for being authentic and speaking his mind no matter what the consequences. The implicit assumption here is that always saying what's on one's mind is a desirable characteristic for effective leaders, particularly given that most voters view politicians as dishonest (Pew Research Center, 2015). Of course, as a general principle, honesty is usually a good thing. Yet, unbridled candidness is generally viewed as rude and disrespectful, and no evidence exists to suggest that effective leaders always says what they think. In everyday life, people view those who say whatever's on their mind as rude, boorish, offensive, or unbalanced. And, we certainly don't like people who have control over important outcomes—our bosses, supervisors, coaches, pastors, military leaders, and elected officials, for example—to always say what they think, particularly when doing so is unnecessarily rude, disrespectful, hurtful, or offensive. It is difficult to know where this implicit leadership assumption comes from.

Trump and his supporters might counter that he is simply resisting pressures to be "politically correct," and certainly political correctness is sometimes pursued in ways that skirt important issues. But what Trump's supporters implicitly view as political correctness is often deemed by others to simply be civility and politeness.

Wealth

Although Americans generally distrust rich people (Parker, 2012), Trump's followers view his status as a billionaire as a strength because they believe that, as president, he's not likely to pursue policies for financial gain. In a phrase, he can't be bought. This belief rests on two implicit assumptions. The first is that a very wealthy person will not do things to acquire even more money. Yet, Trump has obviously spent his adult life behaving in ways that result in financial gain, even past the point where he apparently has more money than he will ever need. In fact, as he admits, Trump has worked hard to influence politicians and government agencies to act in ways that will help him make even more money. So, on examination, the implicit assumption that a wealthy person is immune to financial incentives is obviously not true.

The belief also assumes that money is the only incentive that leads to self-serving political decisions that are not in the public's best interests. Everyone, politicians included, is motivated by many things: to bring attention to themselves or make a splash, to leave a legacy and go down in history, to please other people, to boost their own egos, and so on. These are normal human motives, and they are unavoidable. The point is that many things other than money lead politicians to support actions that are personally beneficial. Thus, the implicit notion that Trump is impervious to extraneous influences seems questionable to many voters who are not his supporters.

Trump Understands

Many Trump supporters perceive that he understands them and their problems in a way that other candidates and elected officials do not (Guilford, 2016). Certainly, his views on illegal immigration, certain economic issues (such as jobs going overseas), and the policies of the Obama administration are consistent with those of his supporters. Yet, inspection of the implicit assumptions underlying this perception raises the question of whether an exceptionally rich businessman from New York City truly understands the daily challenges of most ordinary Americans, particularly those who make up a large segment of Trump's committed supporters, such as low-income voters who live in rural areas. And the question should be particularly discomfiting to voters for whom Trump's stance on other issues—such as religious issues and transgender rights—are clearly contrary to their own.

In brief, many of the reasons that Trump's supporters give for their support are based on implicit assumptions that do not survive explicit scrutiny.

Conclusion

While Trump's committed supporters view him as the only obvious choice in the 2016 election, many others simply can't understand his appeal. In my view, this failure to understand arises because nonsupporters do not share or understand supporters' implicit and explicit beliefs about the nature of the country's problems, the central characteristics of effective leadership, and Trump's qualifications based on his business experience, toughness, authenticity, wealth, and perceived understanding of the voters' problems.

In addition, the 2016 election is different from others in recent memory in that most voters, including some who will vote for Trump, view his behavior as a national candidate as inappropriate, and some see it to be entirely outside the bounds of acceptable behavior. As a result, many view him as inherently unfit for office even if they resonate to some of his ideas. People who have strong negative reactions to Trump's rhetoric and temperament find it difficult to grasp that other people are willing to entrust him with the presidency. In addition, it seems that many observers do not understand the Trump phenomenon because they are unwilling to accept the conclusion that a high percentage of the American electorate have the kinds of implicit and explicit beliefs that underlie his support—beliefs about the nature of the country's problems, the solutions needed to solve them, the characteristics of effective and trustworthy national leaders, and Trump's experiential and temperamental qualifications to be president.

References

Carlyle, T. (1841/2007). *On heroes, hero-worship, and the heroic in history.* Whitefish, MT: Kessenger.

Derue, D. S., Nahrgang, J. D., Wellman, N., & Humphrey, S. E. (2011). Trait and behavioral theories of leadership: An integration and meta-analytic test of their relative validity. *Personnel Psychology, 64,* 7–52.

Doty, R. M, Peterson, B. E., & Winter, D. G. (1991). Threat and authoritarianism in the United States, 1978–1987. *Journal of Personality and Social Psychology, 61,* 629–640.

Epitropaki, O., & Martin, R. (2004). Implicit leadership theories in applied settings: Factor structure, generalizability, and stability over time. *Journal of Applied Psychology, 89,* 293–310.

Evans, J. St. B. T. (2008). Dual-processing accounts of reasoning, judgement and social cognition. *Annual Review of Psychology, 59,* 255–278.

Gallup. (2013, June 12). *Gridlock is top reason Americans are critical of Congress.* Retrieved from http://www.gallup.com/poll/163031/gridlock-top-reason-americans-critical-congress.aspx

Guilford, G. (2016, April 1). Inside the Trump machine: The bizarre psychology of America's newest political movement. *Quartz.* Retrieved from http://qz .com/645345/inside-the-trump-machine-the-bizarre-psycholog-of -americas-newest-political-movement

Gutmann, A., & Thompson, D. (2012). *The spirit of compromise: Why governing demands it and campaigning undermines it.* Princeton, NJ: Princeton University Press.

Hankin, S., & Ivanic, R. (2015, October 19). What voters most want: Honesty or intelligence? *Washington Monthly.* Retrieved from http://washingtonmonthly .com/2015/10/19/what-voters-most-want-honesty-or-intelligence

Hetherington, M, & Suhay, E. (2011). Authoritarianism, threat, and Americans' support for the War on Terror. *American Journal of Political Science, 55,* 546–560.

Hoyt, C. L., Simon, S., & Innella, A. N. (2011). Taking a turn toward the masculine: The impact of mortality salience on implicit leadership theories. *Basic and Applied Social Psychology, 33,* 374–381.

Jost, J. T., Glaser, J., Kruglanski, A. W., & Sulloway, F. J. (2003). Political conservatism as motivated social cognition. *Psychological Bulletin, 129,* 339–375.

Judge, T. A., Bono, J. E., Ilies, R., & Gerhardt, M. (2002). Personality and leadership: A qualitative and quantitative review. *Journal of Applied Psychology, 87,* 765–780.

Junker, N. M., & van Dick, R. (2014). Implicit theories in organizational settings: A systematic review and research agenda of implicit leadership and followership theories. *The Leadership Quarterly, 25,* 1154–1173.

Kahneman, D. (2011). *Thinking, fast and slow.* New York: Farrar, Straus and Giroux.

Kenney, R. A., Schwartz-Kenney, B. M., & Blascovich, J. (1996). Implicit leadership theories: Defining leaders described as worthy on influence. *Personality and Social Psychology Bulletin, 22,* 1128–1143.

Kono, T., Ehrhart, K, H., Ehrhart, M. G., & Schultze, T. (2012). Implicit leadership theories in Japan and the US. *Asia Pacific Journal of Human Resources, 50,* 367–387.

LePine, J. A., Colquitt, J. A., & Erez, A. 2000. Adaptability to changing task contexts: Effects of general cognitive ability, conscientiousness, and openness to experience. *Personnel Psychology, 53,* 563–594.

Lord, R. G., DeVader, C. L., & Alliger, G. M. (1986). A meta-analysis of the relation between personality traits and leadership perceptions: An application of validity generalization procedures. *Journal of Applied Psychology, 71,* 402–410.

Lord, R. G., Foti, R. J., & De Vader, C. L. (1984). A test of leadership categorization theory: Internal structure, information processing, and leadership perceptions. *Organizational Behavior and Human Performance, 34,* 343–378.

Lord, R. G., & Maher, K. J. (1991). *Leadership and information processing: Linking perceptions and performance.* New York: Routledge.

Malone, C. (2016, May 23). Why Donald Trump?: A quest to figure out what's happening in America. *FiveThirtyEight.* Retrieved from http://fivethirtyeight.com/features/why-donald-trump

Mann, R. D. (1959). A review of the relationship between personality and performance in small groups. *Psychological Bulletin, 56,* 241–270.

Nisbett, R., & Wilson, T. (1977). Telling more than we can know: Verbal reports on mental processes. *Psychological Review, 84,* 231–259.

Parker, K (2012, August 27). Yes, the rich are different. Pew Research Center. Retrieved from http://www.pewsocialtrends.org/2012/08/27/yes-the-rich-are-different

Pew Research Center (2003, September 28). Additional findings and analyses. Retrieved from http://www.people-press.org/2003/09/25/additional-findings-and-analyses-8

Pew Research Center (2013, January 17). *Obama in strong position at start of second term: Support for compromise rises, except among Republicans.* Retrieved from http://www.people-press.org/2013/01/17/obama-in-strong-position-at-start-of-second-term

Pew Research Center (2015, November 23. *Beyond distrust: How Americans view their government.* Retrieved from http://www.people-press.org/2015/11/23/beyond-distrust-how-americans-view-their-government

Pollard, M., & Mendelsohn, J. (2016, January 27). RAND kicks off 2016 presidential election panel survey. *The RAND Blog*. Retrieved from http://www.rand.org/blog/2016/01/rand-kicks-off-2016-presidential-election-panel-survey.html

Reuters (2016, May 9). *Top reason Americans will vote for Trump—to stop Clinton*. Retrieved from http://www.reuters.com/article/us-usa-election-anti-vote-idUSKCN0XX06E

Seyranian, V. (2010). Interactionist theories of leadership. In J. M. Levine & M. A. Hogg (Eds.), *Encyclopedia of group processes and intergroup relations* (Vol. 1, pp. 456–459). Thousand Oaks, CA: Sage Publications.

Shondrick, S. J., & Lord, R. G. (2010). Implicit leadership and followership theories: Dynamic structures for leadership perceptions, memory, and leader-follower processes. In G. P. Hodgkinson & J. K. Ford (Eds.), *International review of industrial and organizational psychology* (Vol. 25, pp. 1–33). New York: Wiley-Blackwell.

Simonton, D. K. (2006). Presidential IQ, openness, intellectual brilliance, and leadership: Estimates and correlations for 42 U.S. chief executives. *Political Psychology, 27*, 511–526.

Sloman, S. A. (1996). The empirical case for two systems of reasoning. *Psychological Bulletin, 119*, 3–22.

Tesler, M., & Sides, J. (2016, March 3). How political science helps explain the rise of Trump: The role of white identity and grievances. *The Washington Post*. Retrieved from https://www.washingtonpost.com/news/monkey-cage/wp/2016/03/03/how-political-science-helps-explain-the-rise-of-trump-the-role-of-white-identity-and-grievances

Yukl, G., & Mahsud, R. (2010). Why flexible and adaptive leadership is essential. *Consulting Psychology Journal: Research and Practice, 62*, 81–93.

CHAPTER FOUR

Leadership and Followership: Trump—An Adaptive Mismatch?

Micha Popper

A scene in a Japanese film directed by Akira Kurosawa shows a troop of war-weary soldiers moving toward the next battlefield. The camera lingers on their perspiring faces, tired eyes, and laggard movements. They are totally exhausted. Suddenly, in the distance, they notice their leader standing on a hilltop and waving his hand in greeting. The dramatic effect of the leader's presence is amazing. The soldiers' eyes sparkle, their backs straighten, and their weariness disappears. With renewed energy, they march into the battle. Afterward, the camera turns away from the soldiers and slowly moves in to a close-up of the leader. When the camera hovers over the leader's face, the viewer discovers that he is dead. Someone is supporting him and waving his hand in the air.

This powerful scene illustrates one of the propositions in the psychological literature on leadership, namely, the need for leaders is inherent in humans (Popper, 2012, 2015). Allison and Goethals (2014) and Castelnovo, Popper, and Koren (2016) indicate four sources underlying the yearning for leaders: (1) the need for meaning, (2) an epistemic need, (3) a need for security, and (4) an innate evolutionary code.

The Need for Meaning

A key element in the creation of meaning is related to the notion of "self-concept" (Markus & Kitayama, 1991), which is described by Shamir, House, and Arthur (1993) as a collection of identities under a dynamic hierarchy. Huntington (2004) demonstrates this idea through the story of Rachel Newman published after the collapse of the Twin Towers on September, 11, 2001:

> When I was 19, I moved to New York City. If you asked me to describe myself then, I would have told you I was a musician, a poet, an artist, and, on some political level, a woman, a lesbian, and a Jew. Being an American wouldn't have made my list. In my college class, my girlfriend and I were so frustrated by inequality in America that we discussed moving to another country. On September 11 all that changed. I realized that I had been taking the freedom I have here for granted. Now I have an American flag on my backpack, I cheer at the fighter jets as they pass overhead, and I am calling myself a patriot. (Huntington, 2004, p. 4)

This example clarifies the idea of a collection of different identities inherent in each of us, but it also illustrates how events and people can change the salience of identity categories in the hierarchy of self-identity. Leaders may make such an impact. A person's identification with a certain leader and his or her affiliation with his or her camp can prioritize a certain category in his or her self-concept (Shamir et al., 1993). Manifestations of this argument can be found in the influence of myths and stories about leaders who appear in socialization and identity creation processes (Allison & Goethals, 2014).

An Epistemic Need

The centrality of the epistemic need (i.e., to be capable of understanding) appears as early as the biblical story of the tree of knowledge. Heider (1944) gave this motif researchable psychological expression, arguing that human beings are like a "naive scientist" who wants to understand the causality of events taking place around him or her. Similarly, people formulate hypotheses of cause and effect in their daily lives. This argument led to many studies on the patterns of inference people apply on encountering various stimuli (Hamilton, 1988)—patterns Karl Wieck (1995) characterized by a well-chosen title: "sense-making." From this perspective, leaders provide one of the most accessible and convenient explanations for the occurrence of phenomena that are very complex and difficult to explain. For example, studies in social psychology have identified a phenomenon known in the psychological literature as the "fundamental attribution error": when explaining events, people tend to attribute greater causality to the "actor" than to the circumstances in a given situation (Ross, Amebile, & Steinmatz, 1977). This bias intensifies when circumstances (e.g., social and economic) become more complex. For example, when asked to explain the collapse of the Soviet Union, people tend more to attribute the central factor to Gorbachev (prominent, highly available information) than to delve into longstanding complex processes that existed in the Soviet Union prior to this event (Popper, 2013; Westlake, 2000).

A Need for Security

Security was identified by Maslow (1970) as a basic need common to all creatures. Its centrality in the context of leadership was exemplified by Lipmen-Blumen (2007), who cited statistical evidence from a national survey conducted by the *Los Angeles Times* in 2006. The results showed that when the need for strengthening security conflicts with the values of freedom and human rights, the need for security prevails. Only 40 percent of the respondents thought that human rights should be protected under any circumstances. Regarding voting patterns, the data showed that although 62 percent thought that the state should take other directions than those set by the ruling party (the Bush administration), the majority of this group (46%) declared that they would vote for the party they opposed because it promised them more physical security.

An Innate Evolutionary Code

The claim (like all evolutionary claims) is that millennia of evolution have imprinted in us "software" that dictates many of our reactions. As Zajonc (1980) argues, in many cases, "preferences need no inference." Indeed, there is evidence that feelings precede cognitive functions in the phylogenetic development. For example, it was found that the limbic system, which controls emotional responses, originally carried basic adaptive functions (Izard, 1977). Meltzoff and Moore (1977), for example, showed that infants aged just 12 days—long before they acquire language—can mimic emotional expressions. The supremacy of emotions is also reported in the domain termed in the literature as "leadership emergence," particularly in situations termed "weak psychological situations," such as crises or situations characterized by uncertainty (Mischel, 1973; Pillai, 1996).

Clearly, the evolutionary perspective does not contradict other psychological perspectives (i.e., need for security or epistemic need) but rather complements arguments that rely on central psychological theories such as Freud's (1920) or Bowlby's (1988), according to which the leader under certain circumstances is experienced as a parent figure or as a protecting attachment figure (Popper, 2015). The evolutionary perspective in fact expands the psychological explanations to their primal and collective foundations and therefore can contribute new insights that are not trivial, particularly on the issue of choosing or electing leaders. We turn now to examine the evolutionary logic of this process.

Attraction to Leaders: A Psychoevolutionary Perspective

Recently, the discussion on leadership from an evolutionary perspective has been gaining momentum (Van Vugt & Grabo, 2015). The general claim is that people tend to follow those who they feel might have an "adaptive value." For example, people tend to follow figures sensed as strong and resolute when threatened by war (McCann, 1992) or when experiencing crisis (Pillai, 1996). As summarized by Van Vugt, Hogan, and Kaiser (2008), the same elements that guided our forefathers when they followed those they felt could lead them to the source of water vital to their existence still guide preferences for leaders today. Such a process can be described using Sperber and Wilson's (1995) relevance theory, arguing that hearers/readers will search for meaning in any given communication, and having found a meaning that matches their expectations of relevance, they will stop processing. In other words, there is a "relevance threshold" that determines whether a stimulus merits additional processing. As a psychological situation weakens (in terms of threat or uncertainty), personality differences and differences in income, education, and social status may shrink or even disappear. Then, intellectuals as well as manual workers may find themselves following a leader who represents provision of the basic needs of living creatures everywhere. This initial longing was described by Eleanor Roosevelt in an oft-cited description of her husband's inauguration ceremony as the U.S. president during the Great Depression. "It was quite frightening," she recalled, "when Franklin said in his inauguration speech that he might have to assume presidential powers that are usually assumed by the president in wartime, just in that part of the speech he received the most thunderous applause" (Schlesinger, 1958, pp. 1–2).

This kind of account has been used to explain the rise of leaders like Hitler (Kershaw, 1998), that is, the rise of leaders in extreme situations in which the phylogenetic foundations of followership can be identified more clearly (Van Vugt et al., 2008). Obviously, this is only a partial picture. Comparative studies, for example (Den Hartog, House, Hanges, Ruiz-Quintanilla, & Dorfman, 1999; Gerstner & Day, 1994; Hofstede & Hofstede, 2005), have shown that followers in various cultures have different "leadership schemas" created from exposure to different textbooks, novels, movies, and other channels of socialization (Popper, 2012). This fact often raises questions: Can Hitler occur in any culture? Could Mahatma Gandhi, the most revered leader in Indian history, with his mannerisms, dress, and spiritual messages, be elected in the United States or England? In a more formal phrasing, how can the universal and the local-cultural elements be taken into account in predicting or explaining the appeal of leaders in situations that are not felt as extreme?

The relevance principle previously discussed can provide a conceptual framework for characterizing the selection process of various "leadership signals" in different cultures. For instance, research conducted by Schjoedt, Stødkilde-Jørgensen, Geertz, Lund, and Roepstorff (2010) showed that a devout Christian audience, listening to a priest believed to possess "extraordinary forces," evinced significant deactivation of the social executive functions, the medial dorsolateral prefrontal cortex that is responsible for "learning associations between context, locations, events and corresponding adaptive responses, particularly emotional responses" (Euston, Gruber, & McNaughton, 2012, p. 1507)—indicating yielding control, much like the effect of hypnosis on people. By contrast, when the subjects believed they were listening to a non-Christian preacher, the opposite reaction was reported: an increase in activation of these parts of the brain. Consistent with these findings, when asked later to assess the charisma of the two preachers, the devout Christians perceived the Christian preacher as more charismatic than the non-Christian. Moreover, such differences in the brain's activity were not found in a parallel group of secular people exposed to the same conditions.

The experiment clearly illustrates the idea of filters or "relevance threshold" in different ecologies. Borrowing Hofstede and Hofstede's (2005) metaphor of "the software of the mind," we can argue that there are "cultural cues" that determine the relevance of the messages perceived from leaders or candidates for leadership roles. This process can be likened to a canonical process of a literary work. The need for leaders is universal in all cultures. However, a cultural hero in a certain collective may not be accepted as such in another collective. This is contingent on characteristics of certain cultural leadership schemas.

Why do such processes occur? What is their relevance to the question of attraction to leaders? This question can also be analyzed on the basis of evolutionary interpretation using Tomasello's (2014) two arguments: (1) Humans are more skillful than other species at discerning what others perceive, intend, desire, know, and believe. Human beings possess the foundational skill of understanding intentions. The pinnacle of this ability is understanding beliefs that are indisputably mental and normative. (2) Humans can engage better than other species in complex collaborative activities, such as preparing a meal together or playing a cooperative game. These two dimensions of human expertise—reading intentions and interacting with others culturally—are intimately related. The ability to maintain the type of symbolic communication needed for cooperative activities is also the foundation of individuals' identification and solidarity with the group they feel they belong to, as well as the source of feelings of separation and difference with regard to other groups. These differences might at times seem somewhat vague, but many phenomena confirm their reality, particularly the many types of group biases that humans exhibit, for example, helping in-group more than out-group members, caring more about one's reputation within a group, and so on (Bennett & Sani, 2008). Tomasello and Rakoczy (2003) call this "we" feeling "group mindedness," that is, based not only on intentionality jointly with other individuals at a given moment, but an ongoing "collective intentionality."

There is testimony indicating that developmentally these biases appear very early. For example, an experiment was conducted on extreme influence, termed in the literature as "over-imitation." This is a persistent, accurate imitation of *all* behaviors, including those that are clearly not instrumental to the imitator (a phenomenon that does not exist even among monkeys, which emulate rather than imitate (e.g., Csibra & Gergely, 2011; McGuigan, 2013). In the experiment, children aged four (Kinzler, Corriveau, & Harris, 2011) as well as infants (Buttelmann, Zmyj, Daum, & Carpenter, 2013) were found to prefer to imitate someone from their group to someone from the "other" group. This phenomenon can already be observed at the age of 14 months. As mentioned, this group attunement is unique to humans, as it presumes to promote relative advantages in the struggle among various groups. Thus, the unique human ability of understanding and cooperating with other people is actually also the basis of sectarianism, ethnocentrism, and racism.

The processes of maintaining group identity also mean the creation of certain filters. That is, beyond being drawn phylogenetically to leaders accepted as competent, the attraction to leaders will also be influenced by the unique filters of the individual's culture. In other words, the filters determine the leadership's relevance threshold. As long as the leadership's signals (i.e., leader's image, messages) are sensed as being within the group-mindedness boundaries (Tomasello & Rakoczy, 2003) or reinforcing the group cohesiveness, they will be accepted as enhancing the "we" motif; therefore, they will be accepted as having higher adaptive value.

The link between the discussed concepts—leader's appeal, context, "group mindedness" (Tomasello & Rakoczy, 2003)—and relevance (Sperber & Wilson, 1995) can be illustrated by comparing President Bush's acceptance as a strikingly charismatic leader immediately after the 9/11 events with his acceptance as much less charismatic after Hurricane Katrina in New Orleans (Davis & Gardner, 2012). Unlike the Hurricane Katrina case, which was perceived as a random disaster, the 9/11 events were grasped as a deliberate action against the collective—an attack by an external group (out-group) on major American *symbols* (the Pentagon and the World Trade Center). Under such circumstances, President Bush, just by being the president, was one of the most prominent symbols inspiring the "we" feeling; therefore, the degree of his charisma in the eyes of the collective was, at that moment in time, dramatically intensified.

Given such complex processes, how can we parsimoniously and accurately explain the processes of electing leaders? How can the "tension" between the universal element and the local cultural element be reconciled when discussing preference for leaders?

An integrative conceptual outlook that can deal with such dilemmas distinguishes System 1 from System 2, suggested by Kahneman (2011) and Stanovich and West (2000). System 1 operates automatically and quickly without a sense of control. In Kahneman's terms, this is a system that effortlessly creates impressions and feelings that are sources for many beliefs, preferences, and choices. This system quickly identifies the moods of people with whom we meet, rapidly determines the "chemistry" on a "blind date," and so forth. By contrast, System 2 is slow, allocates attention, examines facts, does calculations, applies cost-benefit analyses, and builds complex ideas—in short, a system characterized by Kahneman as "thorough and diligent." The argument is that electing leaders in political campaigns is essentially a product of System 1, whereas evaluating leaders' work and contributions is based on System 2. In other words, candidates for political leadership positions (e.g., in a U.S. presidential campaign) are not subject to the same criteria we apply, for example, when we evaluate leaders in organizations (Antonakis, Bostardaz, Jacquart, & Shamir, 2016). In the former, case preferences are processed by System 1. Using the metaphor of a camera, System 1 is an automatic snapshot, whereas System 2 is a careful photograph that relies on thorough examinations of such considerations as angles, light, background, and so forth. The automatic processing (as will be elaborated) is related to both phylogenetic biases and culture-bound leadership cues. The political campaign is a unique and prominent event that allows an examination of such processes in a clear and researchable manner.

The Campaign

An example of System 1 "in action" with regard to preferences for leaders was presented in an experiment conducted by Todorov, Mandisodza, Goren, and Hall (2005).The experimenters showed Princeton University students the faces of men for short periods of up to a second and then asked them to rate the faces on various traits, one of which was competence. The faces were not a random sample but those of politicians. Todorov and his colleagues compared the results of elections in different states with the Princeton students' rating, based, as mentioned, on short exposure without a political context (the students did not know who the candidates were). In 70 percent of the ratings for the position of senator, congressman, or governor, the winners in the elections were candidates whose faces the students rated higher in competence.

Addressing the possibility that people relate to general likability rather than to competence, the researchers asked participants to judge various other trait dimensions, such as intelligence and honesty. From a simple halo-effect perspective, competence emerged as the most important trait attribute on which people evaluated candidates for leadership positions. Such remarkable results have been confirmed in Finland, in regional council elections in England, and in various election races in Australia, Germany, and Mexico (Bellew & Todorov, 2007; Olivola & Todorov, 2010). Antonakis and Dalgas (2009) conducted an election game with children and discovered that children and adults were influenced by similar cues in judging competence from facial appearance.

Studies have attempted to explore the elements of this instinct, namely, to figure out what is sensed as "radiated" by the person elected as a leader. Beyond competence, which is the transmission of a sense that the leader can deal successfully with complex problems and challenges (Popper, 2015), researchers at present are attempting to determine whether there are different preferences for leaders under different circumstances (e.g., in war or exerting diplomatic effort). For example, when people were asked to choose a president assuming the country was at war, more people voted for a candidate whose face was perceived as more masculine (Laustsen & Peterson, 2015; Spiska, Dekker, Kruger, & Van Vugt, 2012).

Such studies are at a very initial phase, but we can already discern a sense created by facial cues that is probably more influential than written or oral materials, including parties' platforms. This claim conforms with the centrality attributed to television debates in U.S. political campaigns. An interesting analysis of this argument was presented by Druckman (2003), who analyzed the famous TV debate between Kennedy and Nixon. He found that more people who were listening to the debate on the radio regarded Nixon as the winner, whereas more people who watched the TV debate saw Kennedy as the winner due to his looks.

One way or another, the studies indicate that fact-based assessments or ideological stands apparently have a less decisive role in the preference for leaders. In other words, electing leaders in political campaigns is not necessarily a result of a thorough analysis anchored in System 2. So, to understand the mechanisms underlying preferences for leaders, we have to better grasp how System 1 operates in the campaign context. Specifically, what are the cues that significantly affect preference for leaders?

Research shows that in the context of election of political leaders, certain cues touch biases that are inherent in all of us. When a leader is sensed as competent due to his or her face or the way he or she talks, behaves, or presents a record that is relevant to our concerns, our innate biases lead us to identify the potential leader as an epistemic authority. Such processes are more intense, as mentioned, in weak psychological situations. In most other situations, cues related to the group identity are given greater weight. In the terms discussed, their relevance grows. It is not accidental that Mahatma Gandhi, David Ben-Gurion, and Nelson Mandela were so admired in their collectives. Analysis of their rhetoric, dress, and manner indicates that they relied heavily on central symbols in the collective history. They were admired first and foremost for being symbols of a distinct collective identity (Popper, 2012), and as such they fulfilled the adaptive function of strengthening the sense of "we" (Tomasello, 2014).

Conclusion

Understanding a political campaign from the perspective outlined in this chapter requires analysis of the primary forces underlying preferences for leaders. Such an analysis is based on System 1 and is focused less on leaders' personality and more on the followers' feelings regarding certain leadership cues that the leaders (or the candidates) represent for them. These cues are emotionally connected to biases innate in the voters as individuals and as members of certain (cultural) groups. On the individual level, preference for leaders is primarily related to feelings about the leader's competence—his or her ability to deal with primary adaptive challenges. On the group level, leadership cues are influential when they are felt by members as helping the group to strengthen its coping capabilities as a distinct collective.

Examples that may illustrate the arguments presented are the general election campaign in Israel a year ago and the presidential campaign in the United States. These are good examples, as according to opinion polls in both cases the candidates (Netanyahu and Herzog in Israel and Donald Trump and Hillary Clinton in the United States) were not popular with the public, including significant portions of their own supporters. This paradox can be explained using the arguments and concepts outlined in this chapter. There are certain relevance thresholds in both societies. For many Israelis, a major threshold is associated first and foremost with "security signals" (which are above all military). For example, retired generals have a very high electoral value (beyond a particular personality). Indeed, high-ranking retired officers, particularly combat officers, star in Israeli political life. They have the right leadership cues sensed as essential for dealing with the major adaptive issues facing society.

Netanyahu, for whom the polls and experts predicted a colossal failure in the elections, was most probably favored in the last minute when the voter was faced with his or her primary concerns and biases. Apparently, at the moment of truth (indicated retrospectively in evidence and analyses), Netanyahu's background (he had been an officer in the special forces), his manner of speaking, his age, his experience, and even his voice (this was also an issue during the campaign) were sensed as transmitting more and stronger security signals than his opponent. We may mention that this analysis is relevant to the Israeli context in which the public experiences attributed competence in the area of security as having major adaptive value.

The unexpected rise of Donald Trump (also contrary to predictions of polls and experts) can also be explained in terms of System 1. The fact that Trump is a successful businessman—a billionaire—might signal competence to many. Business acumen might signal that what he has done for his business he will do for the United States. That is, he might be seen as someone who knows how to solve problems. Such an attribution, as noted, has an evolutionary adaptive value, particularly among certain groups in the United States who also see successful businesspeople as American cultural heroes (much like combat officers among certain groups in Israeli society).

So, in a seemingly paradoxical manner, people, as Lipman-Blumen (2007) has shown, may vote for candidates that they clearly do not even like, only because they have an adaptive value determined by emotions derived from innate biases. Such a pattern, as stated, is more evident in situations experienced as crises, uncertainty, or weakness—feelings most probably being experienced nowadays by many in Israel and the United States.

The principles discussed lie within national cultural boundaries. Such an analysis is relatively straightforward in nations with a homogeneous culture. The matter is more complex as regards immigrant societies (like the United States) consisting of various cultural groups. In such cases, group identities might not necessarily match all aspects that opinion leaders expect to be common to all parts of society. As in the case described regarding individuals (Shamir et al., 1993), groups may also have identity hierarchy and can differ in prioritizing identity categories. As discussed, this is reflected more intensively during political campaigns.

As shown in the studies of Kahneman and Tversky, undermining the "rationality myth" is enormously difficult (see Kahneman, 2011) because we (in the West) probably like to perceive ourselves as rational creatures. The possibility that uneducated inferences based on System 1 determine some of the most important decisions we make in our lives is probably hard to digest. Nevertheless, an examination of other forms of analysis is necessary. The direction presented in this chapter not only suggests additional theoretical framework, but may also provide insights that are important for promoting measures needed to prevent, as history has shown, major disasters.

References

Allison, S. T., & Goethals, G. R. (2014). "Now he belongs to the ages": The heroic leadership dynamic and deep narratives of greatness. In G. Goethals, S. Allison, R. Kramer, & D. Mesick (Eds.), *Conceptions of leadership: Enduring ideas and emerging insights.* New York: Palgrave Macmillan.

Antonakis, J., Bostardaz, N., Jacquart, P., & Shamir, B. (2016). Charisma: An ill-defined and ill-measured gift. *Annual Review of Organizational Psychology and Organizational Behavior, 3,* 293–319.

Antonakis, J., & Dalgas, O. (2009). Predicting elections: Child's play. *Science, 232,* 118.

Bellew, C. C., & Todorov, A. (2007). Predicting political elections from rapid and unreflective face judgements. *Proceedings of the National Academy of Sciences of the United States of America, 104,* 17948–17953.

Bennett, H. M., & Sani, F. (2008). Children's subjective identification with social groups: A group reference effect approach. *British Journal of Developmental Psychology, 26,* 381–338.

Bowlby, J. (1988). *A secure base: clinical applications of attachment theory,* London: Routledge.

Buttelmann, D., Zmyj, N., Daum, M., & Carpenter, M. (2013). Selective imitation of in-group over out-group members in 14-month-old infants. *Child Development, 84*(2), 422–428.

Castelnovo, O., Popper, M., & Koren, D. The innate code of charismatic influence. *The Leadership Quarterly* (under review).

Csibra, G., & Gergely, G. (2011). Natural pedagogy as evolutionary adaptation. *Philosophical Transactions of the Royal Society of London B: Biological Sciences, 366*(1567), 1149–1157.

Davis, K. M., & Gardner, W. L. (2012). Charisma under crisis revisited: Presidential leadership, long-term follower effects and contextual influence. *The Leadership Quarterly, 23,* 918–923.

Den Hartog, D. N., House, R. J., Hanges, P. J., Ruiz-Quintanilla, S. A., & Dorfman, P.W. (1999). Culture specific and cross-culturally generalizable implicit leadership theories: Are alternatives of charismatic/transformational leadership universally endorsed? *The Leadership Quarterly, 10*(2), 219–257.

Druckman, J. N. (2003). The power of television images: The first Kennedy-Nixon debate revisited. *Journal of Politics, 65,* 559–571.

Euston, D. R., Gruber, A. J., & McNaughton, B. L. (2012). The role of medial prefrontal cortex in memory and decision making. *Neuron, 76*(6), 1057–1070.

Freud, S. (1920). *A general introduction to psychoanalysis* (American ed., pp. 363–365). New York: Horace Liveright.

Gerstner, C. R., & Day, D.V. (1994). Cross-cultural comparison of leadership prototypes. *The Leadership Quarterly, 5*(2), 121–134.

Hamilton, D. L. (1988). Causal attribution viewed from an information processing perspective. In D. Bar-Tal & A. W. Kruglanski (Eds.), *The social psychology of knowledge* (pp. 359–385). Cambridge, UK: Cambridge University Press.

Heider, F. (1944). Social perception and phenomenal causality. *Psychological Review, 51,* 358–374.

Hofstede, G. (2001). *Culture's consequences: Comparing values, behaviors, institutions, and organizations across nations.* Thousand Oaks, CA: Sage Publications.

Hofstede, G., & Hofstede, G. J. (2005). *Culture and organizations: The software of the mind.* New York: McGraw-Hill.

Huntington, S. (2004). *Who are we?: The challenges to America's national identity.* New York: Simon & Schuster.

Izard. C. E. (1977). *Human emotions.* New York: Plenum Press.

Kahneman, D. (2011). *Thinking, fast and slow.* New York: Farrar, Straus and Giroux.

Kershaw, I. (1998). *1889–1936: Hubris.* London: Penguin Press.

Kinzler, K. D., Corriveau, K. H., & Harris, P. L. (2011). Children's selective trust in native–accented speakers. *Developmental Science, 14*(1), 106–111.

Kirkpatrick, L. A. (2005). *Attachment, evolution, and the psychology of religion.* New York: Guilford Press

Laustern, L., & Peterson, M. B. (2015). Does a competent leader make a good friend?: Conflict, ideology and the psychologies of friendship and followership. *Evolution and Human Behavior, 36,* 286–293.

Lipman-Blumen, J. (2007). Toxic leaders and the fundamental vulnerability of being alive. In B. Shamir, R. Pillai, M. Bligh, & M. Uhl-Bien (Eds.), *Follower-centered perspectives on leadership* (p. 4). Greenwich, CT: Information Age Publishing.

Markus, H., & Kitayama, S. (1991). Culture and self: Implications for cognition, emotion and motivation. *Psychological Review, 98*(2), 224–253.

Maslow, A. (1970). *Motivation and personality.* New York: Harper & Row.

McCann, S. J. H. (1992). Alternative formulas to predict the greatness of US presidents. *Journal of Personality and Social Psychology, 62,* 469–479.

McGuigan, N. (2013). The influence of model status on the tendency of young children to over-imitate. *Journal of Experimental Child Psychology, 116*(4), 962–969.

Meltzoff, A. N., & Moore, M. K. (1977). Imitation of facial and manual gestures by human neonates. *Science, 198,* 75–78.

Mischel, W. (1973). Toward a cognitive social learning conceptualization of personality. *Psychological Review, 80,* 252–283.

Olivola, C. Y., & Todorov, A. (2010). Elected in 100 milliseconds: Appearance-based trait inference and voting. *Journal of Nonverbal Behavior, 34,* 83–110.

Pillai, R. (1996). Crisis and the emergence of charismatic leadership in groups: An experimental investigation. *Journal of Applied Social Psychology, 26,* 544–562.

Popper, M. (2012). *Fact and fantasy about leadership.* Cheltenham, UK: Edward Elgar.

Popper, M. (2013). Leaders perceived as distant or close: Some implications for psychological theory on leadership. *The Leadership Quarterly, 24,* 1–8.

Popper, M. (2015). Followership, deity and leadership. *Journal for the Theory of Social Behaviour.* Retrieved from onlinelibrary.wiley.com/doi/10.1111/jtsb.12096/pdf

Ross, L. D., Amebile, T. M., & Steinmatz, J. L. (1977). Social roles, social controls and biases in social perception processes. *Journal of Personality and Social Psychology, 35,* 485–494.

Schjoedt, U., Stødkilde-Jørgensen, H., Geertz, A. W., Lund, T. E., & Roepstorff, A. (2010). The power of charisma: Perceived charisma inhibits the frontal executive network of believers in intercessory prayer. *Social Cognitive and Affective Neuroscience.* nsq023

Schlesinger, A. M., Jr. (1958). *The coming of the New Deal* (pp. 1–2). Boston: Houghton Mifflin.

Shamir. B., House, R, J., & Arthur, M. B. (1993). The motivational effects of charismatic leadership: A self-concept based theory. *Organizational Science, 4,* 577–593.

Sperber, D., & Wilson, D. (1995). *Relevance: Communication and cognition* (2nd. ed., pp. 2–9). Oxford/Cambridge: Blackwell.

Spiska, B. R., Decker, P. H., Kruger, M., & Van Vugt, M. (2012). Warriors and peacekeepers: Testing a biosocial implicit leadership hypothesis of intergroup relations using masculine and feminine faces. *PLoS One, 7*(1). Retrieved from http://dx.doi.org/10.1371/journal.pone.0030399

Stanovich, K. E., & West, R. F. (2000). Individual differences in reasoning: Implications for the rationality debate. *Behavioral and Brain Science, 23,* 645–665.

Todorov, A., Mandisodza, A. N., Goren, A., & Hall, C. (2005). Inferences of competence from faces predict election outcomes. *Science, 308*(5728), 1623–1626.

Tomasello, M. (2014). *A natural history of human thinking.* Cambridge, MA: Harvard University Press.

Tomasello, M., & Rakoczy, H. (2003). What makes human cognition unique?: From individual to shared to collective intentionality. *Mind and Language, 18,* 121–147.

Van Vugt, M., & Grabo, A. E. (2015). The many faces of leadership: An evolutionary-psychology approach. *Current Directions in Psychological Science, 24*(6), 484–489.

Van Vugt, M., Hogan, R., & Kaiser, R. B. (2008). Leadership, followership, and evolution. *American Psychologist, 63*(3), 182–196.

Weick, K. E. (1995). *Sense making in organizations.* Thousand Oaks, CA: Sage Publications.

Westlake, M. (Ed.). (2000). *Leaders of transition.* London: MacMillan.

Zajonc, R. B. (1980). Feeling and thinking: Preferences need no inferences. *American Psychologist, 35*(2), 151–175.

CHAPTER FIVE

Power, Persuasion, and Bad Leadership

Ronald E. Riggio

At its core, political leadership, or any kind of leadership, is about power and persuasion. Indeed, many definitions of leadership primarily focus on leadership as influence and power. For example, social psychologist Edwin Hollander (1978) defines leadership as "a process of influence between a leader and those who are followers" (p. 1). Zaleznick (1992) suggests that "leadership inevitably requires using power to influence the thoughts and actions of other people" (p. 2). More comprehensive definitions of leadership also incorporate using influence or power to achieve some goals or outcomes (e.g., Hughes, Ginnett, & Curphy, 2009, p. 6). Finally, the most comprehensive definitions of leadership incorporate the idea of "good," or moral, leadership. For example, James MacGregor Burns (1978), in his seminal book *Leadership*, states that the very best leaders adhere to moral principles: "Leadership, in short, is power governed by principle, directed toward raising people to their highest levels of personal motive and social morality" (p. x).

This chapter will examine the role that influence and power play in leadership (particularly, political leadership) and how leaders use their power and influence to attract followers, gain their support, and affect important outcomes. We will also explore the moral or ethical elements of leadership and see how similar forms of power and influence can be used by leaders in "good" and "bad" ways—leading to great accomplishments or immense disasters. This book focuses on the rise of presidential candidate Donald Trump, so it is important to examine the social psychology of the "Trump phenomenon" through the lens of good and bad leadership. At the end of this chapter, we will try to predict, using social psychological principles, the various avenues that the Trump presidency might venture down.

From a scholarly perspective, successful leadership has been viewed in three ways: (1) attaining a position of leadership (what leadership scholars refer to as "leader emergence," or leader "role occupancy"), which refers to getting elected or appointed to a position of leadership; (2) "leader effectiveness," which typically focuses on the achievement of some collective goals or outcomes or some evaluation of the leader's role in achieving outcomes; and (3) "good (or ethical/authentic/moral) leadership," which focuses on doing the "right" things. All too often, little distinction is made between effective and good leadership, but this can create an "ends justifies the means" situation, and that is problematic. If a leader achieves goals but breaks laws, ravages the environment, or alienates and psychologically damages followers, this cannot be labeled "good" leadership. Good leadership should be more than just being an effective leader.

Let's look first at leader emergence. In terms of getting elected or promoted to a leadership position, persuasion and social influence matter. A candidate must first show a desire to attain the position; in political terms, the candidate must "throw his/her hat into the ring." DeRue and Ashford (2010) suggest that leader emergence is a process of "claiming and granting." That is, a leader lays claim to a position, or puts oneself forward, and followers choose to grant, or not grant, that position to the candidate. To appear worthy of the leadership position, the candidate uses persuasion: advancing one's qualifications, suggesting an action plan to achieve desirable goals, articulating a compelling vision of a better future, or promising future rewards to followers. Successful use of persuasion and social influence usually results in attainment of the leadership position.

What about effective leadership? Achieving collective goals also involves the leader's use of persuasion, power, and social influence. A leader can motivate followers through inspirational rhetoric, exhorting them to work hard or emphasizing the benefits associated with goal attainment. The leader can also use authority and power to reward followers for good performance or threaten punishment for failing to reach goals.

What distinguishes effective leadership from good, moral, or ethical leadership? This is tricky. Social psychology has not traditionally dealt with issues of morality or goodness. However, the ethical debacles of the past two decades in government and business, including bribery, lying, and sexual indiscretions by politicians and accounting scandals by corporate giants Enron, WorldCom, and Tyco, triggered a great deal of interest and research on the elements of ethical leadership. Although there have been many attempts to define good or ethical leadership, there are critical elements to consider.

First, good leaders are responsible leaders. That means they focus on doing the right thing, not winning at all costs. Responsible leaders limit collateral damage; they do not achieve goals at the expense of people or the planet. In other words, good and responsible leaders have a sense of stewardship of the people they lead and the community and world in which they live. In the process of achieving goals, good leaders develop followers instead of using and exhausting them. Finally, good leaders leave the team, the organization, or the nation better off than they found them.

Leadership and Power

French and Raven (1959) distinguished five major types, or "bases," of social power. Leaders use these power bases in their interactions with followers to achieve goals. The five power bases are summarized in table 5.1.

Legitimate power is the authority and formal rights that are bestowed on an individual by virtue of the position he or she holds. It is the power inherent in the title or role. A great deal of research in social psychology has demonstrated that legitimate power, or perceived authority alone, can cause followers to obey the leader's commands.

The well-known Milgram (1974) "shock experiments" clearly illustrated how legitimate power can cause a sort of blind obedience. In these experiments, participants played the role of teacher and were supposed to

Table 5.1   French and Raven (1959) Power Bases and Definitions

Power Base	Definition
Legitimate Power	Formal right and authority given by position
Reward Power	Ability to provide resources (money, positions, etc.) to others
Coercive Power	Ability to punish, sanction, or harm others
Expert Power	Power derived because of some valued skill or expertise
Referent Power	Power derived from being admired, liked, or respected by others

teach a learner (actually a confederate in an adjacent room) to memorize pairs of words. Each time the learner made an incorrect response, the teacher was asked to punish the learner with a series of ever-increasing electric shocks. When the confederate learner began to show signs of pain and distress, the teacher often hesitated in administering additional punishment. The teacher was then told by the experimenter, a nondescript man in a white lab coat, who represented the experiment's authority figure, to "please continue." As the shocks increased, the learner screamed in pain and began to protest. Eventually the learner refused to respond. The experimenter urged the teacher to treat nonresponses as incorrect and to continue administering the punishment, giving shocks at levels labeled as "Danger: Severe Shock" and "XXX." The results of the experiment showed that approximately two-thirds of all participants would continue to give dangerous and life-threatening shocks to the helpless learner rather than disobey the legitimate authority of the experimenter.

Leaders, by virtue of the titles and roles that they possess, have a certain amount of legitimate power over followers. High-level leaders, such as presidents of nations, governors of states, and executive officers of corporations, have the authority to issue orders, decide on courses of action, and make appointments and personnel decisions. Take, for example, the U.S. president's powers under crisis situations. Although the president is obliged to seek congressional authority to declare war or deal with other serious emergencies that imperil the nation, U.S. presidents have, in recent years, simply taken action, relying on the legitimate power of the presidency, and there have been few repercussions (Edelson, 2013).

A good leader wields legitimate power fairly and wisely, taking care to never "abuse the authority" associated with his or her position. Yet, leaders learn that followers will often just blindly carry out the leader's directives, and this opens up the possibility of abuse of power. Recent examples include President George W. Bush's authorization of waterboarding as an interrogation technique and President Obama's ordering of the killing of Osama bin Laden—each carried out without congressional consultation or approval, but resulting in few repercussions, owing to a general acquiescence to the president's legitimate power base.

Perhaps the most commonly used power base is reward power. This is the leader's ability to provide rewards to followers in exchange for their devotion, obedience in carrying out the leader's orders, or to simply encourage desirable behavior (e.g., working toward a shared purpose). The strength of a leader's reward power is directly related to the resources, financial and otherwise, that the leader controls. Importantly, a good leader should maintain fair and equitable transactions and not take advantage of followers by asking for a lot with little in return.

Coercive power involves the use of punishment or the threat of punishment. Excessive use of coercive power is most commonly associated with bad leadership. Tyrants, dictators, and despots, ranging from Hitler and Stalin to Pol Pot and Saddam Hussein, are all recognized for their excessive use of punishment in the form of torture, execution, and genocide. Coercive power is an important tool in the leader's arsenal, but it should be used sparingly and fairly (i.e., punishment befitting the crime) because of the human tendency to fight back and resent those who punish.

Expert power is power derived from the leader's possession of knowledge, skills, or experience. In most instances, and particularly in business leadership, expertise is critical. Social identity theories of leadership (e.g., Hogg, 2001) argue that the leader who emerges in a particular collective is the member who is most prototypical of what the group is all about. In the workplace, and presumably in politics, the leader who emerges is often the one with the most experience and expertise. In recent years, however, with the Tea Party revolution and the recent popularity of "outsider" candidates, U.S. voters seem to be rejecting candidates with greater expertise over those who offer an alternative to the traditional, experienced, "insider" politician (see Riggio, 2005). We will return to this topic later.

Referent power is derived from the relationship between the leader and followers. Individuals who are admired, liked, and respected have referent power over others because they choose to allow the individuals to have power over them. The referent power of a leader is most vividly illustrated by leader fame or charisma. The United States has a long history of putting forward celebrated persons for elected office, including the presidency. War heroes, ranging from Washington to Grant to Eisenhower, received a great deal of popular support. For these former army generals, winning on the battlefield led to admiration, which led to their election. Referent power also played a part in the election of appealing and attractive candidates, such as John F. Kennedy, who appeared youthful, vibrant, and handsome (and was also a war hero), and a former motion picture star, Ronald Reagan. Indeed, it has been suggested that perhaps the worst U.S. president, Warren G. Harding, was nominated and elected primarily based on his physical appeal and supposed "presidential" manner (Gladwell, 2005).

It is important to note that unlike the other power bases, referent power is determined by the followers' willingness to devote themselves to a particular leader because of some sort of perceived connection. It could be the excitement and familiarity brought on by a person's celebrity. This would certainly explain the attraction of voters to actors Arnold Schwarzenegger (governor of California); Fred Thompson, George Murphy, and Al Franken (U.S. senators); and Sonny Bono and Fred Grandy (U.S. congressmen), along with President Reagan. More recently, the rise of presidential candidate Donald Trump combines his celebrity (referent power) with some perceived business acumen (expert power) and a "tell-it-like-it-is" style that gains the admiration of a certain portion of voters.

An obvious concern with a leader's use of referent power is that followers can become blindly devoted to the leader, imbuing him or her with extraordinary powers and abilities. Historically, we have even seen leaders deified, as in the current situation in North Korea. An abuse of referent power occurs when a leader allows such nonsense, and it is particularly bad when leaders fuel their followers' devotion by claiming to be something they are not or laying claim to extraordinary powers that the leader could not ever possess (i.e., religious leaders claiming to have the power to heal). A minor version of this occurred in the 2016 presidential campaign, with Donald Trump claiming that he knows how to negotiate and "cut deals" with foreign leaders and that he can build a huge wall at the U.S.-Mexico border to stop illegal immigration.

Leaders, by virtue of their positions and because of leadership dynamics, typically possess a great deal of power, often having significant levels of each of the core power bases. This gives leaders a decided advantage over followers. And, as we have seen, these power bases can be used in both positive and negative ways. But power is not the only weapon wielded by leaders. Leaders also learn specific persuasion and influence techniques designed to influence followers to achieve ends.

Leadership and Influence Tactics

In his book *Influence: Science and Practice*, social psychologist Robert Cialdini (2001) outlines a number of influence tactics that are regularly used by experts in persuasion, such as salespeople, con artists, lobbyists, and the like, to try to persuade others to alter their attitudes or their behavior. These same influence tactics are regularly used by leaders to influence followers, to gain their support and devotion, and to persuade them to take action. Each of these influence tactics involves deeply embedded social and psychological processes that make them very hard to resist. We will explore several of these tactics of social influence and how each can be used in a positive fashion or in a negative way, corresponding to "good" and "bad" leadership tactics.

Perhaps the most common strategy that leaders use to persuade followers to work together is invoking the in-group–out-group bias (or what is commonly called the "we-they" feeling). This deeply seated psychological phenomenon involves calling on followers, the in-group, to pull together to defeat an out-group, the competition or, in extremes, the enemy. In wartime, the enemy is easily defined, and the positive outcome of this process is a sense of cohesiveness among the in-group members as they work hard to fight against the out-group. In business, this is the heart of the competitive, capitalistic system, motivating an organization to work hard to beat out the competition.

Its use in politics is another story. All too often, the out-group is the other political party. It is this in-group–out-group bias that has led to the current state of U.S. politics, with the Republican and Democratic parties using each other as the out-group to motivate and mobilize their own party members. The problem with this process is that the in-group–out-group bias is the root of prejudice and discrimination, and the process has gone to the extreme. What were once adversaries have become bitter enemies. The terms "conservatives" and "liberals" have become insulting epithets designed to vilify the out-group members. The situation in U.S. politics has become so intransigent that it has led to a near complete deadlock, with the two parties in Congress unable to work together on just about anything.

The in-group–out-group bias was well illustrated by the work of Muzafer Sherif and colleagues (Sherif et al., 1961) in their famous Robber's Cave experiment. Using a boy's summer camp, Sherif created arbitrary groups by having boys in different cabins compete against one another in a series of athletic competitions. Over time, the two factions began to vilify each other, leading to hatred, fights, and destructive raids on the other group's cabin. In another well-known demonstration, a fifth grade teacher was able to create a similarly destructive situation by simply dividing the class into blue-eyed and brown-eyed groups of children (ABC News, 1970).

The Cold War, and its labeling of Communist enemies, and the War on Terror are examples of situations where U.S. presidents have used the we-they feeling to advantage in gaining follower motivation and support to fight the enemy. The effects, however, can be harsh and long lasting. Consider that the United States only recently opened relationships with its "Communist" neighbor, Cuba, after six decades of isolation and conflict. Moreover, there is still quite a bit of resistance to opening relationships with Cuba, with lingering fear that the Cuban government is untrustworthy.

U.S. political leaders use the in-group–out-group bias as an influence tactic all the time, and there is nothing particularly wrong with that, as long as the out-group is one that poses a serious threat to the well-being of the nation. A problem occurs, however, when some identified out-group becomes an undeserved scapegoat, with the leader using the group to influence followers. Such is currently the case with groups such as Muslims, Syrian refugees, and Mexican immigrants to the United States, who are labeled "terrorists" or "criminals." We have seen the damaging results of this scapegoating, as the process escalates to violence against Muslim and refugee groups (Abdelkader, 2016). Note that scapegoating is not just a tool used by conservatives. On the Left, we see conservative demonstrators labeled as "racists" or "fascists," and violence has erupted as a result (CBS News, 2016). Both parties have been guilty.

Another leader-influence tactic is the use of fear appeals and the leader's promise of protecting followers from danger. The world can indeed be a dangerous place, and it is a political leader's duty to do all that she or he can to protect followers from harm. Reassurance that the leader can indeed protect followers helps to decrease follower stress and concern. As Franklin Delano Roosevelt famously proclaimed during the time of the Great Depression, "We have nothing to fear, but fear itself." FDR was addressing what he felt were citizens' unfounded fears. When a leader creates an artificial climate of fear (argumentum in terrorem), however, or when a leader promises to protect followers when protection is impossible, this is an unfair and bad leadership practice. The 2016 U.S. presidential campaign was rife with fear appeals, including warnings of terrorist attacks, economic recession, rioting at the convention (Donald Trump), Russian aggression, congressional gridlock (Hillary Clinton), confiscation of firearms, and persecution of Christians (Ted Cruz). Such fear appeals help to solidify follower support for the candidate who promises protection from these dangers. Threats of war, revolution, violence, terrorism, and the like, if not based in reality, represent a bad leadership tactic designed to manipulate followers.

Cialdini (2001) lists "liking" as another influence tactic, whereby the persuader tries to somehow make a connection with the target. One way to do this is to appear to be similar in some way to the target. Politicians regularly try to find common ground on issues when speaking to specific groups of voters. They may try to dress like their potential followers, adopt an accent, mention a fondness for some local custom or tradition, and the like—all in an effort to increase liking by appearing similar to them. This is, of course, is linked to the earlier concept of increasing one's referent power base. While not particularly damaging in and of itself, when followers see a leader as being "like me," it can lead to a sort of blind following, and that can be problematic.

The United States in particular has had an interesting relationship with leaders and leadership. Jim Meindl and associates called this the "Romance of Leadership" (Meindl, Ehrlich, & Dukerich, 1985), which suggests that we have a deep attachment to leaders, and we often believe they are the main key to getting things done. This causes us to overattribute the successes and failures to actions of the leader and to undervalue the contributions of followers. As Americans, we love to place our leaders on a pedestal, but if things go poorly, Americans are just as happy to knock them off by rejecting their reelection or refusing to follow. This romance of leaders increases the incidence of blind following. As we saw in the Milgram studies, people are all too willing to unquestioningly follow the directives of leaders and authorities. This gives rise to conformity. In situations that are ambiguous, or in situations that are high in uncertainty, people look to leaders for direction, but they also look to one another and tend to blindly go along with what the leader tells them to do or follow the course of action of the majority. Cialdini (2001) calls this "social proof." If we don't know what to do in a given ambiguous situation, we look to others for direction and simply go along.

During election times, this tendency to conform and go along with the crowd leads to a bandwagon effect. We saw this in the early days of the 2016 U.S. presidential primaries, with the rising popularity of Donald Trump—a candidate with no government experience and checkered success in the business world. Potential voters, particularly those who were disengaged and disillusioned with the more establishment Republican political candidates (e.g., Jeb Bush, Chris Christie), seemed to jump on the Trump bandwagon as his popularity grew. A similar process occurred in the Democratic Party with Senator Bernie Sanders, who was not a Democrat (although he does, unlike Trump, have significant government experience) but was able to develop growing popular support with disillusioned Democrats, giving the supposed runaway favorite, Hillary Clinton, a competitive race.

The obvious problem with blind following and the bandwagon effect is that it tends to inhibit critical thinking on the part of followers. Uncertain about direction, many of these individuals are drawn to the social proof of the candidate's growing popularity and conform, joining the growing number of voters jumping on the candidate's bandwagon.

One particular influence tactic that can be used by leaders to insidious ends uses a form of the authority/legitimate power base and involves appealing to followers by associating one's leadership with God. Here is a quote by a famous leader that embodies this tactic: "I believe today that my conduct is in accordance with the will of the Almighty Creator." The quote, of course, is by Adolf Hitler. Throughout history, leaders have tried to align themselves with divinity to attract and keep followers, to the point of declaring themselves gods.

A major problem with using the divine as a tool to gain follower support, or to influence them, is twofold: First, it is impossible to determine whether the leader is indeed acting in accordance with the deity's wishes. Second, it takes advantage of followers who are wary of challenging God's commands and therefore obey the leader out of fear of offending God. A bad leader is one who makes demands of followers by claiming that he or she is following God's wishes or that God is somehow in league with the leader. Even worse, a bad leader offers an unfair exchange by promising eternal salvation in exchange for follower loyalty. A good leader uses divine (or ethical, or moral) principles to guide his or her actions as a check to make sure that she or he is doing the right thing. As Abraham Lincoln noted, "My concern is not whether God is on our side; my greatest concern is to be on God's side."

Why Good Leaders Turn Bad

As Lord Acton famously stated, "All power tends to corrupt; absolute power corrupts absolutely." Although this is an extreme statement, when and why does power, and the use of influence tactics, move from good (or at least neutral) to the dark side? We have already suggested that good leaders use power in a responsible way: they try hard to do the right things and avoid such strategies as winning at all costs. Good leaders attempt to minimize the harm that comes from the use of power and influence and are particularly concerned to not unnecessarily damage their constituents in the leadership process. Good leaders do not *use* followers, but they employ them in getting things done. In the end, good leaders should leave followers better off than when they began leading.

So why is power such a corruptible force? Leadership ethicist Terry Price (2006) suggests that as leaders become more powerful, they begin to believe that they are somehow above the law. Powerful leaders can surround themselves with followers who are devoted, compliant, and adoring, and they are perfectly willing to do the leader's bidding. Over time, some leaders begin to take advantage of this situation, eventually believing that the rules that govern others don't apply to them. Political leaders, falling prey to this exception making, may begin to believe that it is okay to take bribes, engage in illicit affairs, or order followers to engage in illegal behavior. We saw this in the 2016 presidential campaign when candidate Donald Trump exhorted his supporters to deal roughly with protesters. "If you see somebody throw a tomato, knock the crap out of them would you? Just knock the hell out of them. . . . I'll pay for the legal fees, I promise." Trump, who has money and power, likely viewed this as not encouraging followers to break the law (assault and battery), which would be a crime, but part of his right as a powerful and wealthy public figure.

Of course, it is also the case that leader personality and character play a part in distinguishing good and bad leaders. For example, it is quite clear that narcissism is related to leader emergence (Grijalva et al., 2015), and this is particularly true for higher-level leadership positions, such as heads of state. It is not hard to imagine that narcissism could be behind the drive to get to a leadership position, and narcissism can provide the individual with the sense of superiority that makes him or her feel worthy of top-level leadership. Maccoby (2003), however, distinguishes between what he calls "productive" and "destructive" narcissistic leaders. Destructive narcissistic leaders lack empathy, are exploitative, are enamored of power, and aim to win at all costs. Productive narcissists get things done, but they are less exploitative. As in many things, leaders who are too extreme—too narcissistic, too self-absorbed, or too powerful—can be dangerous.

Antidotes to Unfair Leader Use of Power and Influence Tactics

What can be done to prevent the rise of bad leaders, and what can be done to keep leader use of power and influence in check? First, systems must be in place to prevent the wrong types of people from attaining positions of leadership. In the business world, this can be accomplished through careful screening and selection processes or by "rehabilitating" leaders through increasing their self-awareness of their inappropriate behavior regarding the use of power and influence (Hogan, Hogan, & Kaiser, 2011). In politics, it is not so easy to control the selection of candidates for leadership positions. Candidates can easily put their names forward and find a reasonable number of voters to support them. So, it is up to the voters/followers themselves to prevent bad individuals from gaining leadership positions. How can this be done?

In her book *The Allure of Toxic Leaders*, Jean Lipman-Blumen (2005) argues that bad leaders could not exist if followers did not support them. One of her solutions is for followers to detect the early signs of leader toxicity and stand up to them. We saw this in the 2016 U.S. presidential election as an anti–Donald Trump movement began. Opponents of Trump point to his hateful rhetoric and scapegoating tactics as a sign that Trump might become a dictator (Loyola, 2016). The anti-Trump movement first started as a grassroots effort and then became stronger and more systematically organized. Historically, the overthrow of many leaders begins with a groundswell of follower resistance.

Ira Chaleff (2009) argues that followers have to be courageous to stand up to their leaders when the leaders do the wrong thing or choose the wrong path. Developing followers who are courageous, ethical, and feel empowered to take action will help in keeping leaders in check. Having systems in place to hold leaders accountable is also important. Johnson (2007) suggests that creating an ethical climate in an organization (or in the governance structure of a political entity), that includes high ethical performance standards, goes a long way in influencing members to engage in moral reasoning and speaking up when potential violations are imminent.

We are seeing a growing concern among leadership scholars to move beyond simple "effective" leadership, to attempting to define and measure "good" leadership. A number of theories have been proposed, including "authentic leadership," which includes leader self-awareness of one's own weaknesses and shortcomings, being fair-minded and open/transparent, and possessing an "internalized moral perspective" (see Avolio & Gardner, 2005; Walumbwa, Avolio, Gardner, Wernsing, & Peterson, 2008). More recent theories include "benevolent leadership" (Karakas & Sarigollu, 2012) and "virtuous leadership" (Riggio, Zhu, Reina, & Maroosis, 2010). These approaches to "good" leadership all emphasize the importance of the character of the leader, drawing on philosophical notions of goodness ranging from the ancient Greeks to Confucianism and Eastern philosophies. The selection of leaders of good character and the ongoing development of leaders' character are essential for promoting good leadership, particularly given the temptations of power and influence that can steer a good leader astray.

Social Psychology and the Trump Phenomenon

The rise of Donald Trump, from celebrity businessman to presidential candidate, owes a great deal to social psychological processes that underlie leader emergence. Trump possesses several of the core leader power bases that appeal to supporters: his supposed business acumen and ability to make deals suggests expertise in running the country; his claims to "make America great again" suggest that there will be financial and emotional rewards (i.e., the pride instilled by Trump's campaign slogan of "Make America great again"); and, like most politicians, his use of coercive power and fear appeals, warning that electing his opponent will spell disaster. Trump makes great use of the in-group–out-group bias by suggesting that we pull together to fend off enemies, ranging from Muslims, to illegal immigrants, to Chinese business enterprise, and these tactics have been successful. In short, these tactics have worked well in securing the Republican presidential nomination (leader emergence). But what about his effectiveness as a leader?

The question that remains is, what kind of president would Donald Trump actually be? Of course, it is impossible to predict, but what might we conclude from the social psychology of good and bad leadership? One possibility (and one that his Democratic and liberal detractors contend) is that he will try to rule in a dictatorial fashion, using immigrants, Muslims, and other groups as a means to build allegiance in his followers, and these scapegoated groups will not fare well. He will use threats of military and financial sanctions to intimidate foreign nations, and he will focus on winning (achieving his goals) without concern for the long-term consequences and collateral damage that will occur.

Another possibility suggested by social psychology, however, is that the power of the role of U.S. president, and the constitutional checks and balances on the president's power, will require Trump to accommodate and alter both his stated priorities (e.g., "building a wall," confronting China on trade) and his divisive tactics (as President Obama famously said, as president "you represent the entire country"). In this case, the seasoned businessman might realize that success requires making compromises and concessions, and he may back off of the blustering and bullying tactics that got him elected and decide to do what it takes to get things done. Only time will tell.

References

ABC News. (1970). Eye of the storm (Video, 16 mm film).

Abdelkader, E. (2016). *When Islamophobia turns violent: The 2016 U.S. presidential elections*. Special report by the Bridge Initiative. Washington, D.C.: Georgetown University.

Avolio, B. J., & Gardner, W. L. (2005). Authentic leadership development: Getting to the root of positive forms of leadership. *The Leadership Quarterly, 16*, 315–338.

Burns, J. M. (1978). *Leadership.* New York: Harper.

CBS News. (2016, May 28). Violence as Trump brings immigration rhetoric to border. Retrieved from http://www.cbsnews.com/news/donald-trump-protesters-violent-california-rally-gop-election-2016.

Chaleff, I. (2009). *The courageous follower: standing up to and for our leaders* (3rd ed.). San Francisco: Berrett-Koehler.

Cialdini, R. B. (2001). *Influence: science and practice* (4th ed.). Needham Heights, MA: Allyn & Bacon.

DeRue, D. S., & Ashford, S. J. (2010). Who will lead and who will follow?: A social process of leadership identity construction in organizations. *Academy of Management Review, 35,* 627–647.

Edelson, C. (2013). *Emergency presidential power: From the drafting of the Constitution to the War on Terror.* Madison: University of Wisconsin Press.

French, J. R. P., & Raven, B. H. (1959). The bases of social power. In D. Cartwright (Ed.), *Studies in social power* (pp. 150–167). Ann Arbor: University of Michigan Press.

Gladwell, M. (2005). *Blink: The power of thinking without thinking.* New York: Little, Brown & Co.

Grijalva, E., Harms, P. D., Newman, D. A., Gaddis, B. H., & Fraley, R. C. (2015). Narcissism and leadership: A meta-analytic review of linear and nonlinear relationships. *Personnel Psychology, 68,* 1–47.

Hogan, J., Hogan, R., & Kaiser, R. B. (2011). Management derailment. In S. Zedeck (Ed.), *APA handbook of industrial and organizational psychology* (Vol. 3, pp. 555–575), *Maintaining, expanding, and contracting the organization.* Washington, D.C.: American Psychological Association.

Hogg, M. A. (2001). A social identity theory of leadership. *Personality and Social Psychology Review, 5,* 184–200.

Hollander, E. P. (1978). *Leadership dynamics: A practical guide to effective relationships.* New York: The Free Press.

Hughes, R. L., Ginnett, R. C., & Curphy, G. J. (2009). *Leadership: Enhancing the lessons of experience.* Boston: McGraw-Hill.

Johnson, C. E. (2007). Best practices in ethical leadership. In J. A. Conger and R. E. Riggio (Eds.), *The practice of leadership* (pp. 150–171). San Francisco: Jossey-Bass.

Karakas, F., & Sarigollu, E. (2012). Benevolent leadership: Conceptualization and construct development. *Journal of Business Ethics, 108,* 537–553.

Lipman-Blumen, J. (2005). *The allure of toxic leaders: Why we follow destructive bosses and corrupt politicians—and how we can survive them.* Oxford: Oxford University Press.

Loyola, M. (2016, February 11). Dictatorship, American style. *National Review.* Retrieved from http://www.nationalreview.com/article/431135/donald-trump-dictatorship-american-style.

Maccoby, M. (2003). *The productive narcissist: The promise and peril of visionary leaders.* New York: Broadway Books.

Meindl, J. R., Ehrlich, S. B., & Dukerich, J. M. (1985). The romance of leadership. *Administrative Science Quarterly, 30,* 78–102.

Milgram, S. (1974). *Obedience to authority: An experimental view.* New York: Harper & Row.

Price, T. L. (2006). *Understanding ethical failures in leadership.* Cambridge: Cambridge University Press.

Riggio, R. E. (2005). It's the leadership, stupid: An I-O psychology perspective on the 2004 U.S. presidential election. *The Industrial-Organizational Psychologist, 42,* 21–26.

Riggio, R. E., Zhu, W., Reina, C., & Maroosis, J. (2010). Virtue-based measurement of ethical leadership: The Leadership Virtues Questionnaire. *Consulting Psychology Journal, 62,* 235–250.

Sherif, M., Harvey, O. J., White, B. J., Hood, W. R., & Sherif, C. W. (1961). *Intergroup conflict and cooperation: The Robbers' Cave experiment.* Norman: University of Oklahoma Institute of Intergroup Relations.

Walumbwa, F. O., Avolio, B. J., Gardner, W. L., Wernsing, T. S., & Peterson, S. J. (2008). Authentic leadership: Development and validation of a theory-based measure. *Journal of Management, 34,* 89–126.

Zaleznik, A. (1992, March–April). Managers and leaders: Are they different? *Harvard Business Review* [originally published in 1977].

CHAPTER SIX

Nationalist Politics: The Role of Predispositions and Emotions

Michael C. Grillo

Here I discuss support for Donald J. Trump in the context of nationalist politics, as it is understood in the fields of international relations and comparative politics. The focus of this chapter is twofold. First, I describe the process through which Trump's nationalist rhetoric can mobilize mass support. And second, I develop and test a causal model of support for Trump. The theoretical approach I use to understand support for Trump is symbolic politics, which holds that the root causes of nationalist mobilization and conflict are antagonistic narratives and predispositions that elicit strong emotional responses in people that guide decision making (Kaufman, 2001; 2006; 2015).

First, I briefly describe the defining features of nationalism and how it applies to Trump's campaign rhetoric. Second, I discuss competing explanations of nationalist/ethnic conflict that have been put forth by political scientists. And third, I develop a modified version of symbolic politics' causal model of nationalist mobilization, which I assess with 2016 American National Election Studies (ANES) pilot data.

Before proceeding, I must preface that the following analysis is preliminary and exploratory for two reasons. First, at the time of writing, the process of Trump's nationalist mobilization was still underway. And second, and relatedly, the data used in this analysis is also preliminary.

Donald Trump's Nationalist Politics

Scholarly definitions of nationalism are many. Broadly speaking, nationalism is a shared identity based on a common homeland and cultural heritage (that can include artifacts such as language, ethnicity, religion, etc.). At the heart of nationalism is the sense that the people (i.e., the nation) must have the ability to live their lives free from outside influence, thus having complete control over their destinies and territories (Hutchinson and Smith, 1994, p. 4). For the majority of nationalist movements, the state should be defined and controlled by the nation so that it reflects its interests (Gellner, 2008; Hobbsbawn, 2012; Smith, 1993). All ethnic and nationalist movements are defined by a myth-symbol complex, which is a set of narratives and other cultural artifacts (e.g., origin myths, language, common culture, etc.) that establishes the nation's identity, criteria for membership, territory, values, and whom the group views as rivals or enemies (Kaufman, 2015; Smith, 1991; 1999). While nationalism is sometimes not defined by racial or ethnic superiority (Greenfeld, 1993), in most instances, nationalism promotes antipathy toward out-groups, thus setting the stage for conflict (Kaufman, 2015; Saideman, 2012).

From this perspective, American nationalism is an interesting case. On the one hand, many have argued that the American case is an example of civic nationalism, where the centerpiece of national identity is not race or ethnicity, but rather shared values such as individualism, egalitarianism, support for democratic institutions, and so on (Pickus, 2009). On the other hand, many racist and white supremacists have argued that the United States is a country that was created by and for white Protestants. Historically, such notions have been used as the basis and justification for discrimination against African Americans and various immigrant groups (Blum, 2015).

When examining his rhetoric, it is apparent that Trump is appealing to the chauvinistic and rancorous side of American nationalism. This is also evidenced by the support he has among key figures in the Ku Klux Klan. His campaign slogan, "Make American Great Again," suggests that the United States is in a state of decline and needs to be revitalized. Through his official campaign Web site and public statements, Trump makes it clear that the source of America's woes are illegal immigrants, Islamic terrorism, the unfair trade practices of other countries, and political correctness that prevents Americans from honestly addressing these problems for what they are. Thus, for Trump, the relative decline of America's power, influence, and quality of life has been caused by these outsiders/others, and his campaign has sought to appeal to mass-level fears, frustrations, and feelings of victimization, especially among the white, middle-aged middle class. Indeed, Trump has written and noted in many speeches that unemployment and wage stagnation among the middle class has been a direct result of immigration and trade policies (Moore & Kudlow, 2015).

Illegal immigration is the issue that Trump has been the most vocal on, and one of the few where he has laid out a clear policy prescription: building a wall on the U.S.-Mexican border and having Mexico fund the project. The majority of Trump's comments regarding immigration have targeted Latinos, with Muslims placing second. His most infamous comment, which he made at the opening speech of his campaign, was how the Mexican government is sending the worst of their population to the United States (e.g., rapists, thieves, and drug dealers). Later in that same speech, he broadened this statement to include Latin American and Middle Eastern countries (*Washington Post*, 2015). Furthermore, Trump has claimed that Mexico is intentionally sending their criminals to the United States because they do not want to support them (Moreno, 2015).

Trump's comments on immigration and other issues have been particularly derogatory toward Hispanics. For example, he tweeted that the majority of violent crimes in the United States are perpetrated by Hispanics and African Americans. In another tweet, he accused primary opponent Jeb Bush of having an affinity for illegals because his wife is Mexican (Moreno, 2015). In response to the announcement of a new Ford plant in Mexico, Trump remarked, "They're going to build a plant and illegals are going drive those cars right over the border.... And they'll probably end up stealing the cars" (Reyson & Brown, 2016). Furthermore, when two of his supporters assaulted a Hispanic man, he initially refused to condemn their actions, instead noting that his supporters "are passionate" (Moreno, 2015).

Another target of Trump for both immigration and terrorism has been Muslims. When interviewed by Anderson Cooper, Trump noted that "Islam hates us" and how "there is an unbelievable hatred of us" (Sherfinski, 2016). When Cooper further pressed the question of whether we are in conflict with radical Islam or the religion as a whole, Trump played up the security dilemma, noting, "It's radical, but it's very hard to define. It's very hard to separate because you don't know who's who" (Sherfinski,

2016). At a campaign rally, he noted how extremely large numbers of Muslims lauded the World Trade Center's destruction on September 11 (Kessler, 2015). Trump has also stated that Muslims should be prohibited from entering the United States. Moreover, he noted how the government should create a database of Muslims living in the United States, requiring that their faith be listed on their identification (Hensch, 2015), and how he would support warrantless searches and shutting down mosques (Obeidallah, 2015).

In regard to external threats, Trump has pointed to the unsavory trade practices of such countries as Mexico and China. On this front, China has been the centerpiece of Trump's rhetoric, arguing that China has "raped" the United States with its policies of currency manipulation and illegal practices in the areas of "export subsidies and lax labor and environmental standards" (BBC, 2016). Trump has tweeted about how China has been taking American jobs, controlled the trade agenda, and negatively affected U.S. markets with their economic policies (Schroeder, 2015). On the issue of trade, Trump promotes a neo-mercantilist model of economic nationalism, where the United States should increase tariffs on foreign goods (as high as 35%), enact policies to prohibit American companies from outsourcing American jobs, and maintain a naval presence in the South China Sea as a deterrent (Trump Official Campaign Web site).

The fact that Trump has become the nominee of the Republican Party, despite not having the support of many party elites and key donors, shows that his nationalist message has resonated with a sizeable segment of the population. This raises the question of how and why a nationalist candidate like Trump has been able to garner so much support. In the following section, I highlight some of the potential answers offered by political scientists.

How and Why Nationalist Leaders Gain Support among the Masses

Within political science, explanations for why nationalist movements develop, mobilize support, and lead to conflict (both violent and nonviolent) are theoretically divided between rationalist and symbolic politics approaches to political behavior. The former group of explanations are based on the assumption that individuals rationally pursue innate material interests (e.g., power, prosperity, safety). Conversely, the latter assumes that nationalist politics are driven by predispositions (e.g., prejudice, ideology, values, biases) that prompt people to emotionally respond to stimuli, which in turn becomes the basis of their decision making. While both of these approaches stress the importance of political leaders in the process of nationalist mobilization and conflict, they approach the place of leaders and followers within the process in different ways.

Rationalist approaches are built upon rational actor assumptions from economics, which have been utilized in various theories (e.g., realism, rational choice, and game theory). While rationalist approaches seek to explain nationalist politics, they interestingly dismiss the notion that nationalism itself, and all the ideas and beliefs associated with it, is the primary source of conflict. Instead, these theories take an "instrumentalist" view of nationalism, which contends that nationalism is just one of many means that individuals and groups can use to achieve their political goals (Fearon, 1995). Hence, individuals rationally choose to align themselves with a nationalist cause, or any other movement, if they see it as a viable way to achieve their material interests, which usually center on economics or security.

The economic explanation is straightforward; individuals and groups will mobilize behind a nationalist cause in response to economic inequality or "relative deprivation" (Gurr, 1970). In terms of security, rationalists contend that nationalist mobilization and conflict are caused by "information failures" and "commitment problems," which are abundant in weak or transitioning states (Lake & Rothchild, 1998; Snyder, 2000). In such states, groups are concerned for their safety and take measures to secure themselves, which then prompts other groups to respond similarly. This creates a security dilemma, where mistrust and uncertainty regarding other groups' intentions lead to conflict (Lake & Rothchild, 1998; Posen, 1993).

Leaders can manipulate this process in two ways. First, they can capitalize on intergroup fears and promote nationalism as a way to either advance or resuscitate their political careers (Snyder, 2000) or distract the masses from their failures (Brass, 1997). Second, they can use peer pressure or rewards and punishments to gain mass support (Hardin, 1995; Kuran, 1998).

While rationalist approaches provide valuable insights about the domestic conditions that make the rise of nationalism and the outbreak of conflict more likely (especially in weak and transitioning states), they fail to account for the fact that nationalism is a strong identity that can influence how individuals and groups see themselves and others, as well as establish group values and interests. Furthermore, by reducing nationalism to one of many sets of ideas that can mobilize people, such accounts cannot explain why rational actors would support nationalism over other personal interests (Kaufman, 2001). Moreover, there is a methodological problem, as researchers mostly rely on elite actions as their source of evidence, from which they infer mass-level motivations.

Contrary to rationalism, symbolic politics contends that the causes of nationalist mobilization and conflict are hostile narratives and predispositions that justify hostility toward rival groups. Leaders present narratives laden with myths and symbols to emotionally rouse the public. These emotional responses in turn prompt individuals to follow nationalist leaders, support discriminatory policies, mobilize, and engage in violence (Kaufman, 2001; 2006; 2015).

According to Kaufman, the key factors of symbolic politics that determine whether groups can mobilize and engage in conflict are "symbolic predispositions, perceived threat, leadership, and organization" (2015, p. 12). These factors form a multistep causal chain where narratives lead to predispositions (specifically prejudice) that cause threat perceptions. Threat perceptions, in turn, trigger public support for mobilization and the creation of organizations that can facilitate it. Political leaders can contribute to this process by manipulating narratives, predispositions, threat perceptions, and support for mobilization via their framing of issues, which can either escalate or deescalate a conflict. Moreover, they can also contribute to the creation of organization to facilitate action, which I will not address here for the sake of efficiency and because of data limitations (Kaufman, 2015, p. 60).

First, there are predispositions, which is the root cause. People can acquire predispositions via socialization from larger narratives. The majority of identity groups (e.g., racial, ethnic, religious) usually have negative predispositions against rival out-groups. Defined, "predispositions are durable inclinations people have to feel positively or negatively about an object" (Kaufman, 2015, p. 13). Predispositions can consist of biases, values, ideology, religious beliefs, and prejudices, which are the most important in symbolic politics. Predispositions are important because they can prompt individuals to emotionally respond to such stimuli as political rhetoric, events, and actions taken by individuals and groups (Kaufman, 2015). For example, if an individual dislikes Muslims and believes that they are inherently violent, this predisposition will influence how they process information about Muslims. Islamic terrorism and anti-Muslim rhetoric will produce negative emotional responses that reinforce threat perceptions, which can lead to support for such measures as imposing a ban on Muslims.

The second factor is threat. A key determinant of whether violent or nonviolent conflict will occur is whether a group believes they are threatened by another. Threat is critical because it shapes whether politics will be driven by personal and ideological concerns (e.g., reducing or expanding government programs) or fear and prejudices (e.g., banning Muslims, building a wall) (Kaufman, 2015). Threat can be realistic (e.g., economic standing, physical safety) or symbolic (e.g., status). If groups genuinely perceive that they are threatened, politics can become dangerous and lead to discrimination or violence. Trump has appealed to both types of threats. On one hand, he has appealed to the loss of America's status in the world, while on the other he has appealed to economic decline and physical threats caused by immigrants and Islamic terrorism.

Third, there have to be credible nationalist leaders that can frame the situation in a way that appeals to people's predispositions (Kaufman, 2015). Trump's background as a wealthy celebrity businessman and political outsider helps him to cast himself as a credible leader who knows how to manage organizations, knows about economics and how to facilitate deals, and cannot be "bought off" like other politicians. In terms of rhetoric, he mostly promotes a "politics of redistribution" (Kaufman, 2015, p. 18) in that the crux of his platform is that America and Americans "are losing" because the current political system is "rigged" against average Americans, where their jobs are either being outsourced to other countries or taken by illegal immigrants. Moreover, he has argued that current policy helps illegal immigrants. Additionally, Trump also makes some appeal to a "politics of protection" (Kaufman, 2015, p. 19), in that he appeals to the security threat posed by Muslims.

It is important to note that in symbolic politics, a leader's success depends on whether his or her rhetoric aligns with the predispositions of his or her potential followers. For example, an experimental study that presented participants with a speech from a fabricated congressional candidate proposing anti-Muslim policies similar to Trump's (e.g., religious markers on IDs, a Muslim ban) found that individuals with a preexisting dislike for Muslims were emotionally moved by the speech, which prompted support for the policies. Conversely, individuals not having anti-Muslim attitudes were turned off by the speech and rejected the policies (Grillo, 2014). Similarly, in the case of Gandhi's campaign for Indian independence, his appeals to Indian unity failed to resonate with Indian Muslims because they were rooted too much in Hindu religious symbolism, which alienated Muslims (Grillo & Kaufman, 2015, pp. 148–175).

Symbolic Politics and Support for Trump

Applying symbolic politics theory to public support for Trump, I have developed and tested a modified version of Kaufman's causal model using public opinion data. My modified theory is based on the assumption that predispositions and emotions also influence how individuals select

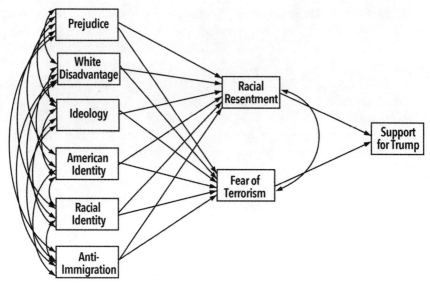

Figure 6.1   Symbolic Politics Causal Model of Support for Trump

leaders. That is, people will support nationalist leaders if they express the same predispositions as they do, which then triggers an emotional response that guides the choice to select one leader over another.

The first step in the model involves predispositions broadly related to prejudice (e.g., minority stereotypes, beliefs that immigration is bad for the United States); status (e.g., beliefs about white disadvantage); and identity (e.g., ideology and racial and American identity). It is important to note that these predispositions are reflective of larger narratives in American politics. The predispositions lead to a negative emotional response (e.g., racial resentment and fear of terrorism), which then leads to support for a nationalist leader (i.e., Trump). Also, note that there are covariances, or relationships, between each of the predispositions and each of the negative emotions (see figure 6.1).[1] Kaufman emphasizes threat perceptions because they are the emotion that leads to violent conflict, but they are not the only emotions that can facilitate mobilization behind a nationalist leader of cause. Others include resentment, anger, frustration, and so on (Grillo, 2014; Petersen, 2002).

Methodology

The theory was tested with a path model on 2016 ANES pilot data. The study was conducted via the Internet in January 2016 and served as a means to vet potential questions for future ANES studies (ANES, 2016). In addition to demographics, the data set includes measures for political party affiliation and ideology, various prejudices, racial resentment, attitudes about white disadvantage, American identity, attitudes about terrorism and immigration, and support for the various presidential candidates.

Respondents

The pilot study had 1,200 respondents who were recruited and randomly selected from a national YouGov panel. The average age of respondents was 48, with the majority being female (630, 53%) and having some college education to a postgraduate degree (687, 57%). Racially, the majority of respondents were white (875, 73%), followed by blacks (135, 11%) and Hispanics (113, 9%). Regarding religious affiliation, the majority were Christian (690, 58%), followed by agnostics, atheists, and those with no affiliation (337, 33%). In terms of party identification, 38 percent identified as Democrat (459), 23 percent as Republican (280), 32 percent as independent (380), and the remaining as other or unsure (81, 7%). Ideologically, on a 7-point scale spanning from 1 (very liberal) to 7 (very conservative), respondents tended to self-identify on the cusp of 3 (closer to liberals) and 4 (neither liberal nor conservative) ($M = 3.95$).

Variables

The dependent variable was support for Trump, which was measured with a feeling thermometer. Values ranged from 1 (very cold or unfavorable feeling) to 100 (very warm or favorable feeling), with 50 representing "no feeling at all" ($M = 41$).

The first set of independent variables measured predispositions related to identity: ideology and American and racial identity. National and racial identity were gauged with questions that asked respondents the importance of their American and racial identity, with scores ranging from 1 (extremely) to 5 (not important at all). On average, American and racial identity were "very important" to participants ($M = 2.14$, $M = 2.80$). These two variables were reverse coded for the analysis so that higher scores indicate higher importance for the identity in question.

The second set of independent variables measured predispositions related to prejudice (i.e., negative attitudes/stereotypes about immigrants and minorities) and status (i.e., belief that whites are at a disadvantage). Prejudice against minorities is a composite measure that combined six stereotype questions for blacks, Hispanics, and Muslims. For each group, respondents were asked, "How well does the word 'violent' *or* 'lazy' describe most members of each group?" Scores ranged from 1 (extremely well) to 5 (not at all well). The scale was created by summing reverse-coded items for each group (α = 0.898) so that higher scores indicate a belief that blacks, Hispanics, and Muslims are violent and lazy (range = 6 to 48, *M* = 31.54). Attitudes against immigrants was gauged with a single measure that asked participants whether it is good or bad that immigrants "legally move to the United States to live and work." Response choices ranged from 1 (extremely good) to 7 (extremely bad). The average response for this item was "kept the same" (*M* = 4.07). White disadvantage is a composite measure that combined the eight questions below assessing the degree to which respondents believe that being white is a disadvantage (α = 0.971). Response options for these measures ranged from 5- to 7-point scales, where lower scores indicate higher quantities (e.g., a great deal, a lot more opportunities). Note that one item was reverse coded for the scale so that higher scores indicate stronger beliefs about white disadvantage (range = 32 to 64, *M* = 48.14).

- Does your skin color make your everyday life easier for you, make it harder, or does it not make any difference?
- How much does being white grant you unearned privileges in today's society?
- To what extent do white people have certain advantages that minorities do not have in this society?
- Does having white skin generally give whites more opportunities in their everyday lives, fewer opportunities, or does it not make any difference?
- Does being white help you, hurt you, or make no difference for you personally in today's society?
- How many advantages do white people have that minorities do not have in this society?
- How many disadvantages do white people have that minorities do not have in this society? (*reverse*)
- Compared to other groups, do white people generally have an advantage, a disadvantage, or does it not make any difference?

The mediating variables were racial resentment and fear of terrorism. Racial resentment is a composite measure that combined the four items below gauging racial resentment. Response options ranged from 1 (agree strongly) to 5 (disagree strongly). The measure was created by summing scores for the four items (α = 0.862). Note that some items were reverse coded so that an increase in the scale indicates an increase in resentment (range = 10 to 26, *M* = 19.35).

- Irish, Italians, Jewish and many other minorities overcame prejudice and worked their way up. Blacks should do the same without any special favors. (*reverse*)
- Generations of slavery and discrimination have created conditions that make it difficult for blacks to work their way out of the lower class.
- Over the past few years, blacks have gotten less than they deserve.
- It's really a matter of some people not trying hard enough; if blacks would only try harder they could be just as well off as whites. (*reverse*)

The second mediating variable was fear of terrorism. This was measured with a single item that asked respondents the degree to which they are worried "about a terrorist attack in the area where you live." Response options ranged from 1 (extremely worried) to 5 (not worried at all). The average score for this variable was between "moderately worried" and "slightly worried" (*M* = 3.79); the majority of respondents fell within the "slightly worried" to "not all worried" categories (64%). This variable was reverse coded so that higher scores show a higher level of worry.

The path model was run in Stata using the SEM builder and was estimated with maximum likelihood estimation. For ease of interpretation, I report standardized regression coefficients, which allows one to compare coefficients to establish which predictors have the most impact on the mediating and dependent variables. To increase the generalizability of the results to the American population, a sampling weight was added to the model to weigh respondents by "age, gender, race/ethnicity, years of education, region, and party identification" (ANES, 2016). Racial identity and attitudes about immigrants had to be excluded from the model because of multicollinearity, though their individual effects will be noted. While collinearity among the variables is expected based on the proposed theory, its degree was high enough to where it distorted estimates for other variables in the model.[2]

Discussion of Results

With the exception of one path, the results supported the posited causal model (see table 6.1). In terms of the first part of the model, all of the predispositions exhibited a positive statistically significant association with racial resentment. Increases in prejudice (i.e., believing that blacks, Hispanics, and Muslims are violent and lazy) and white disadvantage

Table 6.1   Path Model Results

	β	Robust SE	p
Paths to Racial Resentment			
Prejudice*	0.2203	0.0361	0.000
White Disadvantage*	0.2076	0.0283	0.000
Ideology*	0.3822	0.0304	0.000
American Identity*	0.1542	0.0396	0.000
Paths to Fear of Terrorism			
Prejudice*	0.2332	0.0432	0.000
White Disadvantage*	0.0773	0.0348	0.026
Ideology	0.0248	0.0344	0.470
American Identity*	0.1698	0.0344	0.000
Paths to Support for Trump			
Racial Resentment*	0.2211	0.0350	0.000
Fear of Terrorism*	0.1123	0.0294	0.000
SRMR = 0.000, CD = 0.443			*p < .05

(i.e., believing that whites are disadvantaged relative to minorities) were associated with increases in resentment. Likewise, an increase in the importance of American identity was also associated with an increase in resentment. Ideology also exhibited a positive relationship, where increases in conservatism were associated with increases in resentment. In terms of impact, ideology had the greatest impact on resentment, followed by prejudice and white disadvantage.

The causal paths from the predispositions to a fear of terrorism were similar to those for resentment. The only exception was the path from ideology to fear of terrorism was not significant. In regards to impact, prejudice had the greatest impact on fear of terrorism, followed by American identity. Furthermore, all of the predisposition variables exhibited statistically significant covariances with each other, suggesting that the variables are positively related (an increase in one is associated with an increase in the other) (see table 6.2).

In regard to the omitted variables, bivariate regression results suggested that an increase on the legal immigration scale (believing that legal immigration is bad for the United States) had a significant positive relationship on both resentment and fear of terrorism (b = 1.2102, p = 0.000/b = 0.0612, p = 0.005). Racial identity was positively and significantly

Table 6.2   Covariances for Independent and Mediating Variables

	β	Robust SE	*p*
Covariance with Prejudice			
White Disadvantage*	0.1050	0.0406	0.010
Ideology*	0.1828	0.0318	0.000
American Identity*	0.2139	0.0450	0.000
Covariance with Ideology			
White Disadvantage*	0.1415	0.0309	0.000
American Identity*	0.2587	0.0298	0.000
Covariance with American Identity			
White Disadvantage*	0.0752	0.0356	0.035
Covariance with/Fear of Terrorism			
Racial Resentment	−0.0397	0.0371	0.285

*p < .05

associated with fear of terrorism (b = 0.1800, *p* = 0.000). Interestingly, though racial identity exhibited a positive relationship with resentment, it was not statistically significant. In terms of support for Trump, racial identity was also not statistically associated with support for Trump, while attitudes about immigration had a significant positive effect (b = 7.7166, *p* = 0.000). Moreover, bivariate correlations showed that attitudes about immigrants were significantly associated with all predispositions, while racial identity was correlated with all but ideology.[3] The results for race may be because the racial identity of nonwhites reduced its effect on resentment, ideology, and Trump support.

Regarding the second part of the model, resentment exhibited a positive and statistically significant association with support for Trump, where an increase in resentment was related to an increase in support for Trump. Likewise, fear of terrorism had a statistically significant positive relationship with support for Trump. Of the two variables, resentment had the larger impact on support for Trump. However, the covariance between resentment and fear of terrorism was not statistically significant, meaning that these negative emotions are not statistically related (see table 6.2).

The results also suggested that all of the predisposition variables had statistically significant indirect effects on support for Trump (see table 6.3). Conversely, the direct effects of the predispositions on Trump support

Table 6.3   Direct and Indirect Effects of Predispositions on Support for Trump

	Direct Effects			Indirect Effects		
	β	Robust SE	p	β	Robust SE	p
Prejudice	0.2988	0.3862	0.439	0.7678*	0.2741	0.005
White Disadvantage	0.4746	0.3211	0.139	0.5743*	0.1830	0.002
Ideology	2.0342	2.9809	0.495	3.2777*	0.8306	0.000
American Identity	−3.7807	5.4340	0.487	2.8034*	1.0129	0.006

Dependent = Support for Trump   *$p < .05$

were not statistically significant. This suggests that the effects of the predispositions were mediated via racial resentment and fear terrorism. Overall, the model exhibits good fit. The standardized root mean squared residual (SRMR) estimate was 0.000 (values below 0.08 suggest good model fit). The coefficient of determination (CD) showed a medium to strong effect size (0.443), which suggests that the overall model explains about 44 percent of the variation in Trump support.

An earlier analysis of the data used in this study suggested that economic factors are not the driving force of Trump support, but instead it is racial resentment (Klinkner, 2016). Using a different data set, Ehrenfreund and Clemen also found that racial resentment was a driving force of Trump support (Ingraham, 2016). However, they also found that "economic anxiety" and "white status" were also important predictors, but they could not discern "which concern was more important among Trump's coalition" (Ingraham, 2016). Using symbolic politics theory, I sought to establish how racial resentment and concerns about racial status work in a larger causal model of nationalist politics. I demonstrated how predispositions such as attitudes about racial status along with prejudice against minorities, ideology, and American identity lead to negative emotions such as resentment and fear of terrorism that then prompt support for a nationalistic leader such as Trump.

The results from the model suggest that predispositions related to prejudice (negative stereotypes against Hispanics, blacks, and Muslims); status (perceptions of white disadvantage); and identity (ideology and American identity) lead to negative emotions, which then lead to support for Trump. Hence, support for Trump's variety of nationalism is being driven by emotional responses to predispositions. It must be stressed that predispositions for prejudice and white disadvantage are not rational nor based in reality (Rothenberg, 2008). For example, while there are Muslims associated with Al Qaeda, ISIS, and other terrorist groups who are indeed violent, there are about 1.6 billion Muslims in the world, the overwhelming majority of whom are not violent.

Overall, the results suggest that if an individual has the predispositions and negative feelings addressed in the model, they are more likely to support Trump. This counters rational actor approaches contending that nationalist politics are driven by the sagacious pursuit of power, economic well-being, and security. While it can be argued that fear of terrorism is a realistic threat because of recent attacks in Orlando, San Bernardino, and other places, it must be noted that in the current analysis, fear of terrorism in one's local area is driven by predispositions, especially prejudice, and not careful calculation. To further illustrate this point, statistically the chances of being killed by terrorism are extremely low. The average American has a much higher likelihood of perishing from a heart attack, cancer, a car accident, or because of heavy furniture falling on him or her than he or she does from terrorism (Shaver, 2013; Zenko, 2012). Moreover, by weight of comparison, racial resentment has a greater impact on support for Trump than the fear of terrorism.

Though the overall results support the posited causal model, a few additional points should be noted. First, while conservative ideology was statistically associated with racial resentment, it was not with fear of terrorism. There may be a few reasons for this. One may be location. Note that the question asked how worried individuals were about a terrorist attack occurring where they live. Given that terrorist attacks mostly occur in metropolitan areas and that conservatism is far more prevalent outside of major cities, the majority of conservatives may just not be concerned about a terrorist attack happening where they live. Another possibility is that conservatives may not be concerned about a terrorist attack because of sentiments of American power or invincibility. When considering the result for conservatism and fear of terrorism with that of racial resentment, an interesting question does arise. Is support for Muslim bans, refusing Syrian refugees, and other restrictive measures on immigration really about terrorism or crime, or are they driven by racial resentment and fears about the demographic threat posed by immigrants?

Second, it is important to point out that Trump is not creating the narratives and predispositions detailed in this paper. They have been a feature of American politics for a long time and have been festering for quite a while, though Trump has been able to manipulate them. On the one hand, Trump is in a sense bound by the narratives. His platform and rhetoric will resonate with and be embraced by those who have the relevant predispositions and will be rejected by those who do not. On the other hand, Trump's candidacy and rhetoric have provided the context for such ideas to come to the surface. While some may not have publically acknowledged these sentiments before, they can now because Trump is the Republican Party's nominee. Therefore, his ideas now have a sense a legitimacy that they may not have had otherwise. The evolution of this process was evident throughout the primaries. While Trump and his platform may have appeared as an outrageous stunt when he first announced his presidential bid, they gained more legitimacy and acceptability as he starting winning states. Indeed, Trump's success in the primaries created a peer pressure of sorts, as evidenced by the reluctance of many prominent Republicans to criticize his racist and sexist comments. Hence, for individuals who have the predispositions and believe in their corresponding narratives, Trump's candidacy has simply provided an opportunity to publicly display those attitudes with few to no reprisals.

Third, while the fit indices suggest that the proposed causal model has good fit and explains 44 percent of the variation in Trump support, there may be other factors contributing to Trump's rise that have yet to be measured in polls. Some possible factors may include his celebrity status, the fact that he is the epitome of a political outsider, and perceptions that he is a wise businessman/deal maker and thus would be effective in the White House. Others might include Americans' anger with the current state of U.S. government and politics and increased dissatisfaction with career politicians, inter- and intrabranch gridlock, and the overwhelming power of wealthy special interests. Similarly, dissatisfaction with globalization may be another variable, where the outsourcing of jobs, influx of immigrant labor, and the ever-widening rich-poor gap has frustrated many globally and has facilitated the rise of populist nationalist movements throughout Europe. A recent consequence of this growing nationalism was Britain's recent referendum to withdraw from the European Union.

Ultimately, the results of this analysis suggest that public support for Trump's presidency is not rooted in rational concerns for material well-being or economic security, but emotional responses to predispositions, many of which are based on prejudices and ideas about status. Indeed, the other variables noted above do not dispute the findings of this examination, as they are also attitudes rooted in predispositions.

Notes

1. It should be noted that an earlier analysis of Trump support utilizing the same ANES data and some of the variables I examine here noticed that resentment, stereotypes about Muslims, and the belief that Obama is a Muslim were key determinants of support for Trump (Klinkner, 2016). In addition to examining other variables, my analysis differs from the latter in that it seeks to identify and test a causal chain of Trump support based on symbolic politics theory, the research for which has mostly been qualitative and has focused on other countries. I excluded attitudes about Obama from my analysis because symbolic politics emphasizes predispositions about groups.

2. Diagnostics on residuals were also performed. Mean residuals for each of the variables were zero. Additionally, the covariance of residuals was also zero for each variable combination.

3. These estimates were calculated with ordinary least squares regression.

References

American National Election Studies, Stanford University, and University of Michigan. American National Election Study: 2016 Pilot Study. ICPSR36390-v1. Ann Arbor, MI: Inter-university Consortium for Political and Social Research [distributor], 2016-03-16. http://doi.org/10.3886/ICPSR36390.v1

BBC News. (2016, May 2). Trump accuses China of "raping" US with unfair trade policy. BBC News. Retrieved from http://www.bbc.com/news/election-us-2016-36185012

Blum, Edward J. (2015). *Reforging the white republic: Race, religion, and American nationalism, 1865–1898.* Baton Rouge, LA: LSU Press.

Brass, Paul R. (1997). *Theft of an idol: Text and context in the representation of collective violence.* Princeton, NJ: Princeton University Press.

Fearon, James D. (1995). Rationalist explanations for war. *International Organization, 49*(3), 379–414.

Gellner, Ernest. (2008). *Nations and nationalism.* Ithaca, NY: Cornell University Press.

Greenfeld, Liah. (1993). *Nationalism: Five roads to modernity.* Cambridge, MA: Harvard University Press.

Grillo, Michael Charles. (2014). The role of emotions in discriminatory ethno-religious politics: An experimental study of anti-Muslim politics in the United States. *Politics, Religion & Ideology, 15*(4), 583–603.

Grillo, Michael Charles, & Kaufman, Stuart J. (2015). Gandhi's nonviolence, communal conflict, and the Salt March. In Stuart J. Kaufman, *Nationalist Passions* (pp. 148–175). Ithaca, NY: Cornell University Press.

Gurr, Ted Robert. (1970). *Why men rebel.* Princeton, NJ: Princeton University Press.

Hardin, Russell. (1997). *One for all: The logic of group conflict.* Princeton, NJ: Princeton University Press.

Hensch, Mark. (2015, November 19). Trump won't rule out database, special ID for Muslims in US." *The Hill*. Retrieved from http://thehill.com/blogs/ballot-box/presidential-races/260727-trump-wont-rule-out-database-special-id-for-muslims

Hobsbawm, Eric J. (2012). *Nations and nationalism since 1780: Programme, myth, reality*. Cambridge: Cambridge University Press.

Hutchinson, John, & Smith, Anthony (Eds.). (1995). *Nationalism*. Oxford: Oxford University Press.

Ingraham, Christopher. (2016, June 6). Two new studies find racial anxiety is the biggest driver of support for Trump. *The Washington Post*. Retrieved from https://www.washingtonpost.com/news/wonk/wp/2016/06/06/racial-anxiety-is-a-huge-driver-of-support-for-donald-trump-two-new-studies-find

Kaufman, Stuart J. (2001). *Modern hatreds: The symbolic politics of ethnic war*. Ithaca, NY: Cornell University Press.

Kaufman, Stuart J. (2006). Symbolic politics or rational choice? Testing theories of extreme ethnic violence. *International Security, 30*(4), 45–86.

Kaufman, Stuart J. (2015) *Nationalist Passions*. Ithaca, NY: Cornell University Press.

Kessler, Glenn. (2015, November 22). Trump's outrageous claim that "thousands" of New Jersey Muslims celebrated the 9/11 attacks. *The Washington Post*. Retrieved from https://www.washingtonpost.com/news/fact-checker/wp/2015/11/22/donald-trumps-outrageous-claim-that-thousands-of-new-jersey-muslims-celebrated-the-911-attacks

Klinkner, Phillip. (2016, June2). The easiest way to guess if someone supports Trump? Ask if Obama is a Muslim. *Vox*. Retrieved from http://www.vox.com/2016/6/2/11833548/donald-trump-support-race-religion-economy

Kuran, Timur. (1998). "Ethnic dissimilation and its international diffusion." In David A. Lake and Donald S. Rothchild, *The international spread of ethnic conflict: Fear, diffusion, and escalation* (pp. 35–60). Princeton, NJ: Princeton University Press.

Lake, David A., and Rothchild, Donald S. (1998). *The international spread of ethnic conflict: Fear, diffusion, and escalation*. Princeton, NJ: Princeton University Press.

Moore, Stephen, & Kudlow, Larry. (2015, August 27). Is Donald Trump a 21st-century protectionist Herbert Hoover? *National Review*. Retrieved from http://www.nationalreview.com/article/423141/donald-trumps-protectionism-is-worrisome-stephen-moore-larry-kudlow

Moreno, Carolina. (2015, August 31). 9 outrageous things Donald Trump has said about Latinos: "They're bringing drugs. They're bringing crime. They're rapists." *Huffington Post*. Retrieved from http://www.huffingtonpost.com/entry/9-outrageous-things-donald-trump-has-said-about-latinos_us_55e483a1e4b0c818f618904b

Obeidallah, Dean. (2015, November 21). Donald Trump's horrifying words about Muslims. CNN. Retrieved from http://www.cnn.com/2015/11/20 /opinions/obeidallah-trump-anti-muslim

Petersen, Roger D. (2002). *Understanding ethnic violence: Fear, hatred, and resentment in twentieth-century Eastern Europe.* Cambridge: Cambridge University Press.

Pickus, Noah. (2009). *True faith and allegiance: Immigration and American civic nationalism.* Princeton, NJ: Princeton University Press.

Posen, Barry R. (1993). The security dilemma and ethnic conflict. *Survival, 35*(1), 27–47.

Reyson, Jamie, & Brown, Nicole. (2016, March 4). "Donald Trump's memorable, controversial quotes. AM Network. Retrieved from http://www.amny .com/news/elections/donald-trump-s-memorable-controversial-quotes -1.11177219

Rothenberg, Paula S. (2008). *White privilege.* New York: Macmillan.

Saideman, Stephen M. (2001). *The ties that divide: Ethnic politics, foreign policy, and international conflict.* New York: Columbia University Press.

Schroeder, Robert. (2015, August 24). Watch Donald Trump warn China will "bring us down." *MarketWatch.* Retrieved from http://www.marketwatch.com/story /watch-donald-trump-warn-china-will-bring-us-down-2015-08-24

Shaver, Andrew. (2015, November 23). You're more likely to be fatally crushed by furniture than killed by a terrorist. *The Washington Post.* Retrieved from https://www.washingtonpost.com/news/monkey-cage/wp/2015/11/23 /youre-more-likely-to-be-fatally-crushed-by-furniture-than-killed-by-a-terrorist

Sherfinski, David. (2016, March 10). Donald Trump: "I think Islam hates us." *Washington Times.* Retrieved from http://www.washingtontimes.com /news/2016/mar/10/donald-trump-i-think-islam-hates-us

Smith, Anthony D. (1993). *National identity.* Reno: University of Nevada Press.

Smith, Anthony D. (2000). *Myths and memories of the nation.* Oxford: Oxford University Press.

Snyder, Jack L. (2000). *From voting to violence: Democratization and nationalist conflict.* New York: Norton.

Trump, Donald. (2016). Reforming the U.S.-China trade relationship to make America great again. Donald Trump Official 2016 Campaign. Retrieved from https://www.donaldjtrump.com/positions/us-china-trade-reform

Washington Post. (2015, June 16). Full text: Donald Trump announces a presidential bid. *The Washington Post.* Retrieved from https://www.washingtonpost .com/news/post-politics/wp/2015/06/16/full-text-donald-trump -announces-a-presidential-bid

Zenko, Micah. (2012, June6). Americans are as likely to be killed by their own furniture as by terrorism. *The Atlantic.* Retrieved from http://www.theatlantic .com/international/archive/2012/06/americans-are-as-likely-to-be-killed -by-their-own-furniture-as-by-terrorism/258156

CHAPTER SEVEN

Trump:
An Antiestablishment Hero?

Gregg Henriques

For months on the campaign trail, Donald Trump frequently proclaimed that banning Muslims from entering the United States was a necessary step until "we can figure out what is going on." Paralleling this, many individuals in the liberal academic and social circles in which I travel had a very similar sentiment to the rise of Trump himself. That is, they have been dumbstruck about how Trump emerged triumphant out of a competitive field of 17 contenders for the Republican nomination, and they have voiced fantasies that the political process should be put on hold until folks could figure out what was going on. Indeed, when he announced his candidacy in 2015, virtually no serious commentator or established politician gave him any chance of winning, and most viewed his entry into the race simply as an extension of his bid in the prior election and done for purposes of celebrity. It is worth recalling how, at the White House Correspondents' Dinner in 2011, Seth Meyers captured this sentiment: "Donald Trump has been saying he will run for president as a Republican—which is surprising, since I just assumed he was running as a joke."

But against all conventional wisdom and with virtually no initial support from the Republican establishment (and with many prominent Republicans openly criticizing or dismissing Trump as a viable candidate),

Trump proceeded to vanquish one competitor after another and ultimately emerged as the clear choice from the majority of Republican voters to be the nominee. The goal of this chapter is to help the reader understand the psychological, social, and political forces that propelled Trump to success when it initially appeared to be so unlikely. The central thesis of this chapter is that what has driven Trump's unexpected success is that there has emerged a fundamental divide in the American character and identity, namely, a divide between cultural traditionalists and cultural cosmopolitans (Trende, 2016), and that the former are feeling resentful about being unheard and left behind by the political and intellectual establishment; they view Trump as a disruptive force that can break up the current direction of the country and return their sense of identity and value to the place it once rightfully held in American society.

This chapter first articulates why the Trump phenomena requires academic analysis and then proceeds to briefly outline the frame that I am using to understand human behavior more broadly. I then highlight the key elements of Trump's rise, including (1) the divide between cultural cosmopolitans and cultural traditionalists; (2) the reasons why the latter are feeling frustrated, angry, and left behind; (3) the reason that Trump's antipolitical establishment message is absolutely central to his campaign; (4) the nature of Trump's personality and its symbolic value to Trump supporters; and (5) the patterns and concerns of Trump voters that provide aggregate data consistent with the validity of these claims. Finally, I conclude with a comment about Trump's candidacy and why it is so risky.

Understanding What Is Being Explained and Why It Needs an Explanation

If Jeb Bush had won the Republican nomination, there likely would not have been a push to gather academics together and to provide a framework for making sense of this event because we expect there to be a basic alignment with power structures, investment, beliefs, and established tradition. As a candidate, Jeb Bush had this alignment, in terms of political stature, experience, money, backing from the establishment, and name recognition. Trump, of course, was in many ways the opposite. Although he had name recognition and wealth, it was all outside of the political establishment. At the start of the campaign, he had virtually no endorsements or establishment connections and no political experience from which to base his campaign. Thus, his rise is something of a mystery from that perspective.

I also think it is useful to say something about the nature of explanation regarding this kind of event. When attempting to offer scientific explanations for phenomena, the focus is often on control of relevant variables and, especially, prediction. Prediction of future events is the sine qua non of good natural scientific explanation. While this is true for events in the physical sciences, large-scale social phenomena cannot be viewed via the lens of control and prediction, as control is limited and there simply are too many variables that lead to too many possible outcomes that prevent reliable prediction. This is particularly true of things that can be characterized as Black Swan events. A Black Swan is a metaphor for an event that emerges as a surprise and then attempts are made to explain the event after the fact. According to Nicholas Taleb, who authored *The Black Swan* (2010), such an event (1) is a far outlier (i.e., was completely unexpected), (2) has huge consequences, and (3) in retrospect seems to have been at least somewhat understandable. It seems clear that the Trump nomination meets these criteria. But even if they are almost impossible to predict, it is useful to try and explain why they happen after the fact.

So, the question to be addressed here is why did this Black Swan event happen? In what follows, I attempt to root out and highlight the central psychological, social, and political forces that are responsible for Trump's success in acquiring the Republican nomination. But prior to laying out the components that go into my analysis, I will provide a brief background of the conceptual framework that I use to understand human behavior.

A Brief Overview of the Current Framework

I use a new, unified approach to psychology (Henriques, 2011) that pulls together many different threads within the field and related social science perspectives and offers a way to see the whole in a way that is more coherent than the current fragmented arrangement of theories and findings. Although the formal details are beyond the scope of this chapter, I will highlight the core features of the approach central to understanding the forces that are giving rise to the Trump phenomenon. The first is the claim that animal minds (including human minds) can be understood as systems of behavioral investment that calculate the costs and benefits of actions and orient individuals to consider, protect, and advance their interests as they relate to fundamental valued states of being (e.g., states that foster survival and reproduction). The second feature is that, as social mammals, humans are deeply relational creatures who attempt to navigate the social world by attending to their level of social influence and felt sense of relational value (this is defined as the extent to which they feel known and valued by important others). Humans seek relational value in terms of their immediate connections and exchanges with others (such as family members and friends), but also in terms of their group membership and identity. This last point is crucial because it highlights how political groups serve as extensions and affirmations of the self (or not).

Finally, the unified approach characterizes humans as unique animals because of the evolution of human language, which set the stage for humans to give reasons for their actions and the happenings in the world around them. These reason-giving processes gave rise to large-scale systems of explicit, language-based beliefs, which the unified approach characterizes as "justification systems." Political frameworks are seen as large-scale justification systems that attempt to provide individuals with a group identity and a narrative about how the (political) world works and what we should value and the actions we should take to maximize our valued outcomes.

My goal in this chapter is to explicate the forces of human investment, social influence, and justification that have propelled Trump to the nomination. The answer is not to be found in simple theories of rational self-interest or individuals attempting to maximize utility. Rather, what is being played out on the political stage is a battle for the very identity of the United States of America. Specifically, the Trump candidacy, especially when considered against the backdrop of an Obama presidency, is about a battle for the core values (i.e., the interests, investments, and justifications) regarding what the American people stand for and represent.

Cultural Traditionalists versus Cultural Cosmopolitans: A Great Divide in the American Character

At least since the 1980s, there has been a significant and clearly identifiable divide in America regarding cultural and family values. The Moral Majority, founded by Jerry Falwell, provided conservative Christians a clear voice that was defined against secular and progressive social values, and the culture wars that emerged in the wake of the Moral Majority provide a social and historical lineage to the present day. The landscape has changed somewhat in the last decade or so, and I believe the current divide is best captured by the distinction delineated by Sean Trende (2016), who coined the key difference in modern America as that between cultural cosmopolitans and cultural traditionalists.

The essence of the cultural cosmopolitan view is the (apparent) capacity to step outside one's local knowledge and background and explore and embrace diversity. Cosmopolitans are open to the various ethnic, national, and religious ways of being and see their lives as one way of being among many other possible ways. They also tend to be more open to ideas and experiences, are on average better educated than cultural traditionalists, and have values that emphasize multiculturalism, globalization, and an intellectual analysis of the issues, all while being suspicious of claims grounded in local traditional authority. They are also more likely to live in the cities and coastal areas of the country. Unlike traditionalists, cosmo-politans are hesitant to place cultures in explicit hierarchies, although, as will be noted, cosmopolitans are often seen to express contempt or a sense of "elitist" superiority relative to traditionalists.

Cultural traditionalists, in contrast, take pride in their local perspec-tives and hometown values. Embodied in such phenomena as *Duck Dynasty* and such individuals as Sarah Palin, they like getting their hands dirty, telling it like it is in plain language, kicking the tires, and kicking ass when necessary. Although traditionalists exist across all educational and class levels, they are more heavily represented among working-class individuals and on average have lower levels of education than cosmo-politans and tend to live in south, central, and rural America. They are more likely to embrace the idea that America is an exceptional country, and many believe it was blessed by a Christian God as such. Such systems of justification are well represented in an essay by Andrea Lafferty (2016) on why she supports Trump as an evangelical woman:

> Every American woman who professes to believe in God has a responsibil-ity to raise her voice in this election cycle and vote for a candidate who stands ready to restore America and that means American values as the strongest force for good and freedom that modern history has known.
>
> There can be debate and disagreement about Presidents George W. Bush and Bill Clinton but little can be said about any Barack Obama legacy other than he rarely saw anything positive in America past or present. There was never any chance he would make America great *again* because he never thought America was ever great.

As referred to above, a central dynamic between the two groups is that traditionalists resent being looked down upon or perceived as ignorant or racist or hyper-religious by the cultural cosmopolitan elites. In the 2008 campaign, Obama ignited precisely this issue when he explained the mind-set of cultural traditionalists to a cosmopolitan audience at a San Francisco fundraiser, proclaiming that

> You go into these small towns in Pennsylvania and, like a lot of small towns in the Midwest, the jobs have been gone now for 25 years and

nothing's replaced them. And they fell through the Clinton administration, and the Bush administration, and each successive administration has said that somehow these communities are gonna regenerate and they have not.

And it's not surprising then they get bitter, they cling to guns or religion or antipathy toward people who aren't like them or anti-immigrant sentiment or anti-trade sentiment as a way to explain their frustrations.

Crucial to understanding the rise of Trump is that the two parties have different alignments with the values and visions of cosmopolitans and traditionalists. The Democratic Party in general and its leadership in particular are essentially aligned with cultural cosmopolitan values, and over the past two decades, it has become an increasingly cosmopolitan institution. To see this, consider how Barack Obama's life narrative—born of a Kenyan father and white American mother, growing up in Hawaii and Indonesia, becoming the first black person to lead the *Harvard Law Review*, then on to the Senate and finally the presidency—so epitomizes the views and values of cosmopolitan culture.

In contrast, the Republican Party has had a more complicated relationship with cultural traditionalist values. On the one hand, the Republican Party has tried to reach out to cultural traditionalists with emphases on traditional Christian family values. It also attempts to project a strong and proud national identity in terms of international relations, with emphases on American exceptionalism. And the Republican Party clearly aligned itself with traditional whites in the "Southern strategy," which arose in response to the civil rights movement. But it also is the case that most leading establishment Republicans are largely cosmopolitan in their views, education, and many of their values. That is, they are well educated, often advocate for measures such as free trade, are open to diversity, participate in the advancement of technology and globalization, and tend to live in the cities and have much contact with diverse peoples. Think here of Mitt Romney as an individual or of Libertarians as a group; both are largely cosmopolitan in their orientation. Because of this, what has emerged over the past decade or so among many cultural traditionalists is the sense that the Republican Party is often seen as only paying lip service to cultural traditionalist values. A return to Andrea Lafferty's essay makes this point clearly:

> Americans rightly have a healthy skepticism concerning political matters, particularly the Republican Party. While the majority of Americans have dismissed the liberals and their party for some time, they have elected and then reelected Republicans who promised to be different, to reduce the size of government and make Washington work. They weren't different

and they joined right in with the rest of the despised political class. Donald Trump promises he will be different.

The "despised political class" is largely cosmopolitan, and it is the central thesis of this chapter that what is propelling Trump is a wave of anger and frustration directed at the political and intellectual establishment from a group of disaffected traditionalists who feel unheard, unfairly treated, left behind, and betrayed by the dysfunctional establishment.[1] This group believes that the system is rigged by Washington insiders, politically correct academic leftists, and by processes of globalization. They fear that what is happening is a redistribution of power away from traditional places and a shift toward multicultural values and international commerce that threaten both their economic livelihood and their very identity as Americans who take pride in their values and sense of exceptionalism. These individuals seek a strong leader who speaks their plain language and can break up the current establishment and give a metaphorical black eye to the smug cosmopolitan elites who have failed to govern the country effectively. It is this message that Trump has been so successful in selling.

The Decline of Traditional Christian White America

A central claim of the current proposal is that cultural traditionalists, in particular male traditionalists, are experiencing anxiety and anger about the current state of affairs, in large part because they have witnessed a loss of power and prestige. In short, the world is changing in a more cosmopolitan way, and this is exacting an emotional toll and energizing this group toward someone they believe represents real change against these forces. Since the 1960s, the United States has experienced a sea change in power and dominance, especially at the sociocultural normative level (i.e., what is socially justifiable). Throughout the history of our nation (and Western Europe more broadly), the power structures have been dominated by heterosexual, Christian, white males, and this dominance has been legitimized with explicit justification. But (thankfully from the vantage point of cosmopolitanism) the justification for the inherent superiority of this group has been chipped away, from the civil rights movements in the sixties to the feminist movement in the seventies to the LGBT and secular/nonreligious movements of today. Although many see these forces as having moved our society toward justice, it nevertheless is the case that they have come with a loss of relative power and prestige for white male cultural traditionalists.

It is crucial to point out that this is a real phenomenon, and many analyses have been done that reveal just how much is changing for traditional Christian white males. In terms of economic power and prospects, it has been well documented that many working-class jobs have been eliminated and replaced either with technology or via global trade agreements, which have allowed for the production of goods via the cheaper labor markets in the developing countries resulting in the elimination of many good factory jobs in the United States. The 2008 recession created many additional economic pressures and uncertainties, and although the U.S. economy has definitely picked up over the past few years, the recovery has been much weaker for lower- to middle-income workers.

In addition, males are likely to be frustrated because of difficulty in educational achievement. Leonard Sax (2007) documents these difficulties and points out that boys are graduating from high school and college at a substantially lower rate than girls. In addition, there is an emerging sea change with regard to Christianity as well. Robert Jones (2016) documents the political eclipse of white Christian America and how both mainline and evangelical communities have been losing members and influence. Importantly, it is quite plausible that these forces are taking a serious toll on the mental health of white traditionalists. In a revealing analysis of mortality rates, Deaton and Case (2015) documented that there has been a remarkable increase in mortality in middle- and lower-class whites over the past several decades, stemming largely from alcohol and drug abuse and suicide.

The Centrality of Trump's Antiestablishment Message

If there is a significant segment of cultural traditionalists that are feeling left behind, it follows that they would be seeking someone who could upend that establishment and replace it with something that more directly represents their felt sense of identity, values, and interests. And this is Trump's central message, repeated over and over. The establishment is rigged, broken, and corrupt and filled with rules and ideas that are un-American and enacted by incompetents. By the "establishment," I am using the word in two senses. First, I mean the established values of the cosmopolitan class, which can be characterized in terms of (academic) political correctness. The progressive left version of political correctness is the idea that many of society's ills stem from injustices based in hierarchies of sex/gender, race, religion, and sexual orientation and that we must work to change those inequities. In other words, from this perspective, heterosexual Christian white men have dominated, and it is now time to diversify power and privilege. As a consequence, individuals, especially those in public or leadership roles, must be particularly sensitive to issues of hierarchy and injustice, especially involving race, sexual orientation, religion, or disability. The Trump campaign had, as a central message, the idea that this kind of political correctness has gone way too far and needs to be pushed back.

The second meaning of the term "establishment" is in regard to the current political establishment regarding rules of decorum, party alignment, ideology, and the need to play along at least somewhat with the existing structures and expectations of governance. Trump, of course, frequently embraces being an outsider and has regularly promoted the claim that what is needed is someone who has business sense, rather than the knowledge (and constraints and commitments) of a Washington insider. And, true to form, he has run an extremely unconventional campaign in terms of organization, key players, and messaging.

But even more striking has been the way the candidate himself repeatedly behaved in a blatantly antiestablishment fashion. First, he opened his campaign with the claim that many Mexicans illegally crossing the border were "rapists." Shortly thereafter, he proceeded to mock a disabled news reporter. He then shockingly dismissed John McCain's service in Vietnam, saying he preferred heroes who were "not captured." And, on the heels of the attacks in San Bernardino, he famously called for banning Muslims from entering the country. From the perspective of a traditional establishment politician or from the view of a politically correct cosmopolitan, these represent dramatic departures from what is justifiable, and thus many pundits and commentators consistently predicted that these kinds of acts and proposals would get Trump dumped by the electorate. However, these actions not only did not hurt Trump with his supporters, but often strengthened his support. Why? Because they embodied the antiestablishment movement that Trump was tapping into with the cultural traditionalists. In short, what is such a striking affront to establishment cosmopolitans is precisely what Trump is selling to disaffected traditionalists.

Trump's Personality and Why It Appeals to the Cultural Traditionalists

A central theme of this chapter is that people are not, generally speaking, reflective utility maximizers, but instead are largely driven by intuitive factors associated with their interests and influence, which they then develop justifications to legitimize. From this perspective, many of Trump's actions are emotional symbols to his supporters that he can disrupt the corrupt establishment that has left them behind. Indeed, Trump's personality (and persona) can readily be viewed as a symbol that drives his base. Evidence for this is first and foremost found via examining Trump's political ideology.

Political movements are typically founded on justifications about what is happening and what should be done about it that are centered on key beliefs and values that organize the group's understanding of the world. With the exception of his antiestablishment message, this simply is not the case with Trump—he is all over the ideological and political map and clearly has no guiding philosophy. Rather, Trump essentially latches on to issues that are of concern to cultural traditionalists, such as global trade and immigration, and he then makes sweeping claims that if he is elected all will be much better than is currently the case. Indeed, his actual proposals, such as building a great wall on the Mexican border (while having Mexico pay for it), rounding up and exporting 11 million illegal immigrants, banning Muslims from entering the United States, and dramatically altering the global trade arrangements, are consistently evaluated by experts to be illegal, immoral, ineffective, and completely unworkable. The point here is that the Trump phenomenon is clearly not about a rational, justifiable, analytical analysis of the issues, but rather is much better described as a cult of personality. That is, it is what Trump's personality symbolizes that drives his current base.

What, exactly, is it about his personality that is so appealing to some (while being so abhorrent to others)? It is his unabashed egoism and narcissism, coupled with his (apparent) business success. Trump unapologetically views the world through a performance hierarchy. In the real world (or at least what Trump says is the real world), you either get the job done or you don't. His wealth and influence are evidence that he gets things done. Why is he a winner? Because he is better than everyone else, and his intellect, charm and grit are the reasons. Others (i.e., the bimbos and losers out there) fail because they are weak and stupid. In short, Trump is completely and unapologetically defined by egotistical rankism.

But if Trump is so clearly in the top of the economic stratosphere, why would he be appealing to disaffected white cultural traditionalists who feel left behind? When we rally around a candidate, we connect to them, we live vicariously through them, and they represent what we desire. By identifying with someone who has enormous money, power, influence, and access to beautiful women and other powerful people, individuals who are feeling threatened and who long for that sort of power can vicariously connect with the life Trump leads by supporting him. The bottom line is that many white male cultural traditionalists are anxious about the direction the country is taking and see additional threats in a diverse world. As such, there is a yearning for "the good old days" when American white males embraced their exceptionalism and power and did not have to be shy about being "better." They were better because they had more power, which is exactly the kind of logic that Trump symbolizes and endorses.

In 2008, cultural cosmopolitans rallied around Obama because he represented intellect, diversity, globalization, and a complete rejection of the anti-intellectual, cowboy diplomacy of "W." Now we have Trump, who in many ways is the anti-Obama candidate. Trump's campaign slogan, "Make America Great Again," is clearly designed to position Obama as a weak leader who is always making concessions and apologizing for America, rather than boldly advancing our exceptionalism. It is useful to note here that one of Trump's most significant and early moves into politics came as he latched onto challenging Obama's birthplace and for his incessant attacks on Obama as an "other" (i.e., not a real American man). One can argue that Trump, who was a Democrat 10 years ago, becomes a Republican essentially because of "identity politics," and the root of his success is found in that he is so strongly defined against Obama. In sum, this analysis suggests that, for many, the idea of replacing Obama with Trump would be a both a practical and symbolic vindication of white cultural traditionalists over the cosmopolitans.

The Values and Demographics of Trump Voters

The analysis offered here makes a number of hypothetical "predictions" that should be present in the aggregate voting patterns if the analysis has validity. The word "predictions" is in scare quotes because voting data are in large part the phenomenon that one is trying to explain (i.e., the success of Trump in the polls). Thus, I do not mean prediction here in the strong sense of the word of blindly predicting some unknown future event, but rather in the weaker sense of patterned matching. That is, there should be a coherent pattern matching the demographics and values of the aggregate of Trump voters to the analyses that have been laid out here. Specifically, the analysis predicts Trump voters should (1) be heavily skewed in the direction of white relative to nonwhite; (2) be heavily skewed toward males relative to females; (3) live in southern, central, and rural areas (relative to coastal and urban areas); (4) be older; and (5) have somewhat less education and lower socioeconomic status when compared with Clinton supporters (and controlling for relevant variables like ethnicity). In terms of values, Trump supporters should (1) be more oriented toward authority and authoritarianism rather than an informed analytical analysis of the issues; (2) be more closed-minded and defensive than open-minded; (3) be extremely frustrated with the direction of the country; (4) have extremely high disapproval ratings of Obama; (5) have extremely high disapproval ratings of Congress and the direction of the country in general; and (6) feel that they do not have a voice.

At the time of this writing (just prior to the conventions), analyses of voter behavior largely (but not completely) support these claims. For example, a March 2016 analysis found that Trump voters (compared to those supporting the other Republican candidates) exhibited four key characteristics, including (1) being less likely to go to college; (2) being more likely to be authoritarian; (3) being less likely to feel like they have a voice; and (4) being more likely to live in a region that has higher racial tensions. A July 2016 Pew Research poll found a large disparity regarding race, with whites supporting Trump overall (51% to 42%), whereas Hispanic and African Americans showed dominant preferences for Clinton (66% to 24% and 91% to 7%, respectively). Among whites with a college education, a majority supported Clinton (52% to 40%), whereas among whites without a college education, Trump received a clear majority (57% to 36%). In addition, there was a very large gender difference, with women supporting Clinton by a very large margin (59% to 35%) and men showing a preference for Trump (49% to 43%). Finally, there was a clear trend for younger voters to support Clinton (60% to 30%), whereas the oldest voters support Trump (49% to 46%).

It is important to note that not all analyses of voter patterns have been completely consistent with the above predictions. For example, the political polling site *FiveThirtyEight* has offered data showing that the typical Trump supporter has higher levels of income and slightly higher levels of education than the average voter (Silver, 2016). In the end, detailed analyses will need to be conducted after the election to determine exactly who voted for Trump and what their demographic and values tended to look like to determine the full validity of this analysis.

Conclusion: Trump Is an Establishment Disruptor for the Disaffected

This chapter has used a unified approach to human investment, social influence, and justification systems to develop a framework for understanding the rise of Donald Trump. The central thesis offered is that there has emerged a divide in American identity and character between cultural cosmopolitans and traditionalists. The argument has been advanced that traditionalists are feeling particularly resentful and left behind by the current political and intellectual establishment, and they view Trump as a disruptive force that can return their sense of identity and value to the place it once rightfully held in American society. We have explored the characteristics of cultural cosmopolitans and traditionalists, explained why traditionalists are feeling resentful and unheard, and why Trump's outsider status, antiestablishment message, and narcissistic persona have much symbolic value for these voters.

Additionally, central to this analysis is that there is no deep organizing intellectual argument that spells out how a Trump presidency would actually unfold. What we are seeing is the product of the desire of a disaffected group to disrupt what they perceive to be a dysfunctional system; but the narrative of how to effectively reconstruct and reconstitute a more effective political system has been completely absent. In fact, the argument can be made strongly that Trump lacks an intellectual understanding of the issues and the value of intellectual integrity. Thus, a grave fear arises from the current analysis, one that parallels what clinicians often see in the clinic room. That is, feeling unheard, disrespected, and frustrated at the current situation, a group of individuals is engaging in an impulsive and destructive act born out of anger and frustration, rather than a rational analysis of the problem and reasonable solutions. Individuals who do this in their lives end up in treatment because the enacted "solution" fails and ends up bringing far more damaging consequences to them and others around them. Let us hope the same will not be the case for the United States of America.

Note

1. Although not the focus of this chapter, it is central to acknowledge that the current political system is largely polarized and readily characterized as dysfunctional. One does not need to be a traditionalist to have this view. Bernie Sanders' remarkable campaign received much of its fuel from this claim and was very "antiestablishment" in that sense. And this is a view that both Trump and Sanders supporters share.

References

Case, A., & Deaton, A. (2015). Rising morbidity and mortality in midlife among white non-Hispanic Americans in the 21st century. *Proceedings from the National Academy of Sciences*, 112, 15078–15083. doi:www.pnas.org/cgi/doi/10.1073/pnas.1518393112

Henriques, G. R. (2011). *A new unified theory of psychology*. New York: Springer.

Jones, R. (2016). The eclipse of White Christian America. *The Atlantic*. Retrieved from http://www.theatlantic.com/politics/archive/2016/07/the-eclipse-of -white-christian-america/490724/

Lafferty, A. (2016, June). I am an evangelical woman and I support Donald Trump. Fox News. http://www.foxnews.com/opinion/2016/06/30/im-evangelical-woman-and-support-donald-trump.html

Pew Research. (2016, June). Voter general preferences. Retrieved from http://www.people-press.org/2016/07/07/2-voter-general-election-preferences

Sax, L. (2007). *Boys adrift: The five factors driving the growing epidemic of unmotivated boys and underachieving young men*. New York: Basic Books.

Silver, N. (2016, May). The mythology of Trump's working class support. *FiveThirtyEight*. Retrieved from http://fivethirtyeight.com/features/the -mythology-of-trumps-working-class-support/?ex_cid=story-twitter

Taleb, N. (2010). *The Black Swan: The impact of the highly improbable* (2nd ed.). New York: Random House.

Thompson, D. (2016, March). Who are Donald Trump supporters? *The Atlantic*. Retrieved from http://www.theatlantic.com/politics/archive/2016/03/who -are-donald-trumps-supporters-really/471714

Trende, S. (2016, January). Why Trump? Why now? *Realclearpolitics*. Retrieved from http://www.realclearpolitics.com/articles/2016/01/29/why_trump _why_now_129486.html

CHAPTER EIGHT

Intolerant and Afraid: Authoritarians Rise to Trump's Call

Matthew C. MacWilliams

From the moment he announced his candidacy for president, Donald Trump's unvarnished us-versus-them message and unabashed strongman manner electrified some Americans. Activated by Trump's message and bluster, driven by threats real and imagined, and catalyzed by the media's incessant repetition of both, these Americans rallied to Trump's banner, providing him with a resilient base of support that was relatively impervious to attack and large enough—after years of partisan shifts in the electorate—to dominate a multicandidate Republican primary contest.[1]

In a series of articles published in *Politico*, *Vox*, the London School of Economics *USAPP* blog, and *PS: Political Science and Politics*, which analyzed data from a national poll taken in December of 2015, I demonstrated that two variables defined Trump's supporters in a statistically and substantively significant way.[2] Those variables were authoritarianism and a personalized fear of terrorism.

The identification of authoritarianism and fear as the root of Trump's support led to three questions that form the tryptic of topics analyzed in this chapter and go to the heart of the participatory and civil society aspirations of democratic theory. First, I ask, *Did Trump's voters vote "correctly"?* Correct voting is *not* a normative assessment of whether Trump's positions are democratic or autocratic. Instead, correct voting simply means that Trump's issue positions and the issue preferences of his supporters are congruent (Lau and Redlawsk, 2006, p. 15).

In what follows, I demonstrate that Trump supporters share his feelings about Muslims, illegal immigrants, and Syrian refugees. They support a strong executive who takes action when necessary, irrespective of established constitutional limitations on presidential power. And they agree with Trump's calls to close mosques, deport illegal immigrants, ban Muslims from entering the United States, and establish a nationwide database to monitor American Muslims. Trump voters' issue preferences and worldview are simpatico with those articulated by Trump. In the language of political science, the choice of these Americans to support Trump in the Republican primary was both rational (Goldberg, 1969; Krosnick, 1990) and responsible (Key, 1966; Krosnick, 1990).

Second, I ask, *What does the rise of Trump and his rational, responsible, and authoritarian voters mean for the future of American politics and democracy?* I show that Trump supporters' appetite for unconstitutional, antidemocratic solutions extends well beyond the specific proposals advanced by Trump to a fundamental disagreement over the very values on which America's Madisonian democracy is founded.

To many political scientists, the congruency between Trump and his supporters' worldviews and positions on issues is remarkable and raises the third question explored in this chapter, *How did Trump's supporters become so knowledgeable about his stands on a wide range of issues?* I argue the Trump's transformation of political discourse into reality entertainment turned decades of political science theories about information costs and voting behavior on their heads. The cost of learning more about Trump became a benefit—the enjoyment of entertainment—and was no longer a constraint on voters' acquisition of political knowledge and information.

The rational and responsible choice made by Trump's authoritarian and fearful voters, their fervid support for undemocratic values and unconstitutional policies, and the challenge both Trump and his supporters present to theories of voting behavior form the backbone of what follows. I begin with a thumbnail sketch of the authoritarianism of Trump's supporters and define what authoritarianism is, how authoritarians behave, and the relationship between authoritarianism, threat, and intolerance. I also briefly explain how authoritarianism was estimated in the survey that produced most of the data presented in this chapter. Then, I turn to this survey data to explore whether Trump's supporters voted correctly. I examine Trump voters' feelings about groups targeted by him as "the other," their views on presidential power, and where they stand on the key issues on which Trump has staked his presidential campaign.

Next, I review Trump voters' views of fundamental American values and three specific policies that sacrifice those values for what some would argue is increased order and security. Then, I present a more theoretical discussion of how Trump's campaign—and the media coverage and social media commentary it precipitated—may have upended two accepted theories of political behavior before closing with a brief note about an irony of democracy exposed by Trump's success.

Authoritarianism and Trump Supporters

Under the auspices of the University of Massachusetts Amherst, I fielded a national public opinion survey in December 2015 to test my hypothesis that Trump's unvarnished us-versus-them message and bellicose manner activated authoritarians and fearful Americans, driving them to support Trump's candidacy. The poll was conducted online. It sampled 1,800 registered voters.[3] The topline results of the survey compared favorably to the findings of the *New York Times* poll conducted at approximately the same time.

In the survey, I used four child-rearing questions that first appeared on the ANES 1992 survey to estimate an individual's disposition to authoritarianism.[4] The inclusion of these questions on the ANES 1992 survey revived the study of authoritarianism over the last two decades.

Using the child-rearing battery of questions to estimate authoritarianism, my national poll demonstrated that authoritarianism was one of only two variables that are statistically significant and substantive predictors of Trump support among likely Republican primary voters.[5] The other variable was personal fear of terrorism.[6] In other words, American authoritarians and those who were more likely to fear that they or someone in their family will become a victim of terrorism in the next 12 months formed the core of Trump's support. Other variables tested in the model that were not statistically significant predictors of support for Trump included sex, educational attainment, age, church attendance, evangelicalism, ideology, race, and income (see table 8.1).[7]

Individuals with a disposition to authoritarianism demonstrate a fear of "the other" and a readiness to follow and obey strong leaders. They tend to see the world in black-and-white terms and are by definition attitudinally inflexible and rigid. Once they have identified friend from foe, authoritarians hold tight to their conclusions.[8] This intransigent

Table 8.1   Authoritarianism and Fear Predict Support for Trump

Authoritarianism	0.273**
Std. Err.	0.084
Fear of Terrorism	0.150 **
Std. Err.	0.053
Gender	−0.126
Std. Err.	0.200
Education	−0.415
Std. Err.	0.381
Age	−0.013
Std. Err.	0.433
Evangelicalism	0.025
Std. Err.	0.214
Ideology	0.053
Std. Err.	0.214
Church Attendance	−0.387
Std. Err.	0.220
Race	0.253
Std. Err.	0.257
Income	−0.066
Std. Err.	0.43 7
Intercept	−1.917
Std. Err	0.619
R-Squared	0.667
Adj. Count R-Squared	0.037
N	540

Source: University of Massachusetts Amherst, Political Science Department, 12/10/2015 Survey

Note: Estimates produced using logit analysis.

$*p < .05$, $**p < .01$, and $***p < .001$

behavioral tendency of authoritarians may help explain why Trump's support seemed, as a strategist for Marco Rubio complained in *The New York Times*, like "granite."[9]

Much of the extensive scholarly literature on authoritarianism concludes that it is inextricably linked to political conservatism (Adorno et al., 1950; Altemeyer, 1988; Kinder & Kam, 2009; Lavine, Lodge, & Freitas, 2005). But contemporary scholar Karen Stenner makes a critical and welcome distinction between authoritarianism and conservativism. She argues that while authoritarianism is "an aversion" to different "people and beliefs," status quo conservatism "is an aversion to . . . change" (2005, pp. 150–154).[10] Hetherington and Weiler describe the pivotal role authoritarianism can play in politics, arguing that authoritarianism is "a distinct way of understanding political reality" that "shap[es] political behavior and identity" (Hetherington & Weiler, 2009, p. 64).

I submit, as have other students of authoritarianism, that in all of its different manifestations and guises, threat is at the root of authoritarianism. Threat determines where an individual is likely to be located "on the continuum between authoritarian and democratic belief" (Dalton & Klingemann, 2007, p. 189), and it is "one of the strongest predictors of intolerance" (2007, p. 232).

My theory of how threat and authoritarianism interact was critical to the formulation of my hypothesis that authoritarianism and fear are both drivers of support for Trump. It is a hybrid of Stenner's authoritarian dynamic (2005) and Hetherington, Weiler, and Suhay's equally compelling observations about threat and authoritarianism (2009; 2011).[11] On the one hand, I stipulate that those Americans who are predisposed to authoritarianism are also more likely to feel threatened. When they perceive a mortal physical threat or a moral normative danger, their authoritarianism is activated. On the other hand, I contend that nonauthoritarians who perceive such threats will also become more aggressive and behave more like authoritarians. Thus, applying the cartoon character Pogo's well-known aphorism to nonauthoritarian Americans, *We have met the enemy, and when we are frightened, he is us.*

The implications of Pogo's observation to what the *New York Times* labeled Trump's "Campaign of Fear" cannot be underestimated.[12] The more fearful Americans become during an election campaign, the more likely they are to express authoritarian attitudes and be lured by Trump's siren call.

Correct Voting and Trump Supporters

To assess whether voters' support for Trump's candidacy was "correct" (meaning rational and responsible), I analyzed their answers to feeling thermometer questions. I also compared Trump and his voters' views on the constitutional limits of presidential power and examined whether Trump supporters agree with his positions on issues that were at the core of his candidacy.

Feeling thermometer scores are typically reported on a 0–100 scale. A score of 0 represents the coldest or most unfavorable feeling toward a person or a group, while a score of 100 represents the warmest or most favorable feeling. Throughout his campaign, Trump has defined illegal immigrants, Muslims, and Syrian refugees as "the other"—dangerous groups who do not share our values. Theoretically, if supporters of Donald Trump are voting correctly, they should report much lower (unfavorable) feeling thermometer scores for each of these groups than the supporters of other Republican candidates do.

To test this theory statistically, I use a bivariate difference of means test to compare the mean feeling thermometer scores of Trump supporters for illegal immigrants, Muslims, and Syrian refugees with those of supporters of all other Republican presidential candidates. The results are striking. Trump supporters report more unfavorable feelings toward each group targeted by Trump than supporters of the other Republican candidates (see figure 8.1). The difference between the scores is statistically significant at a p-value of 0.0001 or less for each group and ranges between 8 and 13 points on the 100-point scale. On this first measure of rational and responsible voting, Trump and his supporters' views are remarkably congruent.

From his campaign announcement to his acceptance speech at the Republican convention, Trump steadfastly articulated an expansive,

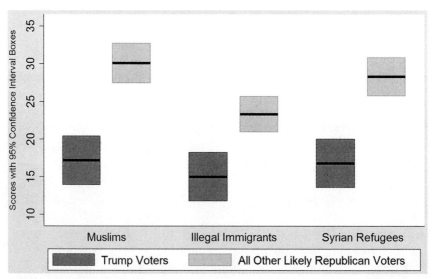

Figure 8.1   Trump Voters versus Other Likely Republican Voters (Feeling Thermometer Scores for Targeted Out-Groups where 0 = Cold/Unfavorable. University of Massachusetts Amherst, 12/10/2015 Survey. N = 588.)

unconstrained, and, many argue, unconstitutional view of the powers of the presidency. At the Republican convention, he proclaimed, "No one knows the system better than me, which is why I alone can fix it."[13]

Trump's call for renewed waterboarding of terrorism suspects ignores American law and the Geneva convention. His proposal to shut down mosques across America violates the First Amendment of the Constitution. And his suggestion that Muslim Americans be monitored and tracked transgresses the equal protection clause of the Constitution as well as other constitutionally protected civil rights. From the movement conservative editorial board of *The National Review* to the editors of the *New York Times*, Trump's expansive views of presidential power have raised concerns among a wide spectrum of America's leaders.[14]

Three questions from my survey demonstrate that Trump voters share his vision of a strong president who, when necessary, need not to be encumbered by constitutional limitations set out in the Constitution. Supporters of Donald Trump are more statistically and substantively likely to agree that "if it is necessary to protect our country the president should limit the voice and vote of opposition parties" than other Republican voters. They think "the president should ignore Congress" if it hinders the work of our government. And they even approve of the president ignoring the Supreme Court if it "hinders the work of our government." Trump voters' support for these unconstitutional grants of power to the president were estimated using an ordinal logit model with independent variables that included support for Trump, sex, education, age, ideology, church attendance, authoritarianism, race, income, and fear of terrorism. The stark, statistically significant differences between the most authoritarian and fearful Trump voters and other Republicans' predicted probability of supporting different aspects of constitutionally unconstrained presidential powers are displayed in figure 8.2.

Importantly, while Trump voters' support for a strongman president is statistically and substantively significant, ideological conservatives are *less likely* to support each of these expansive claims of executive power. This finding comports with Stenner's theory that there is an attitudinal difference between authoritarians and conservatives. In fact, Ted Cruz supporters are statistically more likely to oppose all three of these assertions of expanded presidential power. And their opposition is statistically and substantively significant.[15]

The acid test of correct voting is, of course, whether Trump's voters back his issue positions. I find statistically significant and substantive support for Trump's issue stands among his voters, no matter how controversial the subject. Trump voters are more likely than the supporters of

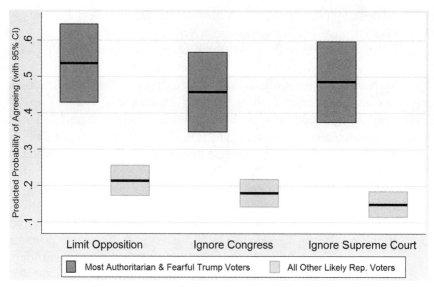

Figure 8.2   **When necessary the President should . . . (University of Mas-sachusetts Amherst, 12/10/2015 Survey. N = 537, except for Limit Opposition question where N = 536.)**

other Republican candidates to agree with the establishment of a force to round up and deport the 11 million immigrants now living illegally in the United States. They back the closure of mosques across America—an obvious abridgement of the first amendment of the Constitution. And they wholeheartedly support banning Muslims from entering the United States and establishing "a nationwide database" that "monitors and tracks all Muslims in America" (see figure 8.3).

Madisonian Democracy and Trump Supporters

So far I have demonstrated that Trump's supporters are rational and responsible voters who are also more likely to be disposed to authoritarian intolerance and afraid they or someone in their family will become a victim of terrorism in the next 12 months. But what does the activation of these voters' authoritarianism by Trump mean for the future of America's Madisonian democracy? While answering this question is beyond the scope of any one survey or this chapter, three general and three specific items asked on my December poll provide a glimpse into the intolerant vein in American politics tapped by Trump.

When asking general questions about attitudes, I find that Trump's supporters are statistically and substantively more likely to agree that

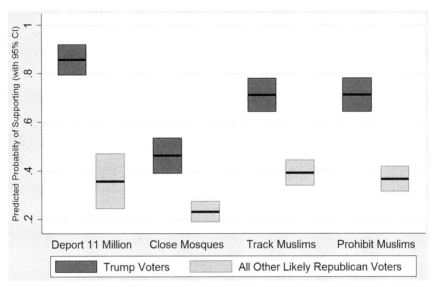

Figure 8.3   Support for Trump's Proposal to . . . (University of Massachusetts Amherst, 12/10/2015 Survey. N ranges from 538 to 542.)

sometimes *other* groups must be kept in their place than other likely Republican voters. They believe those who disagree with the majority are a threat to the interests of our country. And they reject the fundamental concern that a majority can act tyrannically, agreeing that minority rights do not need to be protected from majority power.

Specifically, Trump voters are statistically more likely to favor requiring all U.S. citizens to carry a national identification card and to show it to police upon request. They favor limiting free speech by prohibiting the media from reporting on secret methods the government is using to fight terrorism. But the most worrisome position backed by Trump voters is their statistically significant and substantive support for ending the constitutionally guaranteed writ of habeas corpus. Trump voters, especially those who are the most authoritarian and fearful, are more likely than the supporters of other Republican candidates to favor allowing police and other law enforcement agencies to *arrest and detain indefinitely* anyone in the United States who is *suspected* of belonging to a terrorist organization (see figure 8.4).

The Great Writ found in Article I, Section 9, Clause 2 of the Constitution is one of the fundamental bulwarks of the rule of law and order in America. The willingness of Trump voters to discard it is a warning sign that all is not well with the principles and values on which our democracy rests.

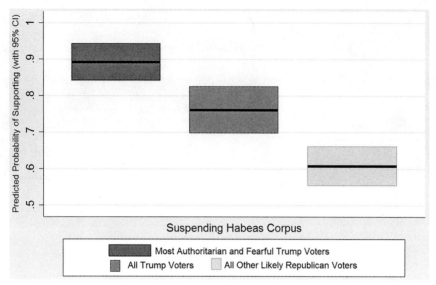

Figure 8.4   Support for . . . (University of Massachusetts Amherst, 12/10/2015 Survey. N = 540.)

Political Knowledge and Trump Voters

At face value, the question of how Trump supporters became so knowledgeable about his worldview and positions on a wide range of issues may seem like an odd inquiry. But "the enduring view" within political science is that "the mass public generally has limited political information and incoherent worldviews" (Hillygus & Shields, 2014, p. 6).

The assessment that most American voters possess shockingly little knowledge about stunningly few issues was first advanced in 1960 by the iconic political science treatise *The American Voter* (Campbell et al., 1960). Philip Converse expanded on *The American Voter*'s findings in a seminal essay two years later (1962). Decades later, Converse's conclusions about the sophistication of the American mass public is one of the established facts of political science. Carpini and Keeter call the persistent disparity of knowledge within the American public across time "intractable" (1997, p. 17), with Converse concluding "we hardly need argue low information levels anymore" (2000, p. 331). To most political scientists, the public is bifurcated into a small, knowledgeable elite and an unsophisticated mass public. The result is a stratified American democracy with a mass, uninformed electorate that is, at best, "more in the shadows [than] in the dark" (Carpini & Keeter, 1997, p. 95).

In campaigns, low information levels persist because "once the marginal cost of new information exceeds the potential gain from that information" voters stop "paying attention" (Lau & Redlawsk, p. 7). Since information costs are said to be high and the marginal utility of acquiring new information about a candidate is low, voters are theorized to make decisions based on constrained bits of information (Downs, 1957); single issues (Conover et al., 1982); easy issues (Carmines & Stimson, 1980); or heuristics that simplify their choice (Popkin, 1991).

Trump's voters may have initially decided to support him based on shards of information, but their exceptional congruency with him on issues and worldview, and their shared enmity to groups targeted by him as "the other," suggests another possibility. I submit that voters' support for Trump is not only correct but also politically informed because the cognitive costs of acquiring information about Trump were actually quite low.

Coverage and talk about Trump has been everywhere—online, in social media, and on television. More importantly, to some, Trump has been entertaining. He transformed political discourse into reality television and in doing so transformed information into entertainment. The cost of learning more about Trump became a benefit to some voters—the joy of being entertained.

Trump's reality-television entertainment approach to politics also turned inside out a recent theory of the use of wedge issues in presidential campaigns. In 2008, Hillygus and Shields offered an insightful analysis of the rapidly evolving world of presidential campaign strategy. They argued that general election candidates for president, who "cannot win the election with their partisan base alone," now employ dog-whistle communications to deliver messages on divisive wedge issues to persuadable voters to win their votes (Hillygus & Shields, p. 5). As such, targeted voters hear a contentious message. Other voters do not. And the candidate blowing the dog whistle wins over persuasion targets without alienating base supporters.

Trump turned the notion of dog-whistle politics on its head, replacing it with what I call bullhorn campaigning. Focusing on divisive and provocative wedge issues and using his bullying strongman persona, Trump forged a messaging bullhorn that dominated media coverage, social media commentary, and interest in the campaign. The result was that Trump's message was ubiquitous. It defined the political contours of the Republican nomination campaign. And it reached and activated American authoritarians who rallied to Trump's clarion call.

The so-called bizarre spectacle of Donald Trump's primary campaign made for electric must-see media that drew eyeballs, drove ratings, and, for legacy broadcast and cable news media operations, generated much-needed revenue.[16] For example, with Trump driving interest in the campaign and the Republican debates, CNN was able to raise its advertising rates for one 30-second spot in the September 2015 debate from $5,000 to $200,000.[17]

Advertising rates across cable news channels rose throughout the fall of 2015 and well into the spring of 2016 as a symbiotic relationship between Trump and the media developed. Trump provided well-timed and compelling content, and the media covered it. Trump rallies were timed to maximize live coverage. Trump tweets and phone calls were geared to shape the media narrative or change it to his liking. All campaigns seek to shape and drive the media narrative to their advantage, but Trump's manipulation of the media has been unparalleled. And the content he offered was red meat that left the milquetoast pronouncements of his opponents on the cutting room floor.

Unable to resist the political reality show that was unpredictably unfolding before them, Americans rubbernecked their way through the nomination process. The media incessantly covered Trump. Media ratings and revenue increased. And from July 15, 2015, on, Trump's campaign vaulted to the top of national polls among Republican primary voters.

Trump's dominance of the media has been as stunning as his unchallenged dominance in national primary polling was remarkable. Every month from June 2015 until the last of his Republican opponents folded on May 3, 2016, Trump's media coverage greatly exceeded the coverage afforded to his opponents (see figure 8.5).

The media followed the ratings and revenue. In doing so, it amplified and mainstreamed Trump's authoritarian, us-versus-them message. And America's authoritarian voters answered Trump's call. But mass media was not the only communication tool that activated voters to support Trump. As Steve Case observed in the *New York Times*, "Trump leveraged a perfect storm. A combo of social media (big following), brand (celebrity figure), creativity (pithy tweets), speed/timeliness (dominating news cycles)."[18] With over 7 million followers on Twitter and Facebook, Trump used the social media platforms of the Arab Spring to cyberbully critics, savage opponents, threaten violence, and foment America's "Authoritarian Spring."[19]

Trump fused mass rally demonstrations of unity and power, the immediacy and unfiltered messaging of social media, and the revenue needs of legacy media to construct a 21st-century, strongman bullhorn not seen before in politics. In doing so, he gutted the opposition, dominated the media narrative, and galvanized a politically informed and loyal cadre of supporters from the ranks of America's authoritarians and fearful.

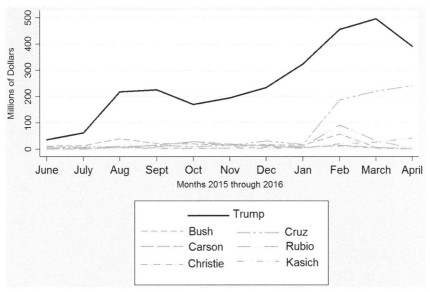

Figure 8.5 Estimated Worth of Presidential Media Coverage (Source of Estimates: MediaQuant)

As Richard Cohen wrote, lamenting the death of liberalism and the ascendance of authoritarianism in the United States and around the globe, "nationalism and authoritarianism, reinforced by technology, have come together to exercise new forms of control and manipulation over human beings."[20]

American Democracy and the Rise of Trumpism

For decades, democratic theorists have derided the apathy and lack of knowledge of America's mass public. Trump's bullhorn campaigning activated and informed some of those Americans, producing supporters who voted correctly and who to this day are abnormally knowledgeable about his policies and politics.

There is an irony, however, to Trump's success in rallying America's authoritarians and fearful. Political scientists have long noted a hidden virtue in the electorate's disinterest in politics. While some Americans are intolerant, they have not "generally act[ed] on their undemocratic beliefs or values" (Taber, 2003, p. 461—referencing Kinder, 1998). Aided and abetted by a willing media, Trump's campaign for the Republican nomination changed that calculus. Intolerant and fearful American authoritarians heard and responded to Trump's clarion call. And their unyielding support made him the Republican nominee for president of the United States.

Trumpism is unlikely to go quietly into the night after the ballots for president are finally counted in November. Trump's support is firmly rooted in an American version of authoritarianism that, once awakened and stoked, is a force to be reckoned with.

Trump's campaign has roused what bears a striking resemblance to another political phenomenon identified by Philip Converse more than a half century ago. In a coda to his essay on the lack of political sophistication of American voters, Converse proposed the existence of what he called "issue publics" (1962). Like Trump's core supporters, members of issue publics are specialists on a limited range of topics, passionate about those issues, and ideologically unconstrained. The specific issue concerns of issue publics (the issues members are interested in) are very accessible to them— just like Trump supporters' remarkable knowledge of Trump's stands on issues. And these issues are "extensively linked to and consistent with [their] basic values" (Krosnick, 1990, p. 70). This is a hauntingly accurate description of Trump voters' attitudes and worldviews found in my survey.

Trump's campaign has activated and energized an issue public. The foundation of Trump's issue public is authoritarian intolerance that knows no racial or ethnic boundaries. Any group targeted as "the other" will become the focus of authoritarian aggression. Authoritarian intolerance is a "violent passion" and a threat to democracy that, as Madison warned in Federalist 63, periodically infects the public. The question before America is, how serious has the infection become?

Notes

1. Retrieved from http://www.nytimes.com/2016/03/16/upshot/measuring -donald-trumps-mammoth-advantage-in-free-media.html?_r=0.

2. See *Politico*, http://www.politico.com/magazine/story/2016/01/donald -trump-2016-authoritarian-213533; *Vox*, http://www.vox.com/2016/2/23/11099644 /trump-support-authoritarianism; London School of Economics *USAPP* blog; and two other posts: http://blogs.lse.ac.uk/usappblog/2016/01/27/donald-trump -is-attracting-authoritarian-primary-voters-and-it-may-help-him-to-gain-the -nomination and *PS: Political Science and Politics* (forthcoming October 2016).

3. The survey included standard demographic questions, feeling thermometers on political figures, groups of people and organizations, screens to identify likely primary and general voters, candidate preference questions, items assessing respondents' worries about the sociotropic and personal threats posed by

terrorism, and a bevy of values and policy questions. The Republican survey population was 558, which included 18 African Americans.

4. The four child-rearing questions used to estimate authoritarianism asks respondents, "Which one do you think is more important for a child to have?" Respondents are then presented with four pairs of answers: "1. Independence or Respect for Elders? 2. Curiosity or Good Manners? 3. Obedience or Self-Reliance? and 4. Considerate or Well Behaved?" Answers in each pair are rotated randomly. In some surveys, respondents are also allowed to answer "Both." Authoritarian answers are Respect for Elders, Good Manners, Obedience, and Well Behaved. Answers are aggregated, and an authoritarian scale is constructed that typically varies from 0 (not authoritarian at all) to 1 (most authoritarian). Developing a 0–1 scale from the child-rearing questions is the approach used by Feldman and Stenner (1997), Stenner (2005), Hetherington and Weiler (2009), and Hetherington and Suhay (2011).

5. Many other theories have been advanced to explain Trump's rise. Byrd and Collingwood argue racial resentment is behind Trump's rise. Clifford Young of Ipsos says it's nativism. Pew Research thinks it is racism and xenophobia. Rahn and Oliver contend economic populism is behind Trump's success. (See https://www.washingtonpost.com/news/monkey-cage/wp/2016/03/09/trumps-voters-arent-authoritarians-new-research-says-so-what-are-they; http://spotlight.ipsos-na.com/index.php/news/its-nativism-explaining-the-drivers-of-trumps-popular-support; and http://www.vox.com/2016/6/7/11875964/donald-trump-racism-charts.)

Following Hetherington and Weiler, I stipulate that authoritarianism is a predisposition that arises causally prior to the political attitudes and behavior that it affects (2009, p. 145). As such, it occurs before ideology, partisanship, and the other *-isms* that have been offered to explain Trump's rise.

6. The question wording is, "How worried are you that you or someone in your family will become a victim of terrorism in the next 12 months?" Possible answers are arrayed on a 7-point scale from "not at all" to "a lot."

7. Only likely Republican primary voters were included in the sample tested.

8. Published in 1950, *The Authoritarian Personality* (Adorno et al., 1950) marks the beginning of the scholarly exploration of authoritarianism. Its core observation that prejudice is a generalized attitude in those individuals who are intolerant—an "entire way of thinking about those who are 'different'" (Myers, 2010, p. 230)—is the foundation on which the numerous studies of ethnocentrism and authoritarianism that followed are based. In short, authoritarianism is the taproot of intolerance.

9. Retrieved from http://www.nytimes.com/2016/01/29/us/politics/marco-rubios-camp-sees-opening-if-donald-trump-wins-in-iowa.html?_r=2.

10. Although authoritarianism and racism are correlated in the United States, they are different. As Stenner notes, authoritarianism is an aversion to different "people and beliefs" (2005). Thus, the sources of authoritarian intolerance are much broader than race.

Stenner's observation is quite important. It creates theoretical space for the empirically undeniable existence of left-wing authoritarian regimes, such as Hugo Chavez's government in Venezuela

11. Stenner argues that normative threat activates authoritarianism. Hetherington, Weiler, and Suhay contend that authoritarians are always vigilant and activated. And threat, particularly personal physical threat, makes nonauthoritarians act more authoritarian.

12. The lead editorial in the *New York Times* the morning after Trump's acceptance speech at the Republican National Convention on July 21, 2016, was titled "Donald Trump's Campaign of Fear." Retrieved from http://www.nytimes.com/2016/07/22/opinion/donald-trumps-campaign-of-fear.html?_r=0.

13. Retrieved from http://www.vox.com/2016/7/21/12253426/donald-trump-acceptance-speech-transcript-republican-nomination-transcript.

14. The editors of America's preeminent conservative journal, the *National Review*, and 20 leading conservatives, including Mona Charen, William Kristol, Edwin Meese III, and John Podhoretz, opposed Trump's nomination, warning of his "free-floating populism with strongman overtones." Retrieved from http://www.nationalreview.com/article/430137/donald-trump-conservative-movement-menace.

15. Rubio supporters' opposition was statistically and substantively significant on two of the three questions. Bush and Carson supporters' support or opposition was not statistically significant on any question.

16. Retrieved from http://www.politico.com/story/2015/06/donald-trump-2016-announcement-10-best-lines-119066.

17. Retrieved from http://fortune.com/2015/09/06/trump-cnn-ad.

18. Steve Case founded AOL; retrieved from http://www.nytimes.com/2016/05/08/us/politics/republican-party-unravels-over-donald-trumps-takeover.html?_r=0.

19. By May 2016, Trump's followers on Twitter and Facebook surpassed 8 million; retrieved from http://www.nytimes.com/2016/02/27/us/politics/donald-trump.html?_r=0; retrieved from http://www.politico.com/story/2016/03/trump-slams-marco-rubio-social-media-220374; retrieved from http://www.commondreams.org/news/2016/03/13/its-not-threat-trump-says-hell-order-supporters-disrupt-sanders-rallies.

20. Retrieved from http://www.nytimes.com/2016/04/14/opinion/the-death-of-liberalism.html.

References

Adorno, T. W., Frenkel-Brunswick, E., Levinson, D. J., & Sanford, R. N. (1950). *The authoritarian personality.* New York: Harper and Row.
Altemeyer, B. (1988). *Enemies of freedom: Understanding right-wing authoritarianism.* San Francisco: Jossey-Bass.
Campbell, A., Converse, P. E., Miller, W. E., & Stokes, D. E. (1960). *The American voter.* New York: John Wiley and Sons.

Carmines, E. G., & Stimson J. A. (1980). The two faces of issue voting. *American Political Science Review, 74,* 78–91.

Carpini, M. X. D., & Keeter, S. (1997). *What Americans know about politics and why it matters.* New Haven, CT: Yale University Press.

Conover, P. J., Gray, V., & Coombs, S. (1982). Single-issue voting: Elite-mass linkages. *Political Behavior, 4*(4), 309–331.

Converse, P. E. (1962). *The nature of belief systems in mass publics* (pp. 206–261). Survey Research Center, University of Michigan.

Converse, P. E. (2000). Assessing the capacity of mass electorates. *Annual Review of Political Science, 3*(1), 331–353.

Dalton, R., & Klingemann, H. D. (Eds.). (2007). *Oxford handbook of political behavior.* Oxford: Oxford University Press.

Downs, A. (1957). *An economic theory of democracy.* New York: Harper and Row.

Feldman, S., & Stenner, K. (1997). Perceived threat and authoritarianism. *Political Psychology, 18*(4), 741–770.

Goldberg, A. S. (1969). Social determinism and rationality as bases of party identification. *American Political Science Review, 63,* 5–25.

Hetherington, M., & Suhay, E. (2011). Authoritarianism, threat, and Americans' support for the war on terror. *American Journal of Political Science, 55*(3), 546–560.

Hetherington, M., & Weiler, J. (2009). *Authoritarianism and polarization in American politics.* New York: Cambridge University Press.

Hillygus, D. S., & Shields, T. G. (2014). *The persuadable voter: Wedge issues in presidential campaigns.* Princeton, NJ: Princeton University Press.

Key, V.O. (1966). *The responsible electorate.* Cambridge, MA: Belknap Press of Harvard University Press.

Kinder, D. R. (1998). Opinion and action in the realm of politics. In D. T. Gilbert, S. T. Fiske, & G. Lindzey (Eds.), *Handbook of Social Psychology* (4th ed., Vol. 1, pp. 778–867). New York: Oxford University Press.

Kinder, D. R., & Kam, C. D. (2010). *Us against them: Ethnocentric foundations of American opinion.* Chicago: University of Chicago Press.

Krosnick, J. A. (1990). Government policy and citizen passion: A study of issue publics in contemporary America. *Political Behavior, 12*(1), 59–92.

Lau, R. R., & Redlawsk, D. P. (2006). *How voters decide: Information processing in election campaigns.* New York: Cambridge University Press.

Lavine, H., Lodge, M., & Freitas, K. (2005). Threat, authoritarianism, and selective exposure to information. *Political Psychology, 26*(2), 219–244.

Popkin, S. L. (1991). *The reasoning voter: Communications and persuasion in presidential campaigns.* Chicago: University of Chicago Press.

Stenner, K. (2005). *The authoritarian dynamic.* New York: Cambridge University Press.

Taber, S. T. (2003). Information processing and public opinion. In D. O. Sears, L. Huddy, & R. Jervis, *Oxford Handbook of Political Psychology* (pp. 433–476). New York: Oxford University Press.

CHAPTER NINE

Death: The Trump Card

Florette Cohen, Sharlynn Thompson, Tom
Pyszczynski, and Sheldon Solomon

Charismatic leaders have a way of appearing in times of great distress.
They usually espouse a decidedly radical vision that promises to
resolve the crisis. Crisis, by definition, is a period of great threat and
uncertainty, a time when the existing leadership seems to falter. It is
also a period in which the society's ordinary coping mechanisms are
out of kilter. It is not, then, all that surprising that a charismatic
leader offering a solution, however radical, is particularly welcome in
difficult times. Of course, one might even argue that, in the turmoil
and anxiety that keep company with crisis, anyone who confidently
proposes a solution is likely to be looked upon as charismatic....
Followers' response to charismatics [is] a devotion born of distress.
—Jean Lipman-Blumen, *The connective edge* (1996, p. 30)

Voice or no voice, the people can always be brought to the bidding of
the leaders. That is easy. All you have to do is tell them they are
being attacked and denounce the pacifists for lack of patriotism and
exposing the country to danger. It works the same way in any
country. —Hermann Göring, leading member of the Nazi Party (in
Gilbert, 1995, pp. 278–279)

The 2016 presidential election promised to be one of the most spirited
affairs in the history of American politics, due in large measure to Donald
Trump securing the Republican Party nomination. To his detractors,

Mr. Trump is a vulgar, sadistic, vindictive, egomaniacal, misogynistic, xenophobic, twittering Mussolini-with-a-spray-tan who makes no pretense of coherence, consistency, or veracity and is thereby unfit for public office. To his supporters, Mr. Trump was a savvy, deal-making, bold, and heroic change agent who was unbeholden to special interests and unrestrained by political correctness. They were enthralled by his vow to "Make America Great Again" by revitalizing the economy, deporting 11 million immigrants, building an impregnable wall to secure the southern border, prohibiting all Muslims from entering the United States, and "bomb[ing] the shit out of ISIS."

Pundits and academics have offered a variety of cogent economic, sociological, and psychological accounts of Mr. Trump's political ascent. However, in our estimation, such explanations are incomplete without examining the role of unconscious death anxiety on human behavior in general and in forging a bond between charismatic leaders and their followers in particular. In this chapter, we present an existential psychodynamic account of the allure of Donald Trump based on terror management theory (TMT; Greenberg, Pyszczynski, & Solomon, 1986; Solomon, Greenberg, & Pyszczynski, 1991; Solomon, Greenberg, & Pyszczynski, 2015). We will provide historical and empirical evidence that support for charismatic leaders, including Mr. Trump, is driven by death anxiety, and we argue that these findings have portentous implications for democracy, regardless of one's political predilections.

Terror Management Theory

TMT is derived from cultural anthropologist Ernest Becker's (1971; 1973; 1975) efforts to explain the motivational underpinnings of human behavior. The theory starts with the assumption that although humans share with all forms of life a basic biological inclination toward self-preservation in the service of survival and reproduction, we are unique in our capacity for abstract and symbolic thought culminating in the capacity for self-reflection (Deacon, 1997); mental time travel (i.e., to ponder the past and anticipate the future; Varki & Brower, 2013); and the fabrication of products of our imagination (e.g., helicopters and symphonies; Rank, 1978). These are all highly adaptive proficiencies; however, they also give rise to the terrifying realization that one's death is inescapable and can occur at any time for reasons that cannot always be foreseen or prevented and that people are ultimately no more consequential or enduring than cucumbers or caterpillars.

According to Becker and TMT, humans "manage" the potentially debil-
itating terror produced by the awareness of death (which originates in
children as young as age two and often occurs in the absence of physical
danger; Solomon, Greenberg, & Pyszczynski, 2015) by embracing *cultural
worldviews*: humanly constructed beliefs about reality shared by people in
groups that provide a sense that one is a person of *value* in a world of
meaning. Cultural worldviews provide meaning by offering an account of
the origin of the universe (i.e., creation myths), prescriptions for appro-
priate conduct, and promises of literal or symbolic immortality to those
who adhere to cultural edicts. Literal immortality entails persisting in
perpetuity in some form, for example, souls, heavens, reincarnations,
afterlives, and ancestral stomping grounds central to most of the world's
religions. Symbolic immortality (Lifton, 1979) is a sense that a vestige of
oneself will endure after one is gone, for example, by having children,
amassing prodigious fortunes, producing great works of art or science, or
being part of a great tribe or nation.

In addition to affording a sense that life has meaning, cultural worldviews enable individuals to perceive themselves as persons of value by
meeting or exceeding standards associated with various social roles
embedded in the culture, for example, saving lives for a nurse, scoring
goals for a soccer player, or making money for a hedge fund manager. *Self-
esteem* results from the belief that one is a valuable member of a meaningful universe, and TMT posits that a primary function of cultural worldviews
and self-esteem is to mitigate anxiety in general and about death in particular. People are, accordingly, highly motivated to maintain faith in their
cultural worldviews and confidence in their self-worth; moreover, they
respond defensively when their sense of meaning or value is undermined.

Support for TMT (recently reviewed in Pyszczynski, Solomon, &
Greenberg, 2015) includes research on the effects of self-esteem on anxiety, the effects of death reminders on faith in one's worldview and the
pursuit of self-esteem, and the effects of threats to one's cultural worldview or self-esteem on how readily death-related thoughts come to mind.
Momentarily heightened, or dispositionally high, self-esteem reduces
anxiety and physiological arousal in response to threat (e.g., watching
gory death images or anticipating electrical shocks; see Pyszczynski et al.,
2004, for a review of this work). To investigate the effect of death reminders (mortality salience, or MS), TMT researchers make mortality salient
by having people write about death, view graphic depictions of death, be
interviewed in front of a funeral parlor, or be subliminally exposed to the
word "dead" or "death." Reminders of death intensify cultural worldview

defense and self-esteem striving. For example, Greenberg et al. (1990) found that following MS, Christian participants had more favorable reactions to fellow Christians and less favorable reactions to Jewish targets; Ben-Ari, Florian, and Mikulincer (1999) found that Israeli soldiers who derived self-esteem from their driving prowess drove faster and more recklessly in a car simulator in response to a MS induction (see Burke, Martens, & Faucher, 2010, for a meta-analysis of MS studies).

Research on the effects of threats to the cultural worldview or self-esteem on the accessibility of death-related thoughts provides additional converging support for the theory. For example, Christian fundamentalists confronted with logical inconsistencies in the Bible (Friedman & Rholes, 2007) and Americans asked to ponder undesired aspects of themselves (Cohen, Ogilvie, & Solomon, 2008) used more death-related words in a word stem completion task (e.g., C O F F _ _ = coffin rather than coffee; G R _ V E = grave rather than grove; see Hayes, Schimel, Arndt, & Faucher, 2010, for a meta-analysis of DTA research). Heightened death-thought accessibility (DTA) in turn instigates cultural worldview defense and self-esteem striving (Pyszczynski, Greenberg, & Solomon, 1999; Hayes et al., 2015).

Charismatic Leaders and Followers

When mortality is salient, voters favor charismatic candidates who make them feel important and needed. After an MS or aversive control induction, Cohen, Solomon, Maxfield, Pyszczynski, and Greenberg (2004) presented participants with statements representing three hypothetical gubernatorial candidates who varied in leadership style. The charismatic candidate's statement asserted each person's importance in a great nation, avowing that "you are not just an ordinary citizen, you are part of a special state and a special nation and if we work together we can make a difference." The other candidates' statements emphasized completing tasks effectively (task-oriented) or the need for leaders and followers to work together and accept mutual responsibility (relationship-oriented). In the control condition, the task-oriented candidate was preferred by the majority of participants, with just 4 percent of the respondents voting for the charismatic candidate; however, 31 percent of the people who were reminded of death before voting chose the charismatic candidate.

Charismatic leaders have long been known to have remarkable effects on followers in certain situations. At the outset of the 20th century, German sociologist Max Weber characterized charisma as "a certain quality of an individual personality, by virtue of which he is set apart from ordinary men and treated as endowed with supernatural, superhuman, or at least specifically exceptional powers or qualities" (1947, pp. 358–359). Moreover, Weber noted that charismatic leaders generally emerge in times of historical upheaval, and, building on Weber's work, Becker (1973) argued that when mainstream cultural worldviews are not serving people's needs for meaning and significance, death fears impel people to embrace charismatic leaders who bolster their self-worth by making them feel that they are valued parts of something great or instrumental in making something great (again).

In accord with this view, Eric Hoffer, in *The True Believer* (1951), reflecting on the rise of charismatic leaders in the 20th century, including Hitler, Stalin, and Mussolini, proposed that the primary impetus for all populist movements is a critical mass of frustrated and disaffected citizens subject to grave economic or psychological insecurity "in desperate need of something ... to live for" (p. 15). This produces unwavering dedication and loyalty to a leader who confidently espouses a cause that infuses their lives with a sense of "worth and meaning" (p. 15) and faith in the future via "identification, the process by which the individual ceases to be himself and becomes part of something eternal" (p. 63).

Charismatic leaders, Hoffer observed, need not be exceptionally intelligent, noble, or original. Rather, the primary qualifications "seem to be: audacity and a joy in defiance; an iron will; a fanatical conviction that he is in possession of the one and only truth; faith in his destiny and luck; a capacity for passionate hatred; contempt for the present; a cunning estimate of human nature; a delight in symbols (spectacles and ceremonials)... the arrogant gesture, the complete disregard of the opinion of others, the singlehanded defiance of the world ... [and] some deliberate misrepresentation of facts" (p. 114).

Finally, Hoffer (as well as Becker, 1975) noted that mass movements require an external enemy to enable the charismatic leader to direct the rage and righteous indignation of the frustrated and disaffected followers toward a tangible scapegoat, an individual or group of individuals designated as an all-encompassing repository of evil that must be subdued or eradicated.

Fatal Attraction in the Wake of 9/11

President George W. Bush's political transformation after September 11, 2001, provides a relatively recent example of how intimations of mortality affect political preferences. The terrorist attacks on the World Trade

Center and the Pentagon posed a profound existential threat to Americans (Pyszczynski, Solomon, & Greenberg, 2003), as they witnessed potent images of death as the Twin Towers collapsed, the Pentagon blazed, and another plane headed toward the capital crashed in rural Pennsylvania. Beyond the literal carnage, three of the foremost symbols of Americans' cultural worldview had been endangered or assaulted: the Twin Towers, the Pentagon, and the White House—representing U.S. economic, military, and governmental power, respectively.

Prior to 9/11, President George W. Bush's presidency was viewed as ineffectual and uninspired, even to many of his Republican supporters. However, within a few weeks of declaring that the nation was at war and warning other nations to join the "crusade" to "rid the world of the evildoers" or face, in Vice President Dick Cheney's words, the "full wrath of the United States" (Purdum, 2001), President Bush's approval ratings reached historically unprecedented heights among Democrats as well as Republicans (Jacobson, 2005). President Bush became a charismatic leader by declaring that God had chosen him to rid the world of evil at a historical moment when Americans were in the throes of existential terror.

To demonstrate that President Bush's popularity and support for his policies in Iraq were influenced by intimations of mortality, Landau et al., (2004) predicted and found that while President Bush and his policies in Iraq were not highly regarded by participants in an aversive control condition, there was dramatically greater support for the president and his Iraq policies following an MS induction. In a follow-up study, participants were exposed to subliminal terrorism primes (the numbers 911 or the letters WTC) or subliminal control primes (numbers and letters of equivalent familiarity), followed by a word stem completion task to assess the accessibility of implicit death-related thoughts. Results indicated greater levels of DTA for participants in the subliminal terrorism prime conditions; for Americans then, even subliminal reminders of the events of 9/11 aroused concerns about mortality. Accordingly, in a third study, participants were randomly assigned to think about death (MS), the events of 9/11 (terrorism prime), or an aversive control topic before rating the president and his policies in Iraq; both MS and terrorism salience produced substantial increases in support for President Bush and his policies in Iraq. Finally, in another study conducted five weeks before the 2004 presidential election, control participants reported they would be voting for Senator Kerry by a 4:1 margin; however, President Bush was favored by a 2.5:1 margin after a MS induction (Cohen, Ogilvie, Solomon, Greenberg, & Pyszczynski, 2005).

Cohen et al. (2005) argued that the 2004 presidential election was decisively influenced by subconscious defensive reactions to relentless reminders of the events of September 11, 2001, by Republican political strategists aided by the release of a video by Osama bin Laden the weekend before the election. Indeed, Senator Kerry came to the same conclusion when reflecting on the election on January 30, 2005, observing that "the attacks of September 11 were the 'central deciding thing' in his contest with President Bush and that the release of an Osama bin Laden videotape the weekend before Election Day had effectively erased any hope he had of victory" (Nagourney, 2005).

Death: The Trump Card

It is [fear] that makes people so willing to follow brash, strong-looking demagogues with tight jaws and loud voices: those who focus their measured words and their sharpened eyes in the intensity of hate, and so seem most capable of cleansing the world of the vague, the weak, the uncertain, the evil. Ah, to give oneself over to their direction—what calm, what relief. —Ernest Becker, *The birth and death of meaning*

Current political, economic, and psychological conditions are conducive for the rise of a charismatic leader who, in more prosperous economic and more stable historical circumstances, might be dismissed as unserious and incapable. Donald Trump entered the political arena at a time when his supporters—a majority of whom are white men without a college degree—are feeling economically and psychologically assaulted and abused (Thompson, 2016). They believe they are under attack by minorities and terrorists and that political correctness has divested them of their voice and their rights. Swelling diversity is perceived as a threat that increases discrimination against whites (Outten, Schmitt, Miller, & Garcia, 2012; Dover, Major, & Kaiser, 2016). The number of jobs available to them are decreasing as more and more occupations require a college education. To his supporters, who are feeling increasingly unrepresented and underserved, Trump is truly offering a way to "Make America Great Again" by emphasizing issues that are important to them. He appeals to people who feel that their country currently has nothing to offer them at a time when they are vulnerable to attacks by globalism, immigrants, and radical Islam, and he provides them a position in a movement that affords a sense of meaning, value, and hope.

Although Trump's proposals are vague, riddled with contradictions, and have no grounding in reality, they do, however, have one thing in common. They are based on anger and fear: fear of terrorism, fear of immigrants, fear of being taken advantage of economically, and fear of government inefficiency and indifference. Yet, Trump does not ask his supporters to briefly consider their own deaths at the beginning of his rallies, project flashes of the word "death" on his screens, nor hold television interviews in cemeteries. How, then, do subconscious fears of death arise that in turn increase support for Mr. Trump?

Recall that research has shown that threatening cultural worldviews, cherished beliefs, or self-esteem increases death-thought accessibility and that heighted DTA instigates cultural worldview defense and self-esteem striving. Moreover, in the aftermath of 9/11, subliminal exposure to the numbers 911 or the letters WTC (World Trade Center) increased DTA, and asking participants to think about death or the events of 9/11 increased support for George W. Bush. Additionally, Cohen, Soenke, Solomon, and Greenberg (2013) found that thinking about a mosque being built in one's neighborhood increased DTA as much as thinking directly about death. And in a similar study, people either wrote about their own deaths, immigrants moving into their neighborhood, or an aversive control condition (Cohen & Solomon, 2016). Again, thinking about immigrants moving into their neighborhood increased DTA as much as thinking about their own deaths. Together, these studies suggest that Muslims (all of whom are assumed to be terrorists or aiding and abetting terrorists) and immigrants, who are often at the center of Mr. Trump's attacks, increase the accessibility of death thoughts and, at least subconsciously, threaten the American worldview.

For Mr. Trump's supporters, threatening shared cultural worldviews increases DTA and heightens insecurity, which in turn increases hostility toward outsiders and creates an ideal opportunity for a charismatic leader to provide a sense of meaning, value, and security (physical and psychological) to his followers. Discussions of terrorism (and of course actual terrorist attacks in Paris, Belgium, San Bernardino, Orlando, and Istanbul), illegal immigrants taking American jobs and receiving government assistance, liberals taking away guns or individual rights, and making statement such as, "If we don't get tough [on terrorism], and we don't get smart—and fast—we're not going to have a country anymore—there will be nothing left" (www.donaldjtrump.com), all threaten American worldviews and reduce the personal sense of importance gained from belonging to a great nation, which is reputedly no longer great at all. This rhetoric also increases unconscious death thoughts, which contribute to increased support for Trump's candidacy for president.

We have recently examined the effect of death reminders on support for Mr. Trump. Cohen and Solomon (2016) assigned participants to write about their own mortality or being in intense pain. Participants were then asked to report: How favorably do you view Donald Trump? To what extent do you admire Donald Trump? To what extent do you have confidence in Donald Trump as a leader? If you vote in the upcoming presidential election, how likely is it you will vote for Donald Trump? Results indicated that participants asked to write about their own deaths had significantly more favorable impressions of, greater admiration for, increased confidence in, and higher likelihood of voting for Mr. Trump than people who wrote about being in pain. And, consistent with Landau et al.'s 2004 finding that MS increased support for President Bush, this effect was obtained regardless of participants' political orientation.

Mr. Trump's supporters feel that America is a country in need of repair. Although they once received a sense of pride and purpose from being part of the American Dream, they now receive it from Mr. Trump's campaign to rebuild a severely damaged America. The pro-Trump movement has become a new worldview, and supporters' self-esteem is bolstered by belonging to it and supporting the sacred mission it promotes. Mr. Trump's supporters now have something to live for, as well as loyalty to Mr. Trump and his movement, and have willingly abandoned logical and critical thought. Despite Trump's reliance on attacking others, the lack of any real policies and effort to make factually accurate statements (indeed, according to *PolitiFact*, over 70% of Trump's statements are patently false), his supporters are able to immerse themselves in the movement and garner pride and hope in a shared vision. As Hoffer put it,

> All active mass movements strive … to interpose a fact-proof screen between the faithful and the realities of the world. They do this by claiming that the ultimate and absolute truth is already embodied in their doctrine and that there is no truth nor certitude outside of it. … It is the true believer's ability to "shut his eyes and stop his ears" to facts … which is the source of his unequaled fortitude and constancy. He cannot be frightened by danger nor disheartened by obstacles nor baffled by contradictions because he denies their existence. (1951, p. 78)

Mr. Trump's political speeches have a general format that is similar in many ways to a good TMT study. First, worldview threat is induced by identifying villains: someone to be afraid of (immigrants), someone who is attacking America (Islamic terrorists), or someone to blame (immigrants, Muslims, politicians). This increases death-thought accessibility. He then tells his supporters that America is no longer great, which decreases collective self-esteem and the sense of personal value that is normally provided by patriotism. Mr. Trump then promises safety from all threats under his presidency and makes each person feel valuable by emphasizing the importance of each supporter, taking on the persona of the charismatic leader who is sought after when mortality is salient. Most notably, Mr. Trump exudes confidence and defiance, is full of anger and contempt, disregards other's opinions, and makes claims that, although demonstrably untrue, feed the narrative that he promotes. Finally, Mr. Trump pounds home the message that together, he and his followers can "Make America Great Again." As researchers who have studied this phenomenon extensively for decades, we would be hard-pressed to design a more effective campaign strategy based solely on TMT.

The fact that subtle, brief alterations of psychological conditions (i.e., asking people to think about terrorism, mosques, immigrants, or their own mortality) is sufficient to bring death thoughts more readily to mind and produce striking differences in political preferences—for charismatic leaders in general, President Bush post-9/11, and Donald Trump in 2016—suggests that close elections could be decided as a result of nonrational terror management concerns. We'd like to think that Americans across the political spectrum would agree that this is antithetical to democracy. History is replete with examples that elections are no guarantee against totalitarian outcomes; indeed, Hitler's party was elected, and his economic policies and blatant anti-Semitism were applauded in the United States by the America First movement, which included Henry Ford and Charles Lindbergh.

The best antidote to this state of affairs may be to monitor and take pains to resist all efforts by candidates to capitalize on hate-based fear-mongering. Also important is to recognize that feeling safe is not the same as being safe. Affirming the virtuousness and power of our culture makes us feel more secure, but when such assertions involve the collateral damage of killing innocent Muslims abroad or discriminating against them at home, it is likely to provoke greater radicalization and hostility toward the United States and other Western targets. Moreover, illusory efforts to feel safer often erode the freedoms that we hold dear and are (quite rightfully) trying to protect.

We concur with social psychologist David Myers (2004), that "it is perfectly normal to fear purposeful violence from those who hate us. When terrorists strike again, we will all recoil in horror. But smart thinkers also will want to check their intuitive fears against the facts and to resist those who serve their own purposes by cultivating a culture of fear." As a culture, we should teach our children and encourage our citizens to vote with their heads rather than their hearts. Hopefully, such measures will embolden people to cast their votes based on the political qualifications and positions of the candidates rather than on defensive reactions to mortal terror.

References

Becker, E. (1971). *The birth and death of meaning: An interdisciplinary perspective on the problem of man.* (2nd ed.). New York: Free Press.

Becker, E. (1973). *The denial of death.* New York: Free Press.

Becker, E. (1975). *Escape from evil.* New York: Free Press.

Ben-Ari, O. T., Florian, V., & Mikulincer, M. (1999). The impact of mortality salience on reckless driving: a test of terror management mechanisms. *Journal of personality and social psychology,* 76(1), 35.

Burke, B. L., Martens, A., & Faucher, E. H. (2010). Two decades of terror management theory: A meta-analysis of mortality salience research. *Personality and Social Psychology Review,* 14(2), 155–195.

Cohen, F., Ogilvie, D. M., Solomon, S., Greenberg, J., & Pyszczynski, T. (2005). American roulette: The effect of reminders of death on support for George W. Bush in the 2004 presidential election. *Analyses of Social Issues and Public Policy,* 5, 177–187.

Cohen, F., Soenke, M., Solomon, S., & Greenberg, J. (2013). Evidence for a role of death thought in American attitudes toward symbols of Islam. *Journal of Experimental Social Psychology,* 49(2), 189–194. doi:10.1016/j.jesp.2012.09.006

Cohen, F., & Solomon, S. (2016). You're hired: Mortality salience increases Americans' support for Donald Trump (forthcoming).

Cohen, F., Solomon, S., Maxfield, M., Pyszczynski, T., & Greenberg, J. (2004). Fatal attraction: The effects of mortality salience on evaluations of charismatic, task-oriented, and relationship-oriented leaders. *Psychological Science,* 15(12), 846–851. doi:10.1111/j.0956-7976.2004.00765.x

Deacon, T. W. (1997). *The symbolic species: The co-evolution of language and the brain.* New York: W. W. Norton & Company.

Dover, T. L., Major, B., & Kaiser, C. R. (2016). Members of high-status groups are threatened by pro-diversity organizational messages. *Journal of Experimental Social Psychology,* 62, 58–67.

Friedman, M., & Rholes, W. S. (2007). Successfully challenging fundamentalist beliefs results in increased death awareness. *Journal of Experimental Social Psychology,* 43(5), 794–801.

Gilbert, G. M. (1995). *Nuremberg diary.* Boston, MA: Da Capo Press.

Greenberg, J., Pyszczynski, T., & Solomon, S. (1986). The causes and consequences of a need for self-esteem: A terror management theory. In

R. F. Baumeister (Ed.), *Public self and private self* (pp. 189–212). New York: Springer-Verlag.

Greenberg, J., Pyszczynski, T., Solomon, S., Rosenblatt, A., Veeder, M., Kirkland, S., & Lyon, D. (1990). Evidence for terror management II: The effects of mortality salience on reactions to those who threaten or bolster the cultural worldview. *Journal of Personality and Social Psychology, 58,* 308–318.

Hayes, J., Schimel, J., Arndt, J., & Faucher, E. H. (2010). A theoretical and empirical review of the death-thought accessibility concept in terror management research. *Psychological Bulletin, 136*(5), 699.

Hayes, J., Schimel, J., Williams, T. J., Howard, A. L., Webber, D., & Faucher, E. H. (2015). Worldview accommodation: Selectively modifying committed beliefs provides defense against worldview threat. *Self and Identity, 14*(5), 521–548. doi:10.1080/15298868.2015.1036919

Hoffer, E. (1951). *The true believer: Thoughts on the nature of mass movements.* New York: Harper and Row.

Jacobson, G. C. (2003). The Bush presidency and the American electorate. Paper prepared for delivery at the conference on "The George W. Bush Presidency: An Early Assessment" at the Woodrow Wilson School, Princeton University, April 25–26, 2003. Retrieved from http://www.wws.princeton .edu/bushconf/JacobsonPaper.pdf

Landau, M. J., Solomon, S., Greenberg, J., Cohen, F., Pyszczynski, T., Arndt, J., Miller, C. H., Ogilvie, D. M., & Cook, A. (2004). Deliver us from evil: The effects of mortality salience and reminders of 9/11 on support for President George W. Bush. *Personality and Social Psychology Bulletin, 30,* 1136–1150.

Lifton, R. J. (1979). The appeal of the death trip. *New York Times Magazine, 7.*

Lipman-Blumen, J. (1996). *The connective edge: Leading in an interdependent world.* Hoboken, NJ: Jossey-Bass.

Myers, D. (2004). It's the mundane stuff that kills. *Los Angeles Times.* Retrieved from http://articles.latimes.com/2004/mar/09/opinion/oe-myers9

Nagourney, A. (2005). Kerry says bin Laden tape gave Bush a lift. *New York Times.* Retrieved from http://www.nytimes.com/2005/01/31/politics /kerry-says-bin-laden-tape-gave-bush-a-lift.html?_r=0

Ogilvie, D. M., Cohen, F., & Solomon, S. (2008). The undesired self: Deadly connotations. *Journal of Research in Personality, 42*(3), 564–576. doi:10.1016/j .jrp.2007.07.012

Outten, H. R., Schmitt, M. T., Miller, D. A., & Garcia, A. L. (2012). Feeling threatened about the future whites' emotional reactions to anticipated ethnic demographic changes. *Personality and Social Psychology Bulletin, 38*(1), 14–25.

Purdum, T. S. (2001, September 17). After the attacks: The White House. *New York Times,* A2.

Pyszczynski, T., Greenberg, J., & Solomon, S. (1999). A dual-process model of defense against conscious and unconscious death-related thoughts: An extension of terror management theory. *Psychological Review, 106*(4), 835.

Pyszczynski, T., Greenberg, J., Solomon, S., Arndt, J., & Schimel, J. (2004). Why do people need self-esteem? A theoretical and empirical review. *Psychological Bulletin, 130*(3), 435–468. doi:10.1037/0033-2909.130.3.435

Pyszczynski, T., Solomon, S., & Greenberg, J. (2003). *In the wake of 9/11: The psychology of terror.* Washington, D.C.: American Psychological Association. doi:10.1037/10478-000

Pyszczynski, T., Solomon, S., & Greenberg, J. (2015). Thirty years of terror management theory: From Genesis to Revelation. In J. Olson & M. Zanna (Eds.), *Advances in experimental social psychology* (Vol. 52, pp. 1–70) San Diego: Academic Press.

Rank, O. (1978). *Truth and reality.* New York: Norton. (Originally published in 1929).

Solomon, S., Greenberg, J., & Pyszczynski, T. (1991). A terror management theory of social behavior: The psychological functions of self-esteem and cultural worldviews. In M. Zanna (Ed.), *Advances in experimental social psychology* (Vol. 24, pp. 91–159). Orlando: Academic Press.

Solomon, S., Greenberg, J., & Pyszczynski, T. (2015). *The worm at the core: On the role of death in life.* New York: Random House.

Thompson, D. (2016, April). Who are Donald Trump's supporters, really? *The Atlantic.* Retrieved from http://www.theatlantic.com/politics/archive/2016/03/who-are-donald-Mr. Trumps-supporters-really/471714

Varki, A., & Brower, D. (2013). *Denial: Self-deception, false beliefs, and the origins of the human mind.* Hachette UK.

Weber, M. (1947). *Max Weber: The theory of social and economic organization.* Trans. A. M. Henderson & Talcott Parsons. New York: The Free Press.

CHAPTER TEN

Insulter Trump: A Bonus for His Followers?

Karina V. Korostelina

Insults

Insults are embedded in relationships between people, organizations, social groups, and even countries. All insults are formed, maintained, and transformed through social relations and help to construct reality through social interaction (Kashima, Fiedler, & Freytag, 2008). Insult involves the active participation of all involved parties and can be understood as a dialogic process (Maitra & McGowan, 2012; Eribon, 2004). Every insult involves a perpetrator, a target, and an audience, even when some insults can just be attributed to the insulting party (Gabriel, 1998). "Intergroup insult, as many other mutual acts, is also constructed on this social boundary and involves (1) the social identity and power positions of both groups; (2) a history of relations between two groups, (3) awareness of the insult by one or both groups, and (4) the socio-cultural meaning of insult accepted in the specific society and culture(s)" (Korostelina, 2014).

There is a belief that people offend each other out of frustration, because of bad manners, or simply as a result of the satisfaction they gain from hurting other people. However, not all insults can be deemed similar (Korostelina, 2014). The specific form of the insult can indicate personal or group incentives, problems in interactions, or grounds for conflict between two parties. In particular situations, people do not generally just offend each other; instead, they use very particular insults that are suited to the occasion.

Insults performed by Donald Trump are commonly perceived to be a representation of his aggressiveness, incivility, and impoliteness. However, you may notice that each of them has a specific purpose. Some insults create a negative image of his opponents or reduce their prospects to achieve their goals. Some insults establish a boundary between Trump and other people or put on them the responsibility for Trump's actions. Some insults increase the power of Trump in comparison to others or delegitimize them. Thus, Trump uses different insults not just to offend others but rather to accomplish a specific aim.

Supporters of Trump receive a benefit from his insults in the same way that he does. Trump's insults help his supporters to achieve high self-esteem and increase their perception of power, to create distance from people they detest, to stress their advantages in comparison with others, to blame others for their own inappropriate actions, and to increase the legitimacy of their views and positions. Trump supporters enjoy his insults and the reactions of those he insults. They use his insults for their benefits and feel more empowered by them. The discussion below provides some insights into how Trump achieves these goals.

Identity Insults

People endeavor to have a positive image of themselves and high self-esteem. The positive feelings about ourselves, and the knowledge that others like and respect us contributes to our self-esteem. To achieve these positive feelings, we compare ourselves to other people or groups and attribute negative features to them. This favorable comparison to others provides us with high self-esteem and a positive view of ourselves (Tajfel & Turner, 1985). Our prejudices and biases result from a comparison with others that presents us as better than them.

Of course, this comparison is much easier for people who reside at the top of a social hierarchy or who have more power and resources in existing social structures. Such individuals can always compare themselves with less advantaged groups, describing them as lazy, unmotivated, and undereducated, for example. We can expect that people who are frequent targets of such attributions (e.g., poor working people, minorities) will be less inclined to use favorable comparisons because they know how unpleasant it is to be the focus of such discriminative labels. Moreover, we can expect that people at the bottom of established social hierarchies have fewer possibilities to increase their self-esteem by comparing them-selves to others. Much research has demonstrated, however, that the opposite is true (Hewstone, Rubin, & Willis, 2002; Mullen, Brown, & Smith, 1992). Why does it happen? Understanding that comparison can be a major source of self-esteem for these groups helps us answer this question. Members of disadvantaged groups have fewer opportunities to see themselves positively based on their achievements or position in soci-ety. Being a member of a disadvantaged group provides people with less satisfaction, security, and positive social identity (Blunz, Mummendey, & Otten, 1995; Leonardelli & Brewer, 2001). To make their identity more positive, they favor their own group and emphasize the negative aspects in others (Otten, Mummendey, & Blanz, 1996; Simon, Aufderheide, & Kampmeier, 2001). Thus, they have a strong need to compare themselves with members of other groups and, in turn, put these groups down in the process. They usually compare themselves to other disadvantaged groups or find new criteria for comparison. For example, members of a losing team can believe that their team is less aggressive or has higher standards in terms of loyalty and sportsmanship than the winning team.

Identity insults help increase self-esteem through favorable comparison, especially for people who have problems with their own self-respect and confidence. These insults make others look flawed, dishonest, and not worthy. Thus, identity insults employed by Trump help his supporters to increase or preserve their self-esteem.

One of the identity insults that Trump has used against a social group targets Mexican immigrants specifically. Utilizing the perception among the American working class that immigrants are taking their jobs, he has used insults to diminish the Mexican immigrant identity. When he announced his candidacy for president, Trump said, "When Mexico sends its people, they're not sending their best. They're not sending you. They're not sending you. They're sending people that have lots of problems and they are bringing those problems with us. They're bringing drugs. They're bringing crime. They're rapists. And some, I assume, are good people" (*Washington Post*, 2015). Trump has not only created a negative image of Mexican immigrants, but he has also compared them to his audience. Stressing twice that "they're not sending you," he connected his support-ers to the idea that they were "better." Thus, he has successfully used identity insult to increase the positive identity and self-esteem of his sup-porters through a negative comparison with Mexican immigrants.

Faced with a forcefully negative reaction to this insult, Trump has con-tinued to defend his position because it provides his supporters with pos-itive feelings of self-worth. When CNN's Don Lemon asked Trump about his use of the term "rapists," Trump cited recent reports that claim that as many as 80 percent of female immigrants crossing the U.S.-Mexico border had been sexually assaulted during the trip. He then went on to deny the comment that it had not happened in the United States: "Well, somebody's doing the raping, Don. I mean, you know, somebody's doing it. Who's doing the raping?" (Miller, 2015). In response to a question by Fox News host Chris Wallace, Trump accused the Mexican government of sending criminals: "And the Mexican government is much smarter, much sharper, much more cunning. They send the bad ones over, because they don't want to pay for them, they don't want to take care of them. Why should they, when the stupid leaders of the United States will do it for them?" (Fox News, 2015). In this identity insult, not only did Trump portray the Mexican government and citizens negatively, but he also attacked the current U.S. leadership. Thus, through favorable comparison, he supported Americans who feel their jobs and security are being threatened and who are unsatisfied with the U.S. government's response to these problems. This repeated insult of Mexican immigrants has the capacity to make them feel better about their economic problems and disadvantaged positions.

Projection Insults

As we discussed above, it is important for people to have a positive identity. It is harder to maintain self-confidence and self-respect if your actions were negative, destructive, or unjust toward others. To justify their behavior, people can project deleterious intentions onto others, stressing that they incited one's own actions.

When people realize that their own behavior is not acceptable, they experience conflicted feelings between their positive self-image and an evaluation of their actions as negative. Facing this cognitive dissonance (Festinger, 1957), they perform irrational and even maladaptive behavior. To reduce cognitive dissonance and restore harmony between their attitudes and beliefs, people can choose several strategies. One approach is to change their self-perceptions, to recognize bad behavior, and to accept new information about themselves that is negative. They can also change or eliminate the behavior that caused cognitive dissonance. For example, people can stop smoking because of the negative effects on their health. A second strategy is to change their perception about the situation, thus justifying their behavior, or by creating new information about it. People who smoke disregard warnings about the lethal effects of the habit and may consider medical research unconvincing. A third strategy is to reduce the importance of the belief or to change it drastically. People can create a new belief that, for them, life with the pleasure of smoking is more important than a longer but more boring life without it. Usually, the tendency to maintain their positive self-image and consistent beliefs prevails over other approaches.

In both situations—projection and cognitive dissonance—people justify their behavior by attributing negative intentions and features to other people or by blaming them for a given situation. This tendency can be explained by the theory of fundamental attribution error (Ross, 1977; Jones & Harris, 1967). It says that we tend to explain our own behavior based on specific situations (situational attribution) while analyzing the behavior of others based on their personal characteristics (dispositional attribution). In other words, when we see the actions of another person, we believe that it reflects their personality rather than the situation the person might be in. When we analyze our behavior, we believe that it is caused by the situation and our surroundings and does not completely reflect who we are as individuals. For example, people tend to justify being late as a result of bad traffic, but see the lateness of others as a result of their irresponsibility. When students receive low grades, they often explain their low mark as the result of an injustice, particularly in the guise of a tough professor. They see the low grades of others as a result of their laziness.

Projection insults help justify negative actions or deny negative characteristics of the insulter by blaming others for situations they created. They reduce their own negative feelings as insulters by accusing others of provoking their conduct.

Trump has been actively using projection insults to defend his biased remarks. He has also used projection insults to justify his humiliating behavior toward women. During an interview with CNN, Elizabeth Beck, a female lawyer, recounted an incident during a deposition in which Trump was present. Beck had requested a short break from the deposition to pump breast milk. She described Trump's reaction to this request as an "absolute meltdown": "He got up, his face got red, he shook his finger at me and he screamed, 'You're disgusting, you're disgusting,' and he ran out of there" (Malec, 2015).

Trump immediately responded, suggesting that Beck's comments were her way of getting back at him for losing a case. In a series of tweets, he accused her of not only being a bad attorney, but also for sharing her stories as retaliation for her losses: "@CNN & @CNNPolitics did not say that lawyer Beck lost the case and I got legal fees. Also, she wanted to breast pump in front of me at dep"; "Lawyer Elizabeth Beck was easy for me to beat. Ask her clients if they are happy with her results against me. Got total win and legal fees"; "CNN & @CNNPolitics Lawyer Elizabeth Beck did a terrible job against me, she lost (I even got legal fees). I loved beating her, she was easy"; and "@CNN Why is somebody (Beck) I beat so soundly all of a sudden an expert on Donald Trump (all over television). She knows nothing about me" (Malec, 2015). The aim of these projection insults was not only to justify Trump's behavior, but also to provide him with an opportunity to reaffirm his winning image. Presenting himself as the target of someone seeking revenge for her losses, Trump sought to secure both validation and empathy from his supporters. These projection insults reassured them that the attacks on Trump were coming from those who had lost to him and that they were thus connected to a powerful winner.

Divergence Insults

Our social life involves a lot of interactions. Sometimes we try to stay close to some people, and at other times, we are eager to distance ourselves from others. We construct space between us, stressing similarities or differences with other people. This space between us is called a social boundary. Building and changing our relationships always involve changes to social boundaries, making them more permeable or impervious (Barth, 1981). To define social boundaries, people emphasize similarities and differences between themselves and others (Horowitz, 1975).

If social borders between individuals or groups are blurred, some people are ready to defend their distinctiveness from others. Why does this happen? People may be concerned about the future or destiny of their group, particularly concerning changes in group values, beliefs, or position within society. They may think that the existence of a small distance between them and others and increasing similarities have the potential to alter their usual way of life, traditions, and customs. They may be afraid of losing their distinctive identity and, as a consequence, provide emotional responses in the form of collective angst.

If boundaries between groups are permeable, members of low-status groups are more likely to move across those boundaries with the view of trying to create contact with a high-status group (Ellemers, Spears, & Doosje, 1997). Group members can feel that by being similar to the out-group, the in-group can lose its very essence. To differentiate themselves from others, people often react by emphasizing different available dimensions of comparison, such as advances in sport or the arts, economic development, human rights, or family values. To preserve the group's uniqueness and its rights, people can attribute negative values to the features of another group, which, in turn, then create negative stereotypes about that group. This can be achieved by highlighting various differences between groups who speak a similar language or have a different dialect.

People can also resist the imposition of values and traditions by others in the form of individuals or groups. People may be afraid that the closer they come to a set of people that that set of people will exercise a stronger influence over them. If people see the lifestyles, beliefs, and ideas of these new persons or groups as alien, negative, or dangerous, they will try to reinforce their own social boundaries to strengthen their own group affiliations.

Divergence insults help increase distance, stress differences, and strengthen social boundaries between groups. They help insulters to protect their group or way of life. Trump has faced a host of criticism for not releasing his tax returns. Since Richard Nixon, every presidential campaign has released full, robust, and complete tax returns. Trump has said he could not release his returns because they were "under audit," although the IRS has denied this claim (Beamon, 2016). Many experts and journalists have discussed why Trump is not releasing his tax information, accusing him of tax evasion (Ellis, 2016). Trump has used divergence insults to distance himself from those who mishandle their taxes. He accused Jeff Bezos, the CEO of Amazon, who owns the *Washington Post* as well as the space exploration company Blue Origin, of not paying fair taxes. Trump stated that Bezos was using his ownership of the newspaper as a "big tax shelter" for Amazon because the paper was "losing a fortune." He also added that if Amazon paid real taxes, its "stock would crumble like a paper bag" (La Monica, 2015). "The @washingtonpost loses money (a deduction) and gives owner @JeffBezos power to screw public on low taxation of @Amazon! Big tax shelter" (La Monica, 2015). In this tweet, Trump aimed to create a division between himself and a public who are fair taxpayers on the one side and people who abuse the tax system and evade taxes on the other. This divergent insult assured his supporters that he has a good tax record and they are on the right side with the tax issue.

Relative Insults

In assessing ourselves and our current situation, we always rely on comparison of our social positions, available resources, and possibilities with what we had in the past and what we expect to have in the future. People feel relative deprivation if they believe that their life situation has worsened or their expectations are not being fulfilled (Davis, 1959; Gurr, 1993; Runciman, 1966). Temporal deprivations are connected with the evaluation of a person's present status and resources against their status and resources at another point in the past (Albert, 1977). Temporal comparisons are especially important during periods of change (Brown & Middendorf, 1996) or economic hardship experienced by people or their groups (Krahn & Harrison, 1992). If this temporal comparison reveals instability whereby there is movement from an improved position or a situation to a rapid decline, people demonstrate a higher inclination toward aggressive behavior (Grofman & Muller, 1973; de la Sabbloniere, Taylor, Prozzo, & Sadykova, 2009). People also compare what they have now with their expectations and develop a feeling that their positions and resources are limited in comparison with that they should have or deserve to have. These comparisons between their actual status and their expectations can lead to a deep feeling of offense (Davis, 1959).

It is important to note that the perception of deprivation or of being disadvantaged is usually based on comparisons of subjective standards against other people and groups rather than with objective reality (Crosby, 1976). It is enough to believe in a worsening situation to start behaving according to this perception. In many cases, people compare themselves with other people or social groups. This appraisal leads them to believe that people or members of other groups have more advantages in terms of societal positions, power, or resources. As the old saying goes, "The grass is always greener on the other side." These perceptions of relative deprivation, whether real or imagined, lead to feelings of victimization and of being disadvantaged and underprivileged. For example, a person can feel deprived if his or her colleague receives a higher salary or if he or she believes that a neighbor has a better car. People can feel deprived if the social status of their ethnic or racial group is lower than they expected. If they believe that another ethnic group has more access to education, jobs, or social services, they blame other ethnic or racial groups in society for impeding the realization of their expectations. Relative insults help restore a perceived imbalance concerning resources or social positions, or challenge a situation that is believed to be unjust. These insults refute specific rights of others and increase perceptions of the privileged position of insulters.

By seeking to protect his image as a winner, Trump was trying to prevent any attempts to alter this perception. He uses relative insults to diminish any and all information that challenges the identity he has constructed for himself as a winner. When the *Wall Street Journal* noted that although Trump was still the front-runner, his nomination was in question, "given the continuing resistance to his candidacy by so many Republicans," he immediately offended the journal in response. He created relative insults in several tweets: "@WSJ is bad at math. The good news is, nobody cares what they say in their editorials anymore, especially me!" and "Please explain to the dummies at the @WSJ Editorial Board that I love to debate and have won, according to Drudge etc., all 11 of them!" (Jerde, 2016). In these tweets, he blamed the magazine for a low level of professionalism and denied its right to discuss the prospect of him winning. At the same time, Trump reinforced his image as a winner and a front-runner among his supporters. These insults simultaneously reassured his supporters that his position as a leader was secure and decreased their concerns about the GOP convention.

Power Insults

Communication among people is shaped by power relations that define the ways in which we see others and ourselves. People behave around other people based on established power balances. One person engaged in an interaction with others may have less, more, or equal power to other people they are interacting with. The classic definition of power characterizes it as the ability of a person or a group to influence the behavior of others or their ability to achieve objectives and goals (Cartwright, 1955; Deustch & Gerard, 1955; Festinger, 1954; French & Raven, 1959; Kelman, 1958).

What does it mean for our relations with others? A group or a person in power can create a situation that precludes other people from satisfying their needs or achieving their goals. For example, people in power can prohibit particular actions or forbid particular places. They can limit time or the ability to travel, remove essential tools required for work, or deny access to information and other resources.

Power also involves dependence and coercion against people's will in the form of seeking to bend their will and change their beliefs through norms and social consensus (Moscovici, 1976). For example, based on social norms of parenting, a father can establish an agreed weeknight and weekend curfew. Based on social norms existing in some societies, a husband can convince his wife to abstain from wearing certain clothes, from socializing with certain people, or from going to certain places. Thus, people in power can create conditions in which people around them in lower power positions feel inferior and inadequately equipped to deal with a current situation to satisfy their needs. Feelings of stress and threat that are induced by this environment depend greatly upon the degree of power that superior individuals or groups of people possess within an existing system of relations. Power insults help redefine existing balances of power when the insulters see a situation as a competition for coercive power. These insults increase the absolute or relative power of insulters in comparison with others.

Trump has frequently employed power insults to restore his perceived supremacy and control. In 1991, Trump was facing a debt of $900 million. He artfully used this large debt as a powerful bargaining chip, forcing the banks to release him from a portion of his personal obligations (Hylton, 1991). He was left with a debt obligation of $550 million and had to give up his 281-foot super-yacht, *Trump Princess*, to pay the creditors. The yacht at that time was one of the largest in the world and was bought by Prince Al-Waleed Bin Talal bin Abdulaziz al Saud, a member of the Saudi royal family, who renamed it *Kingdom 5KR*. Prince Al-Waleed also owned stakes in other properties that belonged to Trump. In his search for revenge and a restoration of the power balance, Trump tweeted an Al-Waleed parody account: "Saudi Arabia should be paying the United States many billions of dollars for our defense of them. Without us, gone!" (Kaczynski, 2015). When the tensions between Iran and Saudi Arabia intensified in the Middle East, Trump again stated that Saudi Arabia should pay the United States. "I would want to protect Saudi Arabia. But Saudi Arabia is going to have to help us economically. They were making, before the oil went down . . . they were making $1 billion a day," he told host Bill O'Reilly on Fox News' *The O'Reilly Factor* (Hensch, 2016). Trump further diminished the power of Saudi Arabia in his interview to NBC's *Meet the Press*. "Saudi Arabia, if it weren't for us, they wouldn't be here," Trump said. "They wouldn't exist" (Knowles, 2015). This redefinition of the power balance between the United States and Saudi Arabia positively resonates with his supporters and provides them with a feeling of supremacy.

Legitimacy Insults

Legitimacy involves respect for and to others rather than a coercion or dominance. It involves the acceptance that particular people in positions of power have a right to influence the opinions and behaviors of other people (Kelman, 2001). Other people are expected to regard and accept this influence because it is based on established norms and values (Kelman, 2001). Legitimacy is also rooted in a shared social identity (Wenzel & Jobling, 2006). Political leaders increase their influence by utilizing the basic norms and values of their group. They constantly legitimize themselves and delegitimize other leaders. Legitimacy insults help legitimize insulters and delegitimize the other side, diminishing the validity of the other side.

Trump has often used legitimacy insults to decrease the validity of his political rivals. During his appearance on CBS's *Face the Nation*, Bernie

Sanders said that Trump supporters should change their preference and join him. Sanders emphasized that the majority of Trump's supporters are working-class people who are angry "because they're working longer hours for lower wages. They're angry because their jobs have left this country and gone to China or other low-wage countries" (Hensch, 2015). Sanders acknowledged that Trump was successful in addressing people's anger and fears but criticized him for converting this frustration into anger against Mexicans and Muslims. Sanders stressed that this tactic was flawed and he had a better approach to address unemployment and the stalled economy. Trump immediately responded with legitimacy insult. He stated, "Wages in our country are too low, good jobs are too few and people have lost faith in our leaders. We need smart and strong leadership now." Trump increased his legitimacy as this type of leader and invalidated Sanders: "Strange, but I see wacko Bernie Sanders allies coming over to me because I'm lowering taxes, while he will double & triple them, a disaster!" (Hensch, 2015). This insult not only increased the authority of Trump among his supporters but also validated their connection to him as a leader who would address their problems. It helped to make them feel that they were on the "right" side.

Trump actively uses insults, repeats the same insults over and over again, and cements them in the minds of people. For example, he created a connection between Hillary Clinton and the notion of deceit. Referring to the e-mail scandal that has surrounded Hillary Clinton while serving as secretary of state, Trump said, "She should not be allowed to run in the election. She should suffer like other people have suffered who have done far less than she has" (Byrnes, 2016).[1] Pointing specifically to the FBI's decision to not recommend criminal charges against Hillary Clinton for her use of e-mail while serving as secretary of state, Trump called it the "best evidence ever that we've seen that our system is totally rigged" (Diamond, 2016). He emphasized that Clinton used enticement to influence the decision: "You are waiting for a decision by the attorney general and you are saying that you are going to give her a job. You are not allowed to do that. That's bribery, folks" (Miller, 2016b). These attacks on Clinton contribute to the increasing perception among some of the American electorate who describe Hilary Clinton as "dishonest," a "liar," that they "don't trust her," and that she has a "poor character" (Howley, 2015; Miller, 2016a).

Being a Bully

Bullying behavior is often formed in relationships between cliques in middle and high school. Many children in large peer groups feel the need to show that they have more rights or privileges than others through mean and physical behavior that often includes offending their peers. This behavior gradually forms during the last years of elementary school and through into middle school (Eder, 1985). In the seventh grade, cliques become more stable and are based on an emerging hierarchy. The highest-status groups usually include cheerleaders, student council members, and athletes. Students are strongly inclined to ensure that they sit with the people they like. They either save seats for friends or prevent certain students from joining their groups. In addition, all the higher-status groups usually sit on one side of the cafeteria. Often, members of these groups are from middle-class families and wear name-brand clothes. The students on the other side of the cafeteria are primarily from lower- and working-class backgrounds.

By eighth grade, stable cliques define the hierarchical structure of students' relations. Most students communicate and sit with the same group for the entire year. The social-class division and preference of seating arrangements generally become more visible now than in seventh grade. Thus, a particular side of the cafeteria is associated with a higher social position within the student hierarchy and is typically used by students to create insults. These insults help students to increase their status in relation to their peers, stressing their privileged position. Children from high-status social groups are the most visible among other students, who will know most of them by name. They also receive the most attention from others in comparison to other students, whose achievements are often ignored.

At the same time, popular students are not well liked by others. Many peers describe popular students as stuck-up and unfriendly and often clearly dislike them. Many of the students who detest popular students are their former close friends who did not become members of high-status groups. Many students also feel offended by the popular peers and members of the top groups because they ignore them. Many students actively dislike the snobbery of popular people and describe them in negative terms (Kwon, Lease, & Hoffman, 2012).

Members of popular cliques believe that they occupy the highest place among their peers. The status provides a feeling of specialness and symbolizes a more privileged position than their less popular peers. Members of the popular cliques take pleasure in putting other students in their place. In one research study, girls were sharing views on their group: "Well, everybody liked us. Everybody thought highly of everyone in the group. A lot of kids were scared of us. Scared that we were going to beat them up or that we wouldn't be friends with them" (Merten, 1997). By establishing the reputation of being mean and powerful, girls in this group were able to preserve their privileged position without using physical violence. But even though they never physically attacked other girls, they actively intimidated peers with threats of violence. Popular students often insult their peers from low-status groups as well. For example, by referring to them as "grits (refers to an inexpensive type of food)" (Eder, 1985).

However, popular girls do not necessarily dislike girls with lower status. Rather, they try to avoid associations with less-popular girls because they may be concerned about their friends' negative reactions to these relations. The members of lower-status groups tend not to be mean or insult the higher-status members because they can easily become angry and mobilize their group against the insulters. Thus, high-status cliques protect members from insults from other members with less social status and thus reinforce their superiority. Being nice is perceived as a threat to the status because polite behavior creates equality (Pokhrel, Sussman, Black, & Sun, 2010).

Trump's actions resemble the behavior of a "popular" person who employs bullying and insults toward lower social status groups. By connecting to Trump, his supporters place themselves into his clique, which gives them a sense of superiority and a privileged position in the social order. They believe their privileged position gives them a right to be mean to other people and insult them. Trump supporters feel empowered by his bullying behavior because they consider it a sign of his popularity.

Conclusion

Trump craftily uses insults and bullying behavior to empower his supporters. By their association to his insults, his supporters increase their self-esteem. and attain a positive social identity. They also validate their bigotry and discriminative actions and distance themselves from people they dislike. Trump insults help his supporters to delegitimize his competitors and strip other groups of their particular rights. They also help his supporters to justify their views and positions and contribute to their feeling of empowerment.

Trump unites the frustrations of his supporters, their anger, and their pursuit for a better America as they see it. The strategy that Trump employs to empower his supporters is clearly described, ironically, by Saul Alinsky, a Jewish American activist who has worked on improving conditions in African American ghettos in Chicago:

> The organizer ... must first rub raw the resentments of the people in the community; fan the latent hostility of many of the people to the point of

overt expression.... An organizer must stir up dissatisfaction and discontent; provide a channel into which people can angrily pour their frustrations. He must create a mechanism that can drain off the underlying guilt for having accepted the previous situation for so long. (Alinsky, 1971)

Similarly, Trump has inflamed the discontent of his followers and provided an outlet for their dissatisfaction and frustration. He identifies "scapegoat" groups and accuses the current political leadership in the United States. As a result, his followers appreciate his aggressive demeanor in the form of insults and bullying. Through Trump's insults and harassment of others, his supporters are acquiring a perception of higher social status and a feeling of being superior within the established social hierarchy. Trump's bullying behavior helps his supporters to regain a feeling of superiority that they feel is slipping away and addresses their feeling of being threatened by other groups in society.

Note

1. The scandal is that she kept official e-mails on a personal server and kept classified e-mails on an unclassified server.

References

Albert, S. (1977). Temporal comparison theory. *Psychological Review, 84,* 485–503.

Alinsky, S. (1971). *Rules for radicals.* New York: Random House.

Barth, F. (1981). *Process and form in social life.* London: Routledge and Kegan Paul.

Beamon, T. (2016, February 26). IRS: Trump can release tax returns while under audit. *NewsMax.* Retrieved from http://www.newsmax.com/Headline/trump-release-taxreturns/2016/02/26/id/716367

Blanz, M., Mummendey, A., & Otten, S. (1995). Perceptions of relative group size and group status: Effects on intergroup discrimination in negative evaluations. *European Journal of Social Psychology, 25,* 231–247.

Brown, R. & Middendorf, J. (1996). The underestimated role of temporal comparison: A test of the life-span model. *Journal of Social Psychology, 136,* 325–331.

Byrnes, J. (2016, May 4). Trump: Clinton "should suffer" for emails. *The Hill.* Retrieved from http://thehill.com/blogs/ballot-box/presidential-races/278636-trump-clinton-should-suffer-for-emails

Cartwright, D. (1959). *Studies in social power.* Research Center for Group Dynamics, Institute for Social Research, University of Michigan.

Crosby, F. (1976). A model of egoistical relative deprivation. *Psychological Review, 83,* 85–113.

Davis, J. A. (1959). A formal interpretation of the theory of relative deprivation. *Sociometry, 22,* 280–296.

Deutsch, M., & Gerard, H. B. (1955). A study of normative and informational social influences upon individual judgment. *Journal of Abnormal and Social Psychology, 51*(3), 629–636.

Diamond, J. (2016, July 5). Trump: FBI decision on Clinton proves "our system is totally rigged." CNN. Retrieved from http://www.cnn.com/2016/07/05 /politics/election-2016-donald-trump-hillary-clinton-fbi

Eder, D. (1985). The cycle of popularity: Interpersonal relations among female adolescents. *Sociology of Education, 58,* 154–165.

Ellemers, N., Spears, R., & Doosje, B. (1997). Sticking together or falling apart: Ingroup identification as a psychological determinant of group commitment versus individual mobility. *Journal of Personality and Social Psychology, 72,* 617–626.

Ellis, R. (2016, March 8). Donald Trump's tax returns and the empty jewelry box scam. *Forbes.* Retrieved from http://www.forbes.com/sites/ryanellis /2016/03/08/donald-trump-and-the-empty-jewelry-box-tax-scam /#24217cd06aa7

Eribon, D. (2004). *Insult and the making of the gay self.* Trans. Michael Lucey. Durham, NC: Duke University Press Books.

Festinger, L. (1954, May 1). A theory of social comparison processes. *Human Relations, 7*(2), 117–140.

Festinger, L. (1957). *A theory of cognitive dissonance.* Stanford, CA: Stanford University Press.

Fox News. (2015, July 13). Trump on "El Chapo" prison break: "I told you so!" Fox News Insider. Retrieved from http://insider.foxnews.com/2015/07/13 /trump-drug-lord-el-chapos-prison-break-mexico-i-told-you-so

French, J. R. P., & Raven, B. (1959). The bases of social power. In D. Cartwright (Ed.), *Studies in Social Power* (pp. 150–167). Research Center for Group Dynamics, Institute for Social Research, University of Michigan.

Gabriel, Y. (1998, November). An introduction to the social psychology of insults. *Human Relations, 51*(11), 1329–1354.

Grofman, B. N., & Muller, E. N. (1973). The strange case of relative gratification and potential for political violence: The V-curve hypothesis. *American Political Science Review, 67,* 514–539.

Gurr, T. R. (1993). *Minorities at risk: A global view of ethnopolitical conflict.* Washington, D.C.: United States Institute of Peace.

Hensch, M. (2015, December 28). Trump: Sanders "a wacko," and I'll get his votes. *The Hill.* Retrieved from http://thehill.com/blogs/ballot-box/presidential -races/264295-trump-sanders-is-a-wacko-so-ill-get-his-voters

Hensch, M. (2016, January 5). Trump: "I would want to protect Saudi Arabia." *The Hill.* Retrieved from http://thehill.com/blogs/ballot-box/presidential -races/264748-trump-we-made-iran-a-power

Hewstone, M., Rubin, M., & Willis, H. (2002). Intergroup bias. *Annual Review of Psychology, 53,* 575–604.

Horowitz, D. L. (1975). Ethnic identity. In N. Glazer & D. Moynihan (Eds.), *Ethnicity, theory and experience.* Cambridge, MA: Harvard University Press.

Howley, P. (2015, December 22. Poll: 59 percent of Americans say Hillary Clinton is dishonest. *Breibart.* Retrieved from http://www.breitbart.com/big-government/2015/12/22/poll-59-percent-americans-say-hillary-clinton -dishonest

Hylton, R. D. (1991, December 31). The year in finance: Newsmakers in; Money movers caught in the turbulent times of the 90s; Donald J. Trump: Bargaining to stay afloat. *The New York Times.* Retrieved from http://www .nytimes.com/1991/12/31/business/year-finance-newsmakers-1991 -money-movers-caught-turbulent-times-90-s-donald-j.html

Jerde, S. (2016, March 17). Trump rails against critical *Wall Street Journal* editorial: "Nobody cares." *Talking Points Memo.* Retrieved from http:// talkingpointsmemo.com.

Jones, E. E., & Harris, V. A. (1967). The attribution of attitudes. *Journal of Experimental Social Psychology, 3*(1), 1–24.

Kaczynski, A. (2015, September 14). Debt-ridden Donald Trump lost his "ship of jewels" to a Saudi prince. *Buzzfeed.* Retrieved from https://www.buzzfeed .com/andrewkaczynski/set-an-open-course-for-the-virgin-sea?utm _term=.vrZz370Xyq#.nn008W6ybl

Kashima, Y., Fiedler, K., & Freytag, P. 2008. *Stereotype dynamics: Language-based approaches to the formation, maintenance, and transformation of stereotypes.* New York and London: Lawrence Erlbaun Associates.

Kelman, H. C. (1958, March 1). Compliance, identification, and internalization: Three processes of attitude change. *Journal of Conflict Resolution, 2*(1), 51–60.

Kelman, H. C. (2001). Reflections on the social and pyschological processes of legitimization and delegitimization. In J. T. Jost & B. Major (Eds.), *The psychology of legitimacy: Emerging perspectives on ideology, justice, and intergroup relations* (pp. 54–73). Cambridge, UK: Cambridge University Press.

Knowles, D. (2015, August 16). Donald Trump adds Saudi Arabia to list of countries ripping off the U.S. *Bloomberg.* Retrieved from: http://www.bloomberg .com/politics/articles/2015-08-16/donald-trump-adds-saudi-arabia-to-list-of-countries-ripping-off-the-u-s-

Korostelina, K. V. (2014). *Political insults: How offenses escalate conflict.* New York: Oxford University Press.

Krahn, H., & Harrison, T. (1992). "Self-referenced" relative deprivation and economic beliefs: The effects of the recession in Alberta. *Canadian Review of Sociology and Anthropology, 29,* 191–209.

Kwon, K., Lease, A. M., & Hoffman, L. (2012). The impact of clique membership on children's social behavior and status nominations. *Social Development, 21*(1), 150–169.

La Monica, P. R. (2015, December 7). Jeff Bezos wants to send Donald Trump into space. CNN Money. Retrieved from http://money.cnn.com/2015/12/07/investing/donald-trump-amazon-taxes

Leonardelli, G. J., & Brewer, M. B. (2001). Minority and majority discrimination: When and why? *Journal of Experimental Social Psychology, 37*, 468–485.

Maitra, I., & McGowan, M. K. (Eds.) (2012). *Speech and harm: Controversies over free speech*. Oxford: Oxford University Press.

Malec, B. (2015, July 29). Donald Trump angrily responds to claim he called a breastfeeding lawyer "disgusting," calls her "terrible." EOnline. Retrieved from http://www.eonline.com/news/681262/donald-trump-angrily-responds-to-claim-he-called-a-breastfeeding-lawyer-disgusting-calls-her-terrible

Merten, D. E. (1997). The meaning of meanness: Popularity, competition, and conflict among junior high school girls. *Sociology of Education, 70*(3), 175–191.

Miller, J. (2015, July 2). Donald Trump defends calling Mexican immigrants "rapists." CBS News. Retrieved from http://www.cbsnews.com/news/election-2016-donald-trump-defends-calling-mexican-immigrants-rapists

Miller, S. A. (2016a, February 23). Americans see a dishonest Democrat they dislike vs. an old socialist, poll shows. *Washington Times*. Retrieved from http://www.washingtontimes.com/news/2016/feb/23/americans-call-hillary-clinton-dishonest-bernie-sa

Miller, S. A. (2016b, July 6). Trump on Clinton dodging charges: "That's bribery, folks." *Washington Times*. Retrieved from http://www.washingtontimes.com/news/2016/jul/6/donald-trump-hillary-clinton-dodging-charges-s-bri

Moscovici, S. (1976). *Social influence and social change*. Published in cooperation with European Association of Experimental Social Psychology by Academic Press.

Mullen, B., Brown, R., & Smith, C. (1992). Ingroup bias as a function of salience, relevance and status: An integration. *European Journal of Social Psychology, 22*, 103–122.

Otten, S., Mummendey, A., & Blanz, M. (1996). Intergroup discrimination in positive and negative outcome allocations: Impact of stimulus valence, relative group status, and relative group size. *Personality and Social Psychology Bulletin, 22*, 567–581.

Pokhrel, P., Sussman, S., Black, D., & Sun, P. (2010). Peer group self-identification as a predictor of relational and physical aggression among high school students. *Journal of School Health, 80*(5), 249–258.

de la Sablonnière, R., Taylor, D. M., Perozzo, C., & Sadykova, N. (2009). Reconceptualizing relative deprivation in the context of dramatic social change: The challenge confronting the people of Kyrgyzstan. *European Journal of Social Psychology, 39*, 325–345.

Simon, B., Aufderheide, B., & Kampmeier, C. (2001). The social psychology of minority-majority relations. In R. Brown & S. L. Gaertner (Eds.), *Blackwell handbook of social psychology: Intergroup processes* (pp. 303–323). Oxford: Blackwell.

Ross, L. (1977). The intuitive psychologist and his shortcomings: Distortions in the attribution process. In L. Berkowitz (Ed.), *Advances in experimental social psychology* (Vol. 10, pp. 173–220). New York: Academic Press.

Runciman, W. G. (1968). Problems of research on relative deprivation. In H. H. Hyman & E. Singer (Eds.), *Readings in reference group theory and research* (pp. 69–76). New York: The Free Press.

Runciman, W. G. (1996). *Relative deprivation and social justice: A study of attitudes to social inequality in twentieth-century England.* Berkeley: University of California Press.

Tajfel H., & Turner, J. C. (1985). The social identity Theory of intergroup behaviour. In S. Worchel & W. G. Austin (Ed.), *Psychology of intergroup relations* (2nd ed.). Chicago: Nelson-Hall.

The Washington Post. (2015, July 15). Full text: Donald Trump announces a presidential bid. Retrieved from https://www.washingtonpost.com/news/post-politics/wp/2015/06/16/full-text-donald-trump-announces-a-presidential-bid

Wenzel, M., & Jobling, P. (2006). Legitimacy of regulatory authorities as a function of inclusive identification and power over ingroups and outgroups. *European Journal of Social Psychology, 36*(2), 239–258.

CHAPTER ELEVEN

Tweeting Morals in the 2016 Election

J. P. Prims, Zachary J. Melton, and Matt Motyl

Using Twitter to Understand Moral Differences Underlying Political Preferences in the 2016 U.S. Presidential Primary

Making predictions about which presidential hopeful will win is difficult in the best of times. The 2016 primaries were particularly capricious. In the early days of the primaries, few would have predicted that Senator Bernie Sanders would be one of the last two Democrats standing, much less that Donald Trump would secure the Republican nomination (Silver, 2015a; Enten, 2015; Rifkin, 2015). Many predicted that establishment candidates like Hillary Clinton and Jeb Bush would win and that the unconventional candidates like Sanders and Trump would drop out without posing a significant challenge to the establishment candidates (Silver, 2015a; Silver, 2015b; Ostroy, 2015).

Their predictions seemed reasonable at the time, as Donald Trump has never held an elected office and has little political experience (Biography. com, 2016). He is a businessman by trade, and, as a political candidate, he throws out radical ideas and supports radical measures to deal with the nation's most important issues. He is not the only candidate to do so. Senator Bernie Sanders spent much of his career as an outsider who supported some radical policies, including universal health care, student loan debt forgiveness, and free college tuition.

However, over the past 40 years, Sanders has not wavered in his political beliefs (Keith, 2015; Horowitz, 2016), and nor has Senator Ted Cruz. Sanders has preached the same far left of center message advocating for social and political change without pause and did not sponsor a single bipartisan bill in 2015 (Govtrack.us, 2016a). Senator Ted Cruz is similar in that he has preached the same conservative message for many years, and sponsored the fewest bipartisan bills of any Senate Republican in 2015 (Flegenheimer, 2016; Govtrack.us, 2016b). Accordingly, both senators may be considered ideologues, as they strictly stick with a particular ideological agenda and will not compromise on that agenda (Tetlock, 1983). Both are loyal to their ideological values and are unwilling to compromise with other ideologies, regardless of the issue.

Hillary Clinton cannot be categorized as an ideologue. While she may not be as bipartisan as she claims, 44 percent of her resolutions and bills had at least one Republican cosponsor (Emery, 2016). She was not always a "liberal" or "progressive" Democrat. When she was younger, she campaigned for Republican presidential nominee Barry Goldwater, but she has adopted a more liberal stance on several issues since 2008 (Biography.com, 2016; Riddel, 2015).

Donald Trump is similar to Clinton in that his political beliefs have wavered, he has identified with both the Democratic and Republican parties, and he has donated a substantial amount of money to Democrats, including Hillary Clinton (Moody, 2016). He changes his position from liberal to conservative and back on a relatively regular basis (Diamond, 2016; Keneally, 2016). His platform is a mixture of liberal and conservative positions (OnTheIssues, 2016). He supports stricter immigration laws and opposes environmental energy reforms, but supports raising taxes on the wealthy and raising the minimum wage. Trump's unexpected popularity may owe itself, in part, to the fact that many voters are not ideologues, and his mix of conservative and liberal positions may be part of his appeal (Sides & Tesler, 2016). This political malleability may have provided Trump an edge over Senator Ted Cruz, helping him to procure the Republican nomination for the presidency (Steinhauer, 2016). The fact that he is not a strict ideologue allows him to appeal to a broader swath of voters, and that may be why Trump supporters expect that he will accomplish more than the other candidates: he is willing to say and do whatever he thinks will solve the nation's problems, regardless of party lines (Li, 2016; *New York Times*, 2016a; 2016b; 2016c). On many issues, Trump has taken extreme positions. His desire to build a wall between the United

States and Mexico and to ban all Muslim immigration are dramatic, but they notably did not prevent him from succeeding in the Republican primary, and indeed may have helped him. While candidates like Sanders and Cruz are consistent ideologues, Trump is more like Clinton; he is ideologically inconsistent.

Radical proposals often tap into important moral concerns that voters have and may mobilize portions of the electorate who may not ordinarily vote because their traditional electoral options do not represent their core moral priorities. Indeed, past research shows that people who do not vote report more moral priorities that deviate from those of their political party compared to people who do vote (Johnson et al., 2014). This ideological partisan divide seems to be rooted in clashing moral priorities (Hunter, 1992; Sowell, 2007). Indeed, these differences in moral priorities predict policy positions above and beyond demographics, including political ideology (Koleva, Graham, Iyer, Ditto, & Haidt, 2012).

Moral foundations theory (MFT) is a relatively new field of research (Haidt & Graham, 2007). It is a social psychological theory that addresses the variations in human moral priorities across groups and cultures. Much of its work has focused on how moral priorities underlie political conflict in the United States. MFT proposes that there are at least five different foundations of moral beliefs: care/harm, fairness/cheating, loyalty/betrayal, authority/subversion, and purity/degradation (Graham et. al, 2013).[1] The care/harm foundation examines the intuition to protect and nurture those who potentially cannot protect themselves. The fairness/cheating foundation examines the intuition to have just/fair outcomes, such as people getting paid equal amounts for equal work. The loyalty/betrayal foundation examines the intuition to remain faithful to one's ingroup and to punish those who are disloyal. The authority/subversion foundation examines the intuition to obey those in some position of power (e.g., military members, parents, police officers, religious leaders). The sancity/purity/degradation examines the intuition to preserve both bodily and spiritual integrity—violations of this foundation could be having sex with a dead chicken or defecating on a religious text.

Previous research has suggested that liberals and conservatives place different emphases on different foundations (Graham, Haidt, & Nosek, 2009). Liberals tend to prioritize harm/care and fairness/cheating foundations, while conservatives prioritize all of the foundations approximately equally. In practice, this means that conservatives generally prioritize harm/care and fairness/cheating less than liberals do, but prioritize loyalty/betrayal, authority/subversion, and purity/degradation more than liberals do.

But Democrats and Republicans are not homogeneous parties composed of individuals who share the exact same moral priorities to the same extent. Different candidates tend to place different emphases on different foundations and attract different supporters within parties. In a survey of supporters of different candidates, Trump supporters prioritized fairness, loyalty, authority, and sanctity and were less concerned about care. Cruz supporters prioritized fairness above all and care the least. Sanders supporters prioritized care and were less concerned about fairness, loyalty, authority, and sanctity (Ekins & Haidt, 2016). Clinton supporters emphasized care more than the average American but were less concerned about fairness, loyalty, authority, and sanctity. Overall, Clinton's and Sanders's supporters showed relatively similar patterns, valuing care and fairness more than in-group loyalty, authority, and purity. Trump and Cruz supporters also showed relatively similar patterns, valuing fairness, in-group loyalty, authority, and purity more than care. In doing so, all of the candidates exemplified the usually favored dimensions of their respective Republican and Democratic political parties (Graham et al., 2009).

Americans have grown increasingly divided along moral and political lines. Text analysis of tweets (short messages posted to Twitter, a popular social media Web site) has found evidence that people who are high in the purity foundation tend to create social networks composed predominantly of other people who are also high on the purity foundation (Dehghani et al., 2016).

The United States of America has become increasingly polarized and segregated in many ways, but particularly in terms of politics and morality. In terms of politics, numerous nationally representative surveys find that liberals and conservatives are endorsing ever-more-extreme positions on cultural issues (Abramowitz, 2012). These divisions go far beyond simple disagreements over which policies are best. Americans actively avoid communicating with and openly discriminate against people with different political beliefs (Goldman & Mutz, 2011; Munro, Lasane, & Leary, 2010). This distance between political opponents can be observed in the media in the form of a separation of liberal and conservative Twitter users in the sharing of political tweets and increasing segregation of political blogs (Adamic & Glance, 2005; Conover et al., 2011).

In addition to avoiding people who disagree with us, we actively seek out people that do agree with us. We consume media that supports and confirms our preexisting beliefs (Stroud, 2008; Garrett, 2009; Iyengar & Hahn, 2009). In other words, we like it when the media that we consume validates our thoughts, beliefs, and feelings. This bias toward consensual validation is exaggerated when people perceive threat, which campaigns sow when discussing the instability of the economy, the influx of undocumented immigrants, or the specter of terrorism (Greenberg et al., 1990; Pyszczynski et al., 1996; Vail, Arndt, Motyl, & Pyszczynski, 2012).

With recent technological innovations, it is easier than ever to do this. There has been an explosion of different news sources catering to any specific audience (Mutz, 2006). We are becoming increasingly segregated in our media consumption, even within our political parties, gradually gathering into segregated clusters of people who agree on almost every issue, while completely disregarding the other side's arguments (Chopik & Motyl, 2016; Frimer, Skitka, & Motyl, under review; Motyl, 2014; Motyl, 2016; Motyl, Iyer, Oishi, Trawalter, & Nosek, 2014). News media itself has become increasingly partisan, making it difficult to find a news source without some sort of political spin (Prior, 2013). This sort of behavior is not conducive to productive bipartisan discussion.

Consumption of highly polarized media may lead to stereotyping of the opposing party. Both liberals and conservatives display stereotypes about the other side's moral beliefs. While people can often predict the direction of Republicans' or Democrats' political beliefs, they often exaggerate the extremity of these beliefs, regardless of whether they are speaking about their own party or the other party (Graham, Nosek, & Haidt, 2012). Stereotypes about the morality of the opposing party are likely associated with stereotypes about the moral worldviews of political candidates and of the people that support them (Crawford, Modri, & Motyl, 2013). Selective media consumption allows people to expose themselves to a single perspective and may lead to negative stereotypes about other candidates and their supporters. For example, selective media consumption may be responsible for the stereotypes that Trump supporters are "crazy" or Sanders supporters are "ignorant kids" (Arceneaux, 2016; Nimmo, 2015).

Believing that the aforementioned data looking at the moral priorities of people who supported the different political candidates were limited, as they relied on the self-reported surveys of volunteers who agreed to participate, we devised a study to conceptually replicate these findings using a more naturalistic methodology: actual speech on Twitter, which has become a popular means of political communication among politically engaged Americans.

Twitter contains immense stores of accessible data that is ripe for textual analysis (Pak & Paroubek, 2010). It allows researchers to collect data on events in real time as events unfold. In this case, Twitter provided a simple method for collecting data on many supporters of the main candidates running for their party's nomination near the end of the primary election season.

As of June 13, 2016, 2:21 PM CST, on Twitter, 9 million people followed Donald Trump's Twitter account, 6.9 million people followed Hillary Clinton, 1.3 million people followed Ted Cruz, and 2.1 million followed Bernie Sanders. To establish a comparison group, we also identified a nonpolitical celebrity (John Stamos), who had a similar number of followers (1.9 million). For each of these five figures, we randomly selected 15,000–20,000 users who followed each of them and downloaded up to 200 of their most recent Tweets. This yielded a sample of 86,061 people who tweeted 141,903,439 words. During data processing, we discovered that 124 of these people followed more than one of the figures. To allow for a clean comparison of followers of each of the candidates, we excluded these 124 people from all subsequent analyses. Our de-identified data can be accessed at osf.io/z4h97.

We conducted a form of text analysis that uses counts of key words and phrases to extract meaningful psychological constructs from large bodies of text (Tausczik & Pennebaker, 2010). Text analysis of tweets can provide insight into who is talking about what and how they are talking about it. Text analysis performed by Sylwester and Purver (2015) has shown several reliable differences in language usage between Democrats and Republicans. For example, Democrats tend to use more anxiety words, while Republicans tend to use more words related to achievement as opposed to more concrete plans. We used this data to test two competing hypotheses: the Party Line hypothesis and the Ideologue hypothesis.

The *Party Line Hypothesis* states that similarities and differences between candidates will fall roughly along party lines. Supporters of Clinton will be most similar to Sanders, and supporters of Cruz will be most similar to supporters of Trump, and vice versa. This difference should be particularly prevalent in terms of morality. Previous research has shown that liberals tend to place the most emphasis on the harm/care and fairness/cheating foundations of morality, and conservatives place similar emphasis on all five foundations (Graham et al., 2009). If this hypothesis is correct, we would expect supporters to speak the most about moral foundations that are consistent with their political ideology. Clinton and Sanders supporters should look similar to each other, as should Cruz and Trump.

According to the *Ideologue Hypothesis*, supporters of the ideologue candidates (Cruz and Sanders) will be more similar to each other than Trump and Clinton supporters, and vice versa. There is support for this hypothesis as well. People with more extreme political views, regardless of their side of the political spectrum, tend to act more similarly to each other than to moderates of their own party (Sidanius, 1984; van Prooijen, Krouwel, Boiten, & Eendebak, 2015; Tetlock, 1983). If this is the case, we would expect Cruz and Sanders to use more party-consistent moral language than Trump and Clinton.

We used the *Moral Foundations Dictionary* for our analyses (Graham, Haidt, & Nosek, 2009). The *Moral Foundations Dictionary* contains words coded to reflect the five moral foundations mentioned earlier: care, fairness, loyalty, authority, and purity. The *Moral Foundations Dictionary* has been used in empirical work to yield results consistent with other methodologies. For example, liberal speakers tended to use words found in the harm and fairness subdictionaries of the *Moral Foundations Dictionary*, whereas conservative speakers tended to use words found in the in-group loyalty, authority, and purity subdictionaries (Graham et al., 2009). We would expect such a pattern of results given conservatives' increased reliance on in-group loyalty, authority, and purity compared to liberals, and liberals' increased reliance on harm and fairness compared to conservatives.

We used the *Moral Foundations Dictionary*'s measure of general morality to determine which Twitter users spoke about morality the most and which spoke about it the least. This subdictionary uses words such as "law," "principle," "piety," and "wrong" to measure how much people speak about morality more generally. Then we turned to the dictionary's foundations for a finer-grain analysis of what types of morality followers were speaking about. The *Moral Foundations Dictionary* is split into two categories: "virtue" and "vice." The "virtue" subdictionary contains words that correspond with the more positive end of the moral foundations spectrum: care, fairness, loyalty, authority, and purity. However, for the purposes of our analysis, we chose to use the "vice" subdictionary.[2]

The "vice" subdictionary is further separated into various subdictionaries that contain words that correspond with the opposite end of the spectrum on the five moral foundations: harm, cheating, betrayal, subversion, and degradation. The harm subdictionary contains words such as "abuse," "kill," "damage," and "abandon" that measure the degree to which people acknowledge the violation of the harm foundation in their everyday lives. The cheating subdictionary contains words such as "bias," "unfair," "dishonest," and "exclude" to measure how often people speak about perceived violations of fair procedures or outcomes. The betrayal subdictionary contains words such as "treason," "desert," "enemy," and "disloyal" to measure how often people exclude others from their in-group in their speech. The subversion subdictionary contains words such as "defy," "unfaithful," "insubordinate," and "riot" to measure how frequently people signal disobedience toward an authority figure in their speech. The degradation subdictionary contains words such as "wicked," "sin," "disgust," and "disease" to measure how sensitive people are to violations of both physical and spiritual integrity.

Preliminary Analyses

All of the means presented below represent the average percentage of words related to that topic out of the total words tweeted per Twitter user. All means have been standardized and centered on the sample mean to make it easier to spot differences between groups. Due to our large sample size, the *p*-values of all of our omnibus tests are less than 0.001 and will not be reported here.

The *Moral Foundations Dictionary* includes a measure of general moral language. There were not many differences between followers of the different candidates in general moral language. Our apolitical baseline used an amount of moral language that was approximately equal to the sample average. Sanders followers, Trump followers, and Cruz followers were all statistically indistinguishable from the baseline (all $ps > 0.15$). Clinton followers used less moral language than the baseline ($p = 0.04$; see figure 11.1).

Moral Foundations

It appears that some candidates use slightly more moral language than others, but it remains unclear what the implications of speaking more about morality are in general. Pluralistic accounts of morality suggest that followers of these candidates may be similarly high in moral language, yet differ in their moral priorities (Graham et al., 2012; Haslam & Fiske, 1999; Shweder, Much, Mahapatra, & Park, 1997). Therefore, we used the *Moral Foundations Dictionary* to assess differences in the moral content of the tweets of the followers of these candidates. Means and standard deviations for all foundations can be found in table 11.1, and Cohen's *d*s for pairwise comparisons can be found in table 11.2.

Harm/care. Baseline participants speak about harm less than followers of all of the political candidates included in the current study (all $p < 0.001$). Based off of previous findings, we would expect that Trump followers would not be very concerned about this foundation compared to our baseline (e.g., Ekins & Haidt, 2016). And Trump followers do speak less about harm than the average Twitter user in our sample, but more than our baseline ($p < 0.001$). Clinton followers speak about it at

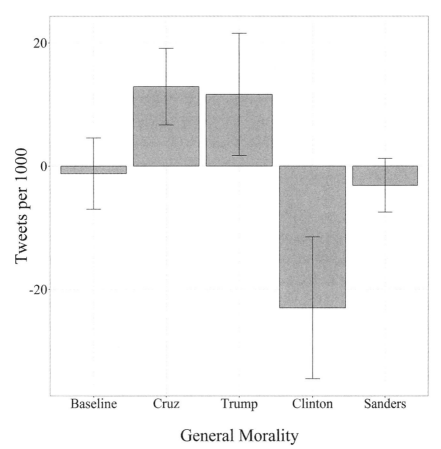

General Morality

Figure 11.1 **A representation of the means for the followers of each candidate for general moral language. "0" represents the mean for the total sample. Bars that fall below "0" are below average, and bars that fall above "0" are above average. Our baseline represents the mean for John Stamos's followers.**

approximately the same frequency as Trump's ($p = 0.07$), and more than our baseline. Both Cruz and Sanders ($p = 0.24$) followers speak the most about harm.

Cheating/fairness. Our baseline participants, as before, speak about cheating the least of all (all $ps < 0.001$). Trump followers speak about cheating more than baseline users, but less than our average user. Clinton followers speak about it slightly more than Trump followers ($p = 0.03$), while both Cruz and Sanders followers ($p = 0.66$) speak about it more than Clinton followers (both $ps < 0.001$).

Table 11.1   Standardized Descriptive Statistics

	Baseline	Cruz	Trump	Clinton	Sanders
General Morality	0.00 (0.79)	0.02 (1.24)	−0.02 (0.87)	−0.03 (1.15)	0.04 (0.85)
Harm	−0.10 (0.78)	0.11 (1.21)	−0.04 (1.09)	−0.06 (0.96)	0.10 (0.88)
Cheating	−0.07 (0.33)	0.06 (1.63)	−0.02 (0.86)	0.0003 (0.91)	0.05 (0.71)
Betrayal	−0.12 (0.46)	0.19 (1.44)	−0.03 (1.03)	−0.05 (0.79)	0.01 (1.00)
Subversion	−0.06 (0.7)	0.11 (1.51)	−0.02 (0.93)	−0.04 (0.85)	0.008 (0.62)
Degradation	0.0001 (0.79)	0.02 (1.24)	−0.02 (0.87)	−0.03 (1.15)	0.04 (0.85)

All variables are centered on the sample mean.

Betrayal/loyalty. Baseline participants speak of betrayal the least (all $ps <$ 0.001). Clinton followers speak about betrayal more than our baseline, but less than the sample average. Trump followers speak about betrayal more than our baseline, and slightly more than Clinton followers ($p = 0.02$). Sanders followers speak about betrayal slightly more than Trump followers ($p = 0.002$), and Cruz followers speak of it most of all ($p < 0.001$).

Subversion/authority. Baseline participants speak about subversion of authority the least (all $ps < 0.03$). Clinton followers speak of it more than our baseline, but less than average. Trump followers speak of about the same amount as Clinton followers ($p = 0.16$). Sanders followers speak about subversion more than Trump's and Clinton's, and slightly above average (both $ps < 0.02$). Cruz followers spoke of it most of all ($p < 0.001$).

Degradation/purity. Baseline participants speak about purity in an amount that was consistent with the sample mean. Trump and Clinton followers both speak about it less than average ($p = 0.43$), and less than baseline followers (both $ps < 0.02$). Cruz and Sanders followers both speak about it more than average ($p = 0.09$). Cruz followers are not statistically different from baseline ($p = 0.07$), but Sanders followers spoke about purity significantly more than baseline followers ($p < 0.001$).

Overall. Trump and Clinton followers show very similar patterns of diction. Both are below average on every foundation. Their more politically polarized counterparts, Cruz and Sanders followers, are above average on most foundations. In other words, followers of the less ideological candidates are more similar to each other than they are to their more extreme counterparts, and vice versa (see figure 11.2). Followers of the candidates are generally more likely to use words related to the five moral priorities than the people who follow our apolitical baseline, though this is not true of general speech about morality.

Table 11.2   Cohen's *d* Scores for All Pairwise Comparisons

	Baseline	Cruz	Trump	Clinton
General Morality				
Cruz	0.02	.	.	.
Trump	0.01	−0.001	.	.
Clinton	−0.02	−0.03	−0.03	.
Sanders	−0.002	−0.02	−0.02	0.02
Harm				
Cruz	0.20	.	.	.
Trump	−0.06	−0.12	.	.
Clinton	−0.04	−0.15	−0.02	.
Sanders	0.23	−0.01	0.13	0.17
Cheating				
Cruz	0.11	.	.	.
Trump	0.07	−0.06	.	.
Clinton	0.11	−0.04	0.03	.
Sanders	0.23	−0.003	0.04	0.06
Betrayal				
Cruz	0.30	.	.	.
Trump	0.13	−0.17	.	.
Clinton	0.12	−0.20	−0.03	.
Sanders	0.19	−0.14	0.04	0.07
Subversion				
Cruz	0.15	.	.	.
Trump	0.05	−0.10	.	.
Clinton	0.03	−0.12	−0.02	.
Sanders	0.10	−0.08	0.04	0.06
Degradation				
Cruz	0.04	.	.	.
Trump	−0.03	−0.04	.	.
Clinton	−0.04	−0.04	−0.009	.
Sanders	0.04	0.02	0.07	0.07

Scores represent row minus column means, so that positive numbers mean that the followers of a candidate in the row scored higher than the followers of the candidate in the column.

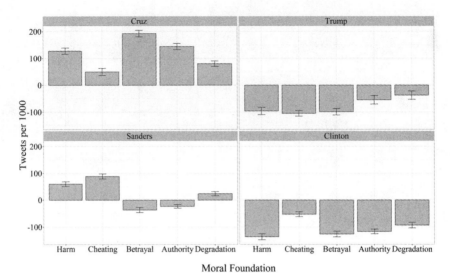

Figure 11.2   **Means and standard errors for the followers of each candidate for their usage of Moral Foundations language. "0" represents the mean for the total sample. Our baseline is composed of the means for John Stamos's followers.**

Conclusion

The common perception of Trump supporters is that they are extreme or even "radical" in comparison to supporters of other candidates (Tesfaye, 2016; Tashman, 2016). Yet, previous analysis of their preferences in terms of different aspects of morality paint them as relatively similar to Ted Cruz's supporters (Ekins & Haidt, 2016).

Our data suggest otherwise. In terms of morality, Trump followers were not outliers. In fact, they rarely stood out on any of the dimensions that we measured. Overall, their moral language was very similar to Clinton followers. Trump and Clinton followers used less morally charged language overall and tended to be low on emotional and trait terms, with some variation on Trump's part.

In terms of morality, our data support the *Ideologue Hypothesis*, and provide little evidence for the *Party Line Hypothesis*. A candidate's adherence to his or her party's values is a more reliable predictor for their follower's speech patterns than their political ideology alone. Followers of less ideological candidates, like Trump and Clinton, use less moral language, while followers of ideologues, like Cruz and Sanders, use more moral language. Their patterns of moral speech are roughly similar to those observed in other studies of liberals and conservatives (Graham et al., 2009). As expected, people who follow a liberal ideologue, like Sanders, write relatively more about care/harm and fairness/cheating. People who follow a conservative ideologue, like Cruz, write relatively evenly on care/harm, loyalty/betrayal, and authority/subversion, though they write relatively less about fairness/cheating and purity/degradation, which deviates somewhat from the usual pattern. This may be because our sample rarely talked about purity/degradation overall. It is possible that any differences were masked by conversational norms on Twitter.

In short, the data provide evidence for both parts of the *Ideologue Hypothesis*: followers of the less ideological candidates, Trump and Clinton, tweeted more similarly, and followers of the more ideological candidates, Cruz and Sanders, tweeted more similarly and in more morally polarized ways.

Our analyses do have their strengths and weaknesses. Our sample is large, and it relies on real behavior as opposed to survey responses, which may be subject to a variety of response biases. However, the effect sizes are small, and we do not know much about these users. We cannot guarantee that there is a perfect correlation between candidates' followers on Twitter and their supporters. Trump was a celebrity long before he was a politician, and many of his Twitter followers may have followed him long before he decided to run for president. But there is evidence that it is possible to reliably estimate Twitter users' ideology based on the people that they follow, so it seems likely that many of them do support him (Barberá et al., 2015). More than that, the diction of his followers resembles that of Clinton followers considerably more than it resembles John Stamos's followers. But John Stamos is just one celebrity. His followers may not be representative of the general population. Further research using multiple control people will be necessary for a more accurate baseline. It is also possible that followers become less morally polarized when their candidates win than when they lose, but, again, further research is required to speak to this point.

For the time being, it appears that the majority of Trump's followers are not as radical as the media suggests (Tesfaye, 2016; Tashman, 2016). Their moral values are more in line with Clinton followers. Trump was a Democrat who is now running as a Republican, and Clinton worked for Republican groups in the past and is now running as a Democrat. This sets them apart from such ideologues as Cruz and Sanders, who have remained on their sides of the aisle for the duration of their political careers. The people who support ideologues like Cruz and Sanders are the ones using extreme moral language, and they are more likely to show party-line differences in the moral foundations than people who support nonideologues like Trump and Clinton. In short, followers of ideologues are more morally polarized than followers of the Democratic and Republican presidential nominees.

What this study shows is that if either Trump or Clinton succeed to the presidency, they may prove themselves to be more pragmatic than Sanders or Cruz might have been, and, importantly, their followers are more likely to permit them some considerable flexibility in their actual policy making than they might have permitted the more ideologically driven Cruz or Sanders.

Notes

1. Discussions on the *YourMorals.org* blog suggest that there may be a sixth foundation pertaining to liberty/oppression, but no peer-reviewed research has yet verified this possible foundation.

2. Additional analyses using the "virtue" subdictionary generally replicate the findings reported in this chapter using the "vice" subdictionary. We also conducted exploratory analyses on several emotion and trait variables from the *Regressive Image Dictionary* (Martindale, 2008). Summaries of all analyses can be accessed at osf.io/z4h97.

References

Adamic, L. A., & Glance, N. (2005, August). *The political blogosphere and the 2004 US election: Divided they blog.* Paper presented at the 3rd International Workshop on Link Discovery, Chicago, IL.

Arceneaux, M. (2016, January 14). Here are the levels of crazy Donald Trump supporters have reached. VH1. Retrieved from http://www.vh1.com /news/236293/crazy-donald-trump-supporters

Barberá, P., Jost, J. T., Nagler, J., Tucker, J. A., & Bonneau, R. (2015). Tweeting from left to right: Is online political communication more than an echo chamber? *Psychological science, 26*(10), 1531–1542.

Biography.com (Eds.). (2016, July 4). "Donald Trump Biography." Retrieved from http://www.biography.com/people/donald-trump-9511238

Chopik, W. J., & Motyl, M. (2016). Ideological fit enhances interpersonal orientations. *Social Psychological and Personality Science.* doi:10.1177/194855061 6658096

Conover, M., Ratkiewicz, J., Francisco, M. R., Gonçalves, B., Menczer, F., & Flammini, A. (2011). *Political polarization on Twitter.* Presented at the Fifth International Conference on Weblogs and Social Media, Chicago IL, August 21–24, 2005.

Crawford, J. T., Modri, S. A., & Motyl, M. (2013). Bleeding-heart liberals and hard-hearted conservatives: Subtle political dehumanization through differential attributions of human nature and human uniqueness traits. *Journal of Social and Political Psychology, 1*(1), 86–104.

Dehghani, M., Johnson, K., Hoover, J., Sagi, E., Garten, J., Parmar, N. J., … & Graham, J. (2016). Purity homophily in social networks. *Journal of Experimental Psychology: General, 145*(3), 366–375.

Diamond, J. (2016, April 1). Abortion and 10 other Donald Trump flip-flops. CNN. Retrieved from http://www.cnn.com/2016/03/31/politics/donald-trump-positions-flip-flops

Ekins, J., & Haidt, J. (2016, February 5). Donald Trump supporters think about morality differently than other voters: Here's how. *Vox.* Retrieved from http://www.vox.com/2016/2/5/10918164/donald-trump-morality

Emery, C. (2016, January 20). Spot check of Hillary Clinton's Senate record fails to support bipartisanship claim. *PolitiFact.* Retrieved from http://www.politifact.com/truth-o-meter/statements/2016/jan/20/hillary-clinton/spot-check-hillary-clintons-senate-record-immolate

Enten, H. (2015, April 30). Enter the Democratic primary's liberal alternative: Bernie Sanders! *FiveThirtyEight.* Retrieved from http://fivethirtyeight.com/features/bernie-sanders-president-announcement-liberal-alternative-2016-democratic-primary

Flegenheimer, M. (2016, April 17). Ted Cruz's conservatism: The pendulum swings consistently right. *The New York Times.* Retrieved from http://www.nytimes.com/2016/04/18/us/politics/ted-cruz-conservative.html

Frimer, J., Skitka, L. J., & Motyl, M. (under review). Liberals and conservatives are similarly motivated to remain ignorant of one another's opinions.

Garrett, R. K. (2009). Echo chambers online? Politically motivated selective exposure among Internet news users. *Journal of Computer Mediated Communication,14*(2), 265–285.

Goldman, S. K., & Mutz, D. C. (2011). The friendly media phenomenon: A cross-national analysis of cross-cutting exposure. *Political Communication, 28*(1), 42–66.

Govtrack.us. (2016a, July 5). Sen. Bernard "Bernie" Sanders. Retrieved from https://www.govtrack.us/congress/members/bernard_sanders/400357

Govtrack.us. (2016b, July 5). Sen. Ted Cruz. Retrieved from https://www.govtrack.us/congress/members/ted_cruz/412573

Graham, J., Haidt, J., & Nosek, B. A. (2009). Liberals and conservatives rely on different sets of moral foundations. *Journal of Personality and Social Psychology, 96*(5), 1029–1046.

Graham, J., Haidt, J., Koleva, S., Motyl, M., Iyer, R., Wojcik, S., & Ditto, P. H. (2013). Moral foundations theory: The pragmatic validity of moral pluralism. *Advances in Experimental Social Psychology, 47*, 55–130.

Graham, J., Nosek, B. A., & Haidt, J. (2012). The moral stereotypes of liberals and conservatives: Exaggeration of differences across the political spectrum. *PloS one, 7*(12), e50092.

Greenberg, J., Pyszczynski, T., Solomon, S., Rosenblatt, A., Veeder, M., Kirkland, S., & Lyon, D. (1990). Evidence for terror management theory II: The effects of mortality salience on reactions to those who threaten or bolster the cultural worldview. *Journal of Personality and Social Psychology, 58*(2), 308.

Haidt, J., & Graham, J. (2007). When morality opposes justice: Conservatives have moral intuitions that liberals may not recognize. *Social Justice Research, 20*(1), 98–116.

Haslam, N., & Fiske, A. P. (1999). Relational models theory: A confirmatory factor analysis. *Personal Relationships, 6*(2), 241–250.

Horowitz, J. (2016, March 25). Bernie Sanders consistent over decades in his call for "revolution." *The New York Times.* Retrieved from http://www.nytimes.com/2016/03/26/us/politics/bernie-sanders-consistent-over-decades-in-his-call-for-revolution.html?_r=0;

Hunter, J. D. (1992). *Culture wars: The struggle to control the family, art, education, law, and politics in America.* New York: Basic Books.

Iyengar, S., & Hahn, K. S. (2009). Red media, blue media: Evidence of ideological selectivity in media use. *Journal of Communication, 59*(1), 19–39.

Johnson, K. M., Iyer, R., Wojcik, S. P., Vaisey, S., Miles, A., Chu, V., & Graham, J. (2014, December 11). Ideology–specific patterns of moral indifference predict intentions not to vote. *Analyses of Social Issues and Public Policy, 14*(1), 61–77.

Keith, T. (2015) Bernie Sanders has stuck to the same message for 40 years. NPR. Retrieved from http://www.npr.org/2015/12/11/459231940/bernie-sanders-has-stuck-to-the-same-message-for-40-years

Keneally, M. (2016, June 16). One year of Donald Trump's campaign: Times he's flip-flopped. ABC News. Retrieved from http://abcnews.go.com/Politics/history-donald-trumps-flip-flopping-issues-presidential-campaign/story?id=39063811

Li, D. (2016, April 5). Here's why people are voting for Trump. *New York Post.* Retrieved from http://nypost.com/2016/04/05/heres-why-people-are-voting-for-trump

Martindale, C. (2007). Creativity, primordial cognition, and personality. *Personality and Individual Differences, 43*(7), 1777–1785.

Moody, C. (2015, July 22). Trump in '04: "I probably identify more as Democrat." CNN. Retrieved from http://www.cnn.com/2015/07/21/politics/donald-trump-election-democrat

Motyl, M. (2014). "If he wins, I'm moving to Canada": Ideological migration threats following the 2012 U.S. presidential election. *Analyses of Social Issues and Public Policy, 14*(1), 123–136.

Motyl, M. (2016). Liberals and conservatives are geographically dividing. In P. Valdesolo & J. Graham (Eds.), *Social Psychology of Political Polarization.* New York: Psychology Press.

Motyl, M., Iyer, R., Oishi, S., Trawalter, S., & Nosek, B. A. (2014). How ideological migration geographically segregates groups. *Journal of Experimental Social Psychology, 51,* 1–14.

Munro, G. D., Lasane, T. P., & Leary, S. P. (2010). Political partisan prejudice: Selective distortion and weighting of evaluative categories in college admissions applications. *Journal of Applied Social Psychology, 40*(9), 2434–2462.

Mutz, D. C. (2006). How the mass media divide us. In D. Brady & P. Divola (Eds.), *Red and blue Nation? Characteristics and causes of America's polarized politics* (pp. 223–248). Washington, D.C.: Brookings Institution Press.

The New York Times. (2016a, February 9). New Hampshire exit poll. Retrieved from http://www.nytimes.com/interactive/2016/02/09/us/elections/new-hampshire-republican-poll.html

The New York Times. (2016b, March 15). Florida exit polls. Retrieved from http://www.nytimes.com/interactive/2016/03/15/us/elections/florida-republican-poll.html

The New York Times. (2016c, March 15). Ohio exit polls Retrieved from http://www.nytimes.com/interactive/2016/03/15/us/elections/ohio-republican-poll.html

The New York Times. (2016d, June 22). Which presidential candidates are winning the money race? Retrieved from http://www.nytimes.com/interactive/2016/us/elections/election-2016-campaign-money-race.html

Nimmo, K. (2015, November 10). Socialism? Young Bernie Sanders supporters are clueless. *Info Wars.* Retrieved from http://www.infowars.com/socialism-young-bernie-sanders-supporters-are-clueless

OnTheIssues. (2016, July 4). Donald Trump. Retrieved from http://www.ontheissues.org/Donald_Trump.htm

Ostroy, A. (2015, November 19). Here's how/why Jeb Bush will win the GOP nomination. *The Huffington Post.* Retrieved from http://www.huffingtonpost.com/andy-ostroy/heres-howwhy-jeb-bush-will-win-the-gop-nomination_b_8598894.html

Pak, A., & Paroubek, P. (2010, May). Twitter as a corpus for sentiment analysis and opinion mining. Paper presented at the International Conference on Language Resources and Evaluation, Valletta, Malta.

Prior, M. (2013). Media and Political Polarization. *Annual Review of Political Science, 16,* 101–127.

Pyszczynski, T., Wicklund, R. A., Floresku, S., Koch, H., Gauch, G., Solomon, S., & Greenberg, J. (1996). Whistling in the dark: Exaggerated consensus estimates in response to incidental reminders of mortality. *Psychological Science, 7*(6), 332–336.

Riddel, K. (2015, October 12). Hillary Clinton flip-flops from 2008 in bid for liberal voters' support. *The Washington Times*. Retrieved from http://www.washingtontimes.com/news/2015/oct/12/hillary-clinton-flip-flops-from-2008-positions-in-

Rifkin, J. (2015, December 30). The worst political predictions of 2015. *Politico Magazine*. Retrieved from http://www.politico.com/magazine/story/2015/12/the-worst-political-predictions-of-2015-213484

Shweder, R., Much, N., Mahapatra, M., & Park, L. (1997). Divinity and the "big three" explanations of suffering. *Morality and Health, 119,* 119–169.

Sidanius, J. (1984). Political interest, political information search, and ideological homogeneity as a function of sociopolitical ideology: A tale of three theories. *Human Relations, 37*(10), 811–828.

Sides, J. & Tesler, M. (2016, March 2). How political science helps explain the rise of Trump: Most voters aren't ideologues. *The Washington Post*. Retrieved from https://www.washingtonpost.com/news/monkey-cage/wp/2016/03/02/how-political-science-helps-explain-the-rise-of-trump-most-voters-arent-ideologues

Silver, N. (2015a, August 11). Donald Trump is winning the polls—and losing the nomination. *FiveThirtyEight*. Retrieved from http://fivethirtyeight.com/datalab/donald-trump-is-winning-the-polls-and-losing-the-nomination

Silver, N. (2015b, April 12). Clinton begins the 2016 campaign, and it's a toss-up. *FiveThirtyEight*. Retrieved from http://fivethirtyeight.com/features/clinton-begins-the-2016-campaign-and-its-a-toss-up

Sowell, T. (2007). *A conflict of visions: Ideological origins of political struggles*. New York: Basic Books.

Steinhauer, J. (2016, January 1). Republican says "malleable" Donald Trump is more electable than a "rigid" Ted Cruz. *The New York Times*. Retrieved from http://www.nytimes.com/politics/first-draft/2016/01/26/republican-says-malleable-donald-trump-is-more-electable-than-a-rigid-ted-cruz/?_r=0

Sylwester, K., & Purver, M. (2015). Twitter language use reflects psychological differences between Democrats and Republicans. *PloS one, 10*(9), e0137422.

Tashman, B. (2016, May 9). Trump's team: The bigoted, unhinged conspiracy theorists benefiting from Donald Trump's campaign. *Right Wing Watch*. Retrieved from http://www.rightwingwatch.org/content/trumps-team-bigoted-unhinged-conspiracy-theorists-benefiting-donald-trumps-campaign

Tausczik, Y. R., & Pennebaker, J. W. (2010). The psychological meaning of words: LIWC and computerized text analysis methods. *Journal of Language and Social Psychology, 29*(1), 24–54.

Tesfaye, S. (2016, February 16). Donald Trump's South Carolina supporters are the most radical yet. *Salon*. Retrieved from http://www.salon.com

/2016/02/16/donald_trumps_south_carolina_supporters_are_the
_most_radical_yet/

Tetlock, P. E. (1983). Cognitive style and political ideology. *Journal of Personality and Social Psychology, 45*(1), 118–126.

Vail, K. E., Arndt, J., Motyl, M., & Pyszczynski, T. (2012). The aftermath of destruction: Images of destroyed buildings increase support for war, dogmatism, and death thought accessibility. *Journal of Experimental Social Psychology, 48*(5), 1069–1081.

van Prooijen, J. W., Krouwel, A. P., Boiten, M., & Eendebak, L. (2015). Fear among the extremes: How political ideology predicts negative emotions and outgroup derogation. *Personality and Social Psychology Bulletin, 41*(4), 485–497.

CHAPTER TWELVE

Dramatic Rationalities: Electoral Theater in the Age of Trump

Mark Chou and Michael L. Ondaatje

In April 2015, just as the campaign for the 2016 U.S. presidential election was kicking off, *The Atlantic*'s Derek Thompson (2015) opined that much of what counts for election coverage today has become "indistinguishable from theater criticism: Its chief concerns are storyline, costumes, and the quality of public performances." According to Thompson, political journalists who cover election campaigns as theater critics not only conflate style with substance, they also popularize the notion that "the best actors will make the best candidates (and, by extension, the best presidents)." Citizens who depend on the media for reliable campaign coverage and substantive analyses of candidates' policies will either be left unsatisfied or none the wiser. In the worst-case scenario, the public will begin to believe that style, performance, and drama are what ultimately matter when it comes to understanding electoral politics. That is bad both for individual citizens and for democracy as a whole.

In a reply to Thompson, Jonathan Bernstein (2015) agreed that there is certainly bad theater criticism coverage of campaign politics. But unlike Thompson, he did not think that theater is an illegitimate lens with which to analyze contemporary elections. As Bernstein saw it, the "problem isn't reporting on candidate rhetoric as if it was theater," because "it is theater!" The problem, for him, is reporters and the media attempting to do something they clearly are ill-equipped to do—in this case, providing good theatrical analyses of electoral drama. Good theater criticism, carried out by qualified analysts, can help peel back the theatrical façade and offer citizens a real glimpse into what it takes to campaign effectively and win votes in modern America.

It is important to take Bernstein's assessment seriously, if for no other reason than to understand the puzzling rise of Donald Trump in 2016. It has now been extensively noted, and derided, just how much Trump owes his success to the entertainment industry. A seasoned performer and reality TV star, he has approached the campaign trail as if it were a stage for his foul-mouthed comedic routine. As James Wolcott (2015) observed in a *Vanity Fair* column,

> Watch Trump on the televised stump or during debates with the sound off (your blood pressure will thank you) and observe how he grips the lectern, employing a battery of shrugs, hand jive, and staccato phrase blurts—it's like being teleported back to an old Dean Martin roast, those medieval days of yore when Foster Brooks hiccupped through his drunk act, Phyllis Diller cackled, or Orson Welles shook from underground rumbles of Falstaffian mirth.

Yet, there is also something that Trump does that goes beyond what these actors from the days of yore did so well. Rick Tyler, the former communications director for Ted Cruz, hit the nail on the head when, leading up to the New Hampshire primary, he tweeted that Trump is "turning the campaign into the latest episode of a reality show." For *Time* columnist Katie Reilly, this is precisely what Trump has done. Writing in January 2016, she quipped that the long-time star of his own reality TV drama *The Apprentice* has his sights set on the "Reality TV Primary" that is so far turning out to be "2016's top-rated show" (Reilly, 2016).

In retrospect, this should have been our cue to start taking the analyses of Bernstein and other theater critics seriously. Writing in the *New York Times* several years ago, columnist Rob Walker (2012) made the very astute observation that reality dramas "are more or less attempts to recreate the core narrative of electoral politics: a bunch of candidates competing and being eliminated until a solitary winner is chosen, by most votes, with a lot of dramatic tension, narrative richness and exciting plot twists along the way." Those who were tempted to write Trump off should have paused on this point, because what he lacked as a statesman, he more than made up for as a first-rate reality entertainer. His act was an important part of what made him appealing; indeed, this was the side of him people clamored to see. Yet too few pundits—more concerned with Trump's populism, ideology, or antipolitics—failed to recognize this key point.

In this chapter, we argue that theatrical insights provide a unique and incisive way to understand the nature of Trump's appeal. Yes, there are many good reasons that explain Trump's appeal—and the appeal of other populists like him throughout Europe, Latin America, and Australasia. But theatrics is an often ignored lens—one that has the potential to help Americans make sense of the dramatic rationalities at play in the 2016 U.S. election and why Trump's "bigotry and bombast," to borrow Hillary Clinton's (2016) words, have had such widespread allure.

Elections and Theater

Although the success of Trump's presidential "act" has thrown up a range of new considerations for scholars to reflect on, theatrics has been an essential aspect of U.S. presidential politics for some time (Chou et al., 2016). Charles Guggenheim, who was Robert Kennedy's former campaign adviser, already knew that many Americans see presidential campaigns as entertainment: "people expect drama, pathos, intrigue, conflict, and they expect it to hang together as a dramatic package" (Guggenheim cited in Davies, 1986, p. 98). But it was not until the Reagan presidency that political campaign strategies became indebted to theater. "Whereas once aspects of theatricality were applied to enhance political expediency," Gautam Dasgupta (1988, p. 78) makes the point that "since Ronald Reagan took office the exercise and implementation of politics has become inseparable from the theatrical act itself." In other words, thanks to Reagan and the legacy he left, political candidates and politicians in America, as well as in other advanced democracies, have increasingly begun to conflate politics with theater. With Reagan's transition from Hollywood to the White House, American politics finally came to terms with how, in a theatricalized society, politicians and office seekers would be rewarded based on their mastery of the stage and screen (Schechter, 1989). Staged in "cinematic terms," as Douglas Kellner (2002, p. 467) puts it, presidencies soon became "played out on a stage where—alongside traditional resources from ideology, ritual, and the values of the older civic cultures—there are scripts, actors, and props which could be seen as 'borrowed' from popular culture" (Richards, 2004, p. 342).

These dynamics are not only entering politics, according to Barry Richards, they are actually "*constituting* everyday politics in the content and channels of political communication, in the dynamics of public opinion, and in the values and decisions of individual citizens" (2004, p. 342). When this happens, performance, narrative, plot, and pathos begin to matter as much as policy platforms, and they are carefully crafted and managed by candidates, political parties, media consultants, pollsters, and television producers. Without a convincing performance, presidential hopefuls know they risk losing the focus of would-be voters. Without a compelling personal story and uplifting vision for the nation, the public simply will not go to the trouble of going to the polls, no matter how good a candidate's policies are. For its part, the media also shapes the performances of candidates through its coverage of certain types of campaign events. Communicating politics to a broad audience often means portraying candidates and their campaigns simplistically and embellishing dramatic narrative trajectories where at all possible. This is done because politics that is entertaining draws a larger audience than politics that is not.

Recalling a Chris Matthews interview with Bob Schieffer during the 2004 U.S. election, Lance Bennett (2005, p. 172) observed that "most campaign events—from the chicken dinners to the televised debates—are dramatic productions: highly rule-governed, and carefully scripted, staged, and managed." What the voter sees, and may think as unstaged, has actually been primed and framed a particular way to send a particular message. As a 2016 *Wired* magazine exposé showed, the stage at both the 2016 Republican and Democratic National Conventions spoke volumes about the person standing on them. Whereas one was designed for a "celebrity," the other was a platform for "a team" (*Wired*, 2016). Like more conventional forms of theater, these staged productions represent a type of symbolic action and social communication. Particular messages, codes, and rationalities are crafted and then communicated from sender (i.e., the performers, producers, and stage managers) to receiver (i.e., the audience or voting public).

Sometimes these messages, codes, and rationalities, and what lies behind them, are easier to spot—such as during key debates when, for theater scholar Ian Watson (2006, p. 341), "every effort is made by the parties involved to control the staging in favor of their candidate and limit his opponent." However, at other times, such as when candidates seemingly kiss a baby in the crowd at random or meet with victims of a natural disaster, supposedly away from the glare of cameras, the script and stage can be harder to identify. Yet, the text and subtext are always there, coded into the candidate's public appearance and media representation.

Precisely because presidential election spectacles are now so highly dramatized and mediated affairs—with codes and symbols, texts and subtexts—the notion that all citizens will be able to understand and critically engage what is staged for them requires careful scrutiny. The common assumption is that citizens know all too well that politics is performance and elections are theater. Not only do they know this, the assumption is that they also know how to spot what is real from what is staged and to read a performance for what it in fact means.

These are assumptions that may need to be reassessed in the age of Trump. A credentialed reality TV performer, the Republican nominee has taken performance politics to new heights. This was effectively the revelation of Trump's top aide, who, in April 2016, disclosed to a group of leading Republican officials that his candidate was "projecting an image" during the early phases of the election campaign. The "part that he's been playing" was not real, assured Paul Manafort. Come the general election, Americans should expect to see a more "presidential" act. That was his take-home message to the Republican National Committee: the part Trump has been playing is evolving.

Understandably, commentators were quick to pounce on Manafort's revelations, which were leaked subsequent to his April 22 meeting with RNC officials. Trump is a con man, argued Eric Levitz (2016)—the Republican establishment has just spent millions of dollars trying to prove it. Americans should "get a grip," pleaded Danielle Allen (2016), and they should "take on board the difference between cosmetology and statesmanship." But that, in this instance, may be easier said than done. As earlier incidents have shown, it is not always easy figuring out when the Republican nominee is acting and when he is not. For example, it was revealed back in March 2016 that many of the sexist comments that Trump had allegedly made were actually made by Trump the reality TV character, not Trump the presidential candidate. As the tagline of one opinion piece asked, "Is this Trump, or Trump's TV character?"

Indeed, just hours after Manafort promised RNC officials that America would soon see "the real person," Trump was already at it again, telling supporters at a Harrisburg rally that what they were seeing was in fact real. Ever the performer, Trump's message was clear: "I just don't know if I want to do it yet," referring to party pressure to make him appear more presidential. Then at a Waterbury rally, the Republican candidate was heard saying to his crowd of adoring fans, "If I acted presidential, I can guarantee you this morning, I wouldn't be here."

According to Robert Brown (2005, p. 79), "the metaphors of theater, stage, acting and audience offer political communication theorists a useful way of assessing the behavior of political candidates and their partisan loyalists and voting constituencies." Yet, making sense of such metaphors is no easy task for political communication experts let alone everyday citizens. Yes, citizens in advanced democracies are generally becoming more media savvy. The trouble is that today, "when we speak of 'dramatic' events in a political campaign, the 'staging' of a rally or of a 'media event,' we are no longer so sure that we're talking about two exclusive realities, one real and the other laden with illusion," as dramaturgy expert Art Borreca (1993, p. 60) puts it. Even the most politically savvy citizen could do with a helping hand in these circumstances to illuminate how political reality is now inseparable from political illusion.

For Jill Dolan, in order for citizens to competently perform their roles as citizens, they need a guide or toolkit to help them comprehend how exactly politics is conveyed through gesture, production, and narrative—in other words, those things that are revealed only through a performative lens. This is a public service that politically engaged theater scholars and theatrically minded political analysts can perform. As Dolan puts it,

> Those of us actually trained to look critically at performance, to study its links to ideology and culture, can offer ourselves as experts who study the election and the debates through a performative lens—not one that stresses entertainment value, but one that looks at gesture, narrative manipulations, contexts, and "spin" with an eye toward the politics they convey. (Dolan, 2001, p. 6)

While it is easy to see how elections are theatrical or to be captivated by dramatic campaign media coverage, most of us, including the many political analysts who rely on theatrical metaphors, still lack the "skills of performance criticism" to differentiate between what is important and what is not. Even when election observations come close to resembling theater criticism, they often rely on problematic dualisms that separate politics from aesthetics and elections from entertainment.

As the German theater expert Joachim Fiebach (2002, p. 34) once argued in relation to 9/11, a "theater scholar's business should be to watch as closely as possible and to *critically* dissect ... how television stages the terrifying deeds, how the majority of the people directly or indirectly afflicted react to them, how political leaders respond to them." Theater scholars can play an equally important role when it comes to dissecting contemporary presidential election campaigns.

Electoral Dramaturgy: The Art of Watching Elections

But the question is how? This is obviously difficult to answer because there are many possible answers out there. But one realm of inquiry that should be increasingly relevant for the public is what is known as electoral dramaturgy. This may sound rather technical and scholarly, but at its core, this realm of inquiry offers strategies to decode the range of meanings found behind the everyday symbols, rituals, gestures, and performances that make up all human interaction, including political interaction.

Human communication is dramaturgical to the extent that our actions are always enacted, performed, and regulated; their meanings stem from the locations, gestures, language, emotions, and objects we use, consciously or otherwise. In the political realm especially, symbols, rituals, gestures, and actions always have embedded in them particular connotations and meanings. After all, politics is about power and how individuals and institutions use that power to evoke certain actions and reactions in others. Electoral dramaturgy is concerned with how politicians and office seekers do this through a performative lens.

It is important to note that, dramaturgically, the notion of the self is always a construct, identity is something that has to be performed, and communication is about strategic impression management. The point is that what appears natural is rarely thus. What seems a foregone conclusion may in reality be propped up by the most fragile of performances. Dramaturgy lets observers peer behind the scenes and see social reality as a construction that has to be meticulously curated and continuously performed.

A dramaturgical analysis, as T. R. Young and Garth Massey (1978, pp. 78–79, 89–90) argue, borrows from the "technologies of social science, mass communication, theatre and the arts" to upend the "systematic evasion of reciprocity" promulgated by the "vast cadre of skilled artists, musicians, photographers, writers, producers, poets, editors, engineers, and publicists who substitute a world of make believe for a world of serious social endeavor." Simply put, what dramaturgy offers election watchers is the skillset to be able to step into the shoes of the performer—the political candidate—and the crew of directors, producers, consultants, and managers who help them stage their political persona.

Many tools and techniques are available to the dramaturgically minded election watcher. Bruce Gronbeck (1984) has argued that there are at least six aspects of dramaturgy embedded in most presidential campaigns that citizens should recognize. The first is that all humans are social actors. We live in collectivities and accord to communal rituals. We are socialized to act out certain behaviors and conventions, and we understand that there may be negative repercussions if we do not. This is true in all realms of social life, including the political realm. Second, as social beings, humans are "acculturated" to "play certain roles in certain situations" (Gronbeck, 1984, p. 494). Depending on the circumstance, in other words, we expect individuals to perform certain rituals if their actions and social status are to be seen as legitimate by us and others.

Third, while playing these roles or performing these rituals, Gronbeck contends that it is customary for individuals to adopt the predetermined script that society has deemed suitable for that particular situation or circumstance. This is done to allow others to comprehend the ritual's meaning and to act appropriately in response. What this means is that the social order is both predetermined but also continuously negotiated. Indeed, Gronbeck's fourth point is precisely this: social reality is something that humans together articulate, agree upon, and then perform over time. Only then will individual actions take on the status of social ritual.

The fifth dramaturgical aspect he highlights is that humans create and then dwell in "symbolic environments" that "dictate our behavior, control the way we perceive and react to our own and others' behaviors, and set our own and others' expectations for each other" (Gronbeck, 1984, p. 494). In other words, acts will only have the intended effect if they operate within the parameters of their social environment. Finally, Gronbeck concludes by outlining the theory of enactment, which speaks to the "culturally sanctioned languages or codes" that are often implicit when we "'naturally' assume culturally sanctioned roles and role relationships with others" (1984, p. 494). Through "embodiment" of these roles and relationships, we thus "enact" socially acceptable languages and codes.

One might ask, what has any of this to do with presidential campaigns and campaign communication? For Gronbeck (1984, p. 495), what these dramaturgical insights help election watchers do is "specify the cultural-political rules which are embodied—even 'given silent expression'—in the stump speeches, advertisements, pamphlets, billboards, and placards which surround us every leap year." A dramaturgical awareness of this sort helps observers peel back campaign performances and staged events to their constituent parts. While most modern-day citizens will have learned about, and taken part in, presidential election rituals at some point during their lives, the symbolism and codes embedded in these events are often taken for granted and thus rarely questioned. Citizens learn to accept and play along with what is staged for them. But how often do citizens really interrogate the social meanings behind these performances and rituals? That is the question electoral dramaturgy helps citizens ask and answer.

Gronbeck's analysis is important, but electoral dramaturgy does not stop there. In another important contribution to the field, Robert Brown (2005) insisted that there are several more dimensions to this that citizens should recognize in political candidates on the campaign trail.

Drawing on the pioneering work of Erving Goffman (1959), Brown reveals that a candidate's success depends to a large extent on whether he or she possesses or can attain dramaturgical discipline. Put in less technical terms, the better a candidate is at fashioning and staying in character for the campaign's duration, the more likely he or she is to win votes. While dramaturgical discipline comes easy to some, no presidential hopeful can expect to create a viable presidential self without a team of skilled advisers, handlers, media and communications experts, pollsters, and other supporting staff. Together with the candidate, these experts present the presidential self to the public and, most importantly, to prospective donors and voters.

Yet, what the public often does not realize is just how difficult dramaturgical discipline is to maintain and how fragile the presidential self can be. As a construct propped up by a believable and well-maintained dramaturgical discipline, it can easily unravel, and at any time. As Brown (2005, p. 80) writes, "in a U.S. presidential campaign, the candidate's self is particularly fragile, subject to an endless series of investigations, interrogations, credibility tests, and performance miscues." For this reason, candidates can spend millions of dollars of their campaign funds controlling and protecting their image. Citizens who realize this fact may be better equipped to call to account candidates whose presidential self lacks legitimacy or credibility. By tuning out or, worse still, viewing some presidential campaigns as "comic opera or bathetic melodrama," they can undermine and even derail a candidate's run.

One strategy citizens can employ to scrutinize a candidate's dramaturgical discipline, Brown argues, is to note where and when the candidate employs a primary frame as to a keyed frame. Whereas the former is used to denote what is actually the case, the latter is used to denote something other than what appears to be the case. He draws on Goffman's example of two animals fighting to demonstrate what he means by this. According to Goffman (1974), when two animals actually fight, this is an example of a primary frame: the fight is real, not pretend. On the other hand, when two animals play fight, this is an example of a keyed frame: the fight looks real, but it is pretend. Goffman's point, according to Brown, is that it is sometimes difficult for the untrained observer to distinguish a primary from a keyed frame. Yet, a competent observer must be able to see what is real from what merely looks real—and when and why these shifts take place. The same is true when observing presidential candidates and their dramaturgical presentation of the presidential self on the campaign trail.

In short, what electoral dramaturgy does is offer a series of useful analytical devices to the citizen when viewing campaign theater. Done right, it can wrest some of the power currently monopolized by political candidates, their crews of experts, and the media. Ultimately, as Borreca (1993, p. 73) puts it, the function of this type of dramaturgy is to "take us to a state of reflective thinking where the use of dramaturgical terminology is not a reflex but a choice, which grasps both political phenomena as well as what dramatic terms are doing to the very structure of how we think about those phenomena."

So these are the questions for us: What is something we might learn about Trump if we watched him through a dramaturgical lens that would otherwise be missed? What insights can dramaturgy offer citizens who might otherwise mistake his theatrics as buffoonery?

Given the political symbolism coded into human actions and expression, a dramaturgical analysis would pause to reflect on Trump's dramaturgical discipline to determine whether he has been putting on an act and what that act might tell us about the man himself. Of course, at first glance, Trump's presidential persona might not look all that hard to place. He is an antipolitician and Washington outsider who swears and hurls insults at the "enemies" of predominantly white male working-class America. He entertains as he reassures a demographic that, having lost out to "globalization, low-wage immigrant labor, and free trade," is fearful and angry about what the future holds (Packer, 2016). From this perspective, it is clear who Trump is. He is antipolitical and authoritarian—which is just as well because so are his supporters. He sees an enemy (many in fact), and his supporters see in him a savior.

Yet, through a dramaturgical looking glass, it is possible to see that Trump is not exactly the man he appears to be. Yes, there is no doubting that his style is all "bashing and pummeling," to quote David Brooks (2016). But that may be a less accurate statement of who Trump really is than what his fan base desires to see in him—because that is what they see in themselves. It is important that his supporters see in "the say-anything billionaire an image of their aspirations" if they are to champion him (Packer, 2016). This is something that he has only been too happy to oblige. Manafort was not wrong: this is the real act Trump has been putting on.

But how can we be sure? As Goffman said, reality can be a complex thing. Sometimes what looks real actually only obscures reality. Though what Trump has said—that America has seen the real him—seems much more believable than Manafort's revelation, which frankly sounds conspiratorial, it is helpful to distinguish what is real from what merely looks real. In other words, we need to distinguish primary frames from keyed frames. What distinguishes one from the other? According to Goffman, the distinction is subtle but distinct: when actors key, they tend to employ playfulness, irony, and exaggeration in the context of a primary frame to subtly distract an audience (see Brown, 2005). Even with no more theater insights, it is enough to speculate from this that Trump probably has been guilty of employing keyed frames during his campaign. After all, who has been more playful, ironic, and hyperbolic in this year's election than the Republican nominee?

But with a dash more theater expertise, a sneaking suspicion can actually be confirmed. Here, theater buffs would probably have detected in Trump and his campaign to date some semblance of melodrama—a theatrical genre known for its overly dramatic portrayals of good and evil as well as its appeals to our emotions through stirring images, music, and gestures. This is not just a turn of phrase. As the melodrama specialist Elisabeth Anker (2016) shows, "Trump's melodramatic promise is this: you may feel weak and injured now, but my state policies will soon overcome terrifying villains and allow you to experience your rightful, and unbound, power." Trump's melodrama includes flamboyant facial expressions and striking body movements set to musical accompaniment. Some observers have also noted Trump's "splenetic" gestures and his "battery of shrugs, hand jive, and staccato phrase blurts" (Tomasky, 2016; Wolcott, 2015). This not only exposes Trump's tell or keyed frame, to use Goffman's term. It also complements Trump's message.

Melodrama offers a black-and-white universe, where moral and political discrepancies are often hyperbolized for dramatic effect (Brooks, 1995; Anker, 2014). This is what his "Make America Great Again" campaign has been all about. Building the wall, keeping Muslims out, demonizing China, provoking ISIS, championing the rights of "everyday" Americans—all these are "policies" that would fit perfectly within a melodramatic paradigm. These are the theatrical techniques that Trump used in

2016—deliberately or not—as he won over millions of voters whom he could not be any more different from.

Conclusion

The case we have made in this chapter is simple: presidential elections have become increasingly dramatized affairs. The campaign trail is now a highly theatricalized stage where would-be presidents must perform their politics for the public to see. Though this is nothing new, Trump's run in the 2016 election has made it more important to revisit and revise our view on the theater of elections. Understanding that the public often does not always fully appreciate the distinction between what is staged and what is not, that they are instead vulnerable to manipulative narratives and emotional appeals, we argued that they need insights and tools from the world of theater to understand the political theater that presidential elections have become.

Like Kellner (2002), we believe that the performance a political candidate gives can play a determining factor in whether he or she goes on to win office and from there leave a positive or negative political legacy. Equally, we also agree with Kellner when he concedes that politics is more than narrative, drama, and performance. Real things, of real consequence, must never be ignored. To this extent, there are many reasons for Trump's success in 2016. Trump continues to be seen as a beacon of hope for many Americans who have suffered through more than half a decade of economic uncertainty and cultural anxiety. Undoubtedly, part of this has to do with Republican Party alarmism and fearmongering. But this does not discount the fact that the lives of millions of Americans—on both sides of the political spectrum—have gotten demonstrably worse in the past several years. Millions more feel alienated from the political process and used by "establishment" politicians who do not seem to care about anything other than their own best interests. During such uncertain times, populist leaders have always stood out from the pack.

Yet, to say this is not to deny that "publics see presidencies and administrations in terms of narrative and spectacle," nor that theatrical attempts to engage "contemporary politics can help us understand, critique, and transform our political system" (Kellner, 2002, p. 485). If ours is an age of so-called monitory democracy, where part of a citizen's duty is to keep a literal eye on the performance of power, then we need more political analysts and theories to show us how to see and observe politics. This is also why we need theater—the art of learning how to watch human action. With these types of insights, we may just be able to get to the bottom of the next electoral drama.

References

Allen, D. (2016, April 29). Donald Trump's "presidential" performance is only skin deep. *The Washington Post.* Retrieved from https://www.washingtonpost .com/opinions/when-presidential-is-only-skin-deep/2016 /04/29/0747adca-0d44-11e6-a6b6-2e6de3695b0e_story.html?utm_term= .adf3519e9508

Anker, E. (2014). *Orgies of feeling: Melodrama and the politics of freedom.* Durham, NC: Duke University Press. Retrieved from http://dailynous.com /2016/03/14/philosophers-on-the-2016-u-s-presidential-race/#Anker

Bennett, W. L. (2005). News as reality TV: Election coverage and the democratization of truth. *Critical Studies in Media Communication, 22*(2), 171–177.

Bernstein, J. (2015, April 28). Politics is theater—and sometimes we need to cover it that way. *Mother Jones.* Retrieved from http://www.motherjones .com/kevin-drum/2015/04/theater-criticism-2016-elections

Borreca, A. (1993). Political Dramaturgy: A dramaturg's (re)view. *The Drama Review, 37*(2), 56–79.

Brooks, D. (2016, February 26). The governing cancer of our time. *The New York Times.*

Brooks, P. (1995). *The melodramatic imagination: Balzac, Henry James, melodrama, and the mode of excess.* New Haven, CT: Yale University Press.

Brown, R. E. (2005). Acting presidential: The dramaturgy of Bush versus Kerry. *American Behavioral Scientist, 49*(1), 78–91.

Chou, M., Bleiker, R., & Premaratna, N. (2016). Elections as theater. *PS: Political Science and Politics, 49*(1), 43–47.

Clinton, H. (2016, July 29). Democratic National Convention acceptance speech. *Vox.* Retrieved from http://www.vox.com/policy-and-politics/2016/7/28 /12319246/read-hillary-clinton-dnc-speech-2016-democratic -convention

Dasgupta, G. (1988). The theatricks of politics. *Performing Arts Journal, 11*(2), 77–83.

Davis, P. J. (1986). The drama of the campaign: Theatre, production and style in American elections. *Parliamentary Affairs, 39*(1), 98–114.

Dolan, J. (2001). Rehearsing democracy: Advocacy, public intellectuals, and civic engagement in theatre and performance studies. *Theatre Topics, 11*(1), 1–17.

Fiebach, J. (2002). Theatricality: From oral traditions to televised "realities." *Sub-Stance, 31*(2&3), 17–41.

Goffman, E. (1959). *The presentation of self in everyday life.* New York: Doubleday.

Goffman, E. (1974). *Frame analysis: An essay on the organization of experience.* Boston: Northeastern University Press.

Gronbeck, B. E. (1978). The functions of presidential campaigning. *Communication Monographs, 45*(4), 268–280.

Kellner, D. (2002). Presidential politics: The movie. *American Behavioral Scientist, 46*(4), 467–486.

Levitz, E. (2016, April 22). Team Trump assures the GOP establishment that the Donald is a con man. *New York.* Retrieved from http://nymag.com/daily/intelligencer/2016/04/trump-to-gop-you-can-trust-me-im-a-con-man.html

Packer, G. (2016, May 16). Head of the class. *The New Yorker.* Retrieved from http://www.newyorker.com/magazine/2016/05/16/how-donald-trump-appeals-to-the-white-working-class

Reilly, K. (2016, January 20). The presidential race is now a reality TV primary. *Time.* Retrieved from http://time.com/4186326/donald-trump-sarah-palin-ted-cruz-duck-dynasty-2016-election

Richards, B. (2004). The emotional deficit in political communication. *Political Communication, 21*(3), 339–352.

Schechter, J. (1989). Politics as theater: Or, how I too lost the election in 1988. *The Drama Review, 33*(3), 154–165.

Thompson, D. (2015, April 20). When political journalists play theater critic, they miss the real drama of elections. *The Atlantic.* Retrieved from http://www.theatlantic.com/politics/archive/2015/04/statler-and-waldorf-on-the-campaign-trail/390894

Tomasky, M. (2016, March 24). The dangerous election. *The New York Review of Books.* Retrieved from http://www.nybooks.com/articles/2016/03/24/the-dangerous-election

Walker, R. (2012, January 4). Electoral politics and reality TV. *The New York Times Magazine.* Retrieved from http://www.nytimes.com/2012/01/08/magazine/electoral-politics-and-reality-tv.html

Watson, I. (2006). Theatre and the presidential debates: The role of performance in voter choice. *New Theatre Quarterly, 22*(4), 336–351.

Wired. (2016, July 26). The hidden meanings behind the set designs of the RNC and DNC. *Wired.* Retrieved from https://www.wired.com/2016/07/hidden-meanings-behind-set-designs-rnc-dnc

Wolcott, J. (2015, December). How Donald Trump became America's insult comic in chief. *Vanity Fair.* Retrieved from http://www.vanityfair.com/culture/2015/11/wolcott-trump-insult-comic

Young T. R., & Massey, G. (1978). The dramaturgical society: A macro-analytic approach to dramaturgical analysis. *Qualitative Sociology, 1*(2), 78–98.

CHAPTER THIRTEEN

Mindfulness: A Tool for Thoughtful Politics

Christopher S. Reina

Mindfulness as the Trump Card

In this chapter, I leverage insight and research from psychology, neuroscience, and mindfulness to shed light on how Donald Trump has exploded into the political scene and taken the GOP by storm, despite offering little in terms of actionable plans or strategy to accomplish any of the bold claims he makes beyond relying on his own grandiose persona. Specifically, I discuss two key factors regarding our default way of viewing and responding to the world that have created an opportunity for the "Trump phenomenon" to occur. Second, I discuss how emotions and worldviews can spread between individuals. Third, I discuss why focusing on outcompeting others is not an effective long-term strategy for our political leaders. Finally, I explain how we can overcome our default mindless processing to engage more fully with higher-level rational thinking that emphasizes the connections *among* people rather than the differences *between* us.

Setting the Stage for the Trump Phenomenon

The prevailing view of human behavior has been adapted from Darwin's theory of natural selection (Darwin, 1859), which suggests that our default way of operating is one of self-preservation and of ensuring that our own needs are met to continually survive in a world where only the strongest competitor prevails. We have built our societies based on competition and the view that resources are scarce; thus, we must fight to amass as many resources as we can. Below I shed light on how two fundamental mechanisms that reinforce this view—the innate human tendency toward fight-or-flight responding and ego-based self-preservation—operate together to influence our behaviors and ultimately inform the way we approach our organizations, our relationships with others, and our politics.

Mechanism 1: Human Fight-or-Flight Response

The fight-or-flight response in humans refers to our ability to successfully respond to an imminent threat (Cannon, 1932). The importance of this mechanism cannot be understated. When a danger presents itself, we do not have time to think or delay our action and must simply act in the way that best increases our chance of survival. For example, imagine a hunter in the jungle coming face-to-face with a ferocious predator. The amygdala, or area of the brain that detects threats, would activate (likely even *before* the predator physically presented itself) by raising the hairs on the back of the neck, subconsciously alerting us to the possibility that something may not be right in the environment. This activation triggers the hypothalamus to increase the heart rate to ensure that the muscles receive more blood and oxygen to prepare the body for physical action (Andreassi, 2013; Klein, 2013).

The hypothalamus would also trigger the release of three separate hormones from the adrenal glands. The first hormone, adrenaline, quickly prepares us to either fight or get away from the harmful situation. It gives us a surge of energy, increases the heart rate, tenses muscles, and produces sweat. A second hormone, norepinephrine, shifts blood flow away from areas where it is not immediately needed to deal with the stressor (like the digestive system, for example) and diverts this blood flow to the muscles while also heightening our awareness and focus, which makes us more responsive. A third hormone, cortisol, is released and ensures that our blood pressure and fluids remain at an optimal level to work through the harmful situation. Together, these complex reactions comprise the stress response that occurs when a fight-or-flight scenario arises (Andreassi, 2013; Klein, 2013).

So what is the problem with the fight-or-flight mechanism operating? It seems that it exists for a good reason, to ensure that we survive, right? Of course the answer is yes, but the problem arises in that in recent times, we are continually operating in a state of constant fight or flight. Political rhetoric and incendiary comments, as well as the availability of 24/7 news that constantly repeats headlines, keep listeners in a state of relentless fear and worry about their future. In other words, the news and social media outlets constantly stir up unrest and ensure that "problems" are always at the forefront of individuals' minds. This taps into the fight-or-flight response mechanism, which reinforces the need to either escape from or attack an enemy that is relentlessly threatening our safety and security. Quite simply, by suggesting that America is no longer great anymore and that we are being threatened from all sides (e.g., terror attacks, incompetent political leadership, other religions, other cultures who are taking our jobs), the effect on the human body and mind is that we are constantly existing in fight-or-flight mode.

When we constantly operate in fight-or-flight mode, our bodies are continually releasing the hormones to bring about the physiological changes discussed above. Over extended periods of time, this is very harmful for our bodies. Studies have shown that the continual release of hormones during the fight-or-flight response leads to reduced ability to fight infection (Saper, 2002), autoimmune disorders, susceptibility to cancer, and reduced ability to function at a high level due to energy drain (McEwen, 1998). Beyond the damaging effects to our physical well-being, the fight-or-flight response also impacts our cognitive abilities. In times of stress, our amygdala is highly activated, which impacts our ability to carry out complex and rational thinking (see Phelps, 2006). The significance of this, of course, is that whenever we see and hear incendiary language on social media that creates fear and anxiety, it taps into our fight-or-flight responses, which suppresses the higher-level thinking needed to effectively interpret and rationally respond to complex situations.

As I will discuss later in the chapter, being mindful means living life in the present moment. This becomes very difficult when we are bombarded with sensationalized news, negativity, and fear; instead, we focus on the past (i.e., "we never had terrorism in the past" or "undocumented workers didn't steal our jobs in the past") or focus on the future (i.e., "when this current president is out of office, the United States will be better off" or "this is the worst president in U.S. history!"). When we hear this rhetoric, it creates constant anxiety because we cannot exist anywhere other than in the present. Our minds race and we get ourselves worked up about what we *perceive* to be true while our minds are living in the past or in the future. This state of mind characterized by fear and unrest, anxiety, and agitation does not promote harmonious relationships, nor does it promote high-level, long-term problem solving and decision making—all of which we expect in our political leaders.

Mechanism 2: The Human Ego

A second default mechanism that is operating that influences human behavior is the ego. The ego is the voice in our head that is always talking to us and guiding our behavior (Brown, Ryan, Creswell, & Niemiec, 2008). Like the fight-or-flight mechanism, the ego seeks to protect us at all costs. The ego assumes all incoming information is self-relevant and makes up stories about this information. For example, when someone changes lanes in front of us on the highway, the voice in our head makes up a story automatically—and this story impacts how we act and feel afterward. The problem with this ego-based processing is that every story revolves around us by default such that everything becomes personal (Leary, Adams, & Tate, 2006).

When considering the current political climate, it is quite easy to observe the ego in action. To test whether the ego is operating, one must look no further than considering an individual's response to a stimulus. Does the individual get angry and attack someone verbally? Does the individual have to always be right or make an argument personal? If any or all of these occur, it is likely that the individual is operating from a place of ego. The ego cannot stand to be wrong and will go at great lengths to win. Although ego operates within all individuals, the ego is especially active in narcissistic individuals. Narcissists desire to be the center of attention; demonstrate arrogance, self-absorption, and dominance; and continually seek to reinforce their inflated self-view to dominate and control others (Miller et al., 2011). Due to their bullying behaviors, narcissistic individuals are viewed by others as being fierce competitors and strong leaders, but this strength is paradoxically laced with vulnerability and the need to continually prove value. This need for "more" suggests that the ego is engaged and battling for control and ensures that narcissistic individuals continually seek to win at all costs. And whenever there is a "loss" of some sort (e.g., losing a debate, losing percentage points in a poll, receiving negative press), the ego seeks to protect itself by employing one or more defense strategies.

One approach is firing back with an aggressive attack to take the offensive (Morf, Weir, & Davidov, 2000; Raskin & Terry, 1988; Rhodewalt & Morf, 1998). A second option is rationalizing that the event was not able to be controlled (i.e., the result could not be helped) or manipulating the situation or the rhetoric about the situation to enhance one's own self-image (Van Dijk & De Cremer, 2006). A third approach is to dig in further to reinforce the comment or action that caused the issue in the first place. To be "right," narcissists ignore others' thoughts, feelings, and feedback, which is why narcissists are often seen as lacking empathy (Judge, LePine, & Rich, 2006). This leads to the individuals escalating their commitment even more to justify their behavior despite the disdain they cause in others (Bradlee & Emmons, 1992). In all three defense strategies, the main goal is to protect self and win at all costs because losing damages feelings of self-worth and signals to the narcissist that he or she has less value.

We have seen Donald Trump behave in ways consistent with all three approaches (i.e., lashing out at other politicians on Twitter, rationalizing that poll numbers are incorrect, and continuing to advocate for banning all Muslims from entering the United States). Mr. Trump has also been referred to as "remarkably narcissistic" by Howard Gardner, a psychologist at Harvard (McAdams, 2016), and a simple Google search using the words "Trump" and "narcissist" returns over 635,000 results. As a final example, Mr. Trump's recent Tweet, "Appreciate the congrats for being right on radical Islamic terrorism" in the wake of the Orlando mass shooting at a gay nightclub, brutally illustrates his need to be right no matter the situation or at what cost.

When the self-protective mechanism of the ego is operating at full capacity for a narcissistic individual, its influence does not stop with the narcissist himself or herself. Given our highly connected society and the fact that we constantly interact with others, the needs of the ego adversely affect others as well. Indeed, research suggests that narcissistic CEOs who exhibit a high tendency for pursuing self-enhancing goals and maximizing personal admiration at the expense of others, adversely impact their colleagues (Reina, Zhang, & Peterson, 2014). While the fight-or-flight mechanism and the ego mechanism operate in tandem *within* individuals to produce thoughts, emotions, and behaviors, it is also important to discuss how these thoughts, emotions, and behaviors spread *between* individuals.

The Sharing of Emotions between Individuals

Although it seems quite obvious that political figures would impact the hearts and minds of the general public, the reason why this impact occurs may be less obvious. It is well-known and accepted that germs spread between individuals through various physical methods of transmission (i.e., coughing or via food). However, when it comes to emotions and our ways of thinking and feeling about the world, there is also a method of transmission that explains how individuals' thoughts and emotions can spread to others. Emotional contagion, the process by which emotions are transferred automatically and unconsciously between individuals (Hatfield, Cacioppo, & Rapson, 1994), has typically been studied using survey-based methods to assess the degree of emotional spread between people (i.e., asking one individual how they feel emotionally after inter-acting with another individual). However, it has been suggested more recently that work in neuroscience can help us better understand how this process functions (Peterson, Reina, Waldman, & Becker, 2015; Reina, Peterson, & Waldman, 2015). At a very basic level, neuroscientific evi-dence suggests that the pattern of neuronal firing in the brain of a given individual *mirrors* the neuronal firing patterns of another individual he or she is observing or interacting with (see Iacoboni, 2009, for a review). This is fascinating given that the observing individual is not performing the activity or actually feeling the emotions himself or herself but rather simply *observing* or being in the presence of another individual who is performing the activity or experiencing a certain emotion.

At the level of our neurons, and without any of our conscious effort or awareness, our brains quite literally play along with those whom we come into contact. When considering the word choice, the tone, the underlying emotion, and the repetition that accompany the onslaught of information continually being directed toward us, it becomes obvious that during election years, and especially during the current political landscape where fear is high and emotions are strong, there is quite a bit of contagion occurring between individuals. Further, we potentially interact with hun-dreds of individuals daily through social media, which further amplifies the contagion taking place. Given the explosion of social media and the trend toward an ever-increasing online presence, further understanding how our thoughts, emotions, and behaviors are influenced by the influx of information taken in from our social networks will continue to be vitally important (Christakis & Fowler, 2013; Coviello et al., 2014).

Why Simply "Winning" Is Not an Effective Long-Term Solution

Now that I have reviewed two processes that naturally occur within humans to shed some light on how we tend to process information and have discussed how our emotions and thoughts can become shared, I seek to explain how Mr. Trump's popularity has risen and why his approach based solely on "winning" is not an effective long-term strategy for leading a nation.

One main reason that Mr. Trump has exploded onto the political scene is that in the business realm, we celebrate individuals who proclaim that they are the fiercest competitors who negotiate the biggest, best deals and claim the lion's share of (or *all* of) the value there is to gain in a given deal. Mr. Trump certainly has not been shy about touting his accomplishments and his claimed ability to win. Winning engages our fight-or-flight response and our egos; no one wants to be viewed as a "loser" or as second best. Using simple rhetoric, Mr. Trump appeals to our basic human tendencies to discern between self and other and to ensure that the self prevails over the other by engaging fight-or-flight and ego-based processing and behavior.

In the language of business negotiations, Mr. Trump's negotiation strategy is consistent with *distributive* negotiation, which assumes resources are scarce and thus the only way to "win" is to claim as much value as possible (Lewicki, Saunders, & Barry, 2011). This is the type of strategy we often think about by default when we hear the word "negotiation." The problem with this approach is that it does not highly value or acknowledge the importance of the long-term relationship. It effectively elevates the importance of completing the task (e.g., securing resources), but it does not emphasize the importance of the relationship. If the long-term relationship is of little importance, then a distributive negotiation tactic may be ideal. However, if the long-term relationship matters (as it most definitely does with politics on the world stage), a second type of negotiation approach referred to as *integrative* negotiation, in which resources are viewed as dynamic and not fixed in supply, will likely be more effective because all negotiating parties can claim value. When all involved parties claim value, they feel positive about the experience, which increases the likelihood that future deals can be made (Lewicki et al., 2011). This approach to negotiation builds trust by cultivating and valuing authentic relationships, and the relationship is viewed as equally important as the task.

Because the Western worldview reinforces the importance of winning and dominating, we tend to gravitate toward distributive negotiating, and, thus, we find rhetoric by individuals whom we identify as being fierce competitors appealing. However, claiming maximum value over time leads to animosity among negotiating partners, which has detrimental long-term consequences. When individuals or nations only look out for their own self-interests at the negotiating table, negotiations are likely to end in an impasse or a situation in which no workable solution is reached. When this occurs, other parties at the negotiating table lose trust and faith in the negotiating process and in the other negotiating parties, which contributes to a "distributive spiral," thus diminishing the chance that future deals will take place (O'Connor & Arnold, 2001).

When running a business (or the United States), a distributive negotiating strategy may work for the short-term, but it is not a viable long-term strategy because the world is inherently more connected than it is separate and relationships matter a great deal. A reputation characterized by ego, the need to dominate, and self-interest persists long after a single negotiation is complete and signals to other negotiating parties that relationships are not valued. Thus, a sole focus on claiming value and constant winning fails to recognize that our own well-being is intimately connected to the well-being of others with whom we share the world and reinforces the idea that it is acceptable to take from others without also giving back.

Another reason that distributive negotiation may be appealing is because it creates an us-versus-them mentality. Simply, this means that two groups are formed, an in-group and an out-group, where the in-group receives preferential treatment relative to the out-group (Sherif, Harvey, White, Hood, & Sherif, 1961). When the task of claiming value has primacy over the relationship, the negotiator will likely claim more value in the short-term, and this is made easier when negotiating with a member of the out-group. It is well accepted that an individual negotiating with a family member or friend will (and should!) claim less of the monetary value from the negotiation. For example, a woman selling her car to a friend (a member of the in-group) may agree to sell it for $2000 less than she would to a stranger because she (a) values the friendship and (b) values knowing that the car will be well taken care of by her friend. In this scenario, the monetary value claimed by the seller may be less, but the total value gained (task plus relationship) would be the same.

Even though the total value claimed in the negotiation may well be the same, we tend to fixate on maximizing the monetary value and view relationship-based negotiating as less desirable. Given this preference, it follows that if we can successfully view the other negotiating party as a member of the out-group (i.e., stranger or foe) rather than a similar in-group member (i.e., friend, family, or ally), it becomes easier to negotiate a good deal because we do not have to value the relationship. While this may indeed allow us to claim more value in the short-run, it comes at a long-term cost. This explains why divisive language, future visions of physical barriers separating people, and banning Muslims from entering the United States effectively creates an us-versus-them scenario that may be appealing as a short-term solution. However, it ignores the long-run implications of such actions and the signals it sends to the world about what we value as a nation. In this regard, the long-term implications of fear-inducing us-versus-them thinking would diminish our respect and standing in the world community, would go against the values that have made the United States great in the first place (i.e., diversity and rejection of intolerance), and would not allow us to nurture the relationships needed to continually make the world a better place to live.

Mindfulness as the Trump Card

Now that I have discussed some of the factors that have opened the door to the "Trump phenomenon" and given a brief example that demonstrates these factors in action while also building the case for why this type of thinking is not an effective long-term strategy, I seek to explain how we can move forward together by harnessing the power of mindfulness to escape our default unconscious ways of operating characterized by fight-or-flight and ego-based processing.

Overcoming the Automaticity of Human Behavior

Building walls, excluding others, and blaming individuals in the out-group has been a common approach throughout history to keep the power concentrated in the hands of the dominant in-group. To retain power, individuals have exerted their own power over others to reinforce the status quo. Whenever power and control are involved, the struggle always involves the ego and the need to reinforce dominance *over* some-one or something. Recent political discourse has brought this phenomenon to the forefront of our attention; individuals in the dominant in-group categorize, demonize, berate, or diminish (exert power over) others to reinforce their own (and the dominant group's) sense of self-worth and importance.

Why is it so easy to fall into this way of thinking? As long as we look at people and categorize and judge, rationalize and stereotype, and assume and label, we exaggerate the differences *between* us rather than the similarities *among* us, thus creating in-groups and out-groups (Sherif et al., 1961). We seek to divvy up pieces of the pie such that those who are more [*insert adjective here*] receive the larger pieces of the pie in the life-size game of distributive negotiation. We fail to see similarity and opportunity to expand the pie so everyone can get a larger piece through integrative solutions. As previously discussed, if this way of seeing the world is what we do by default, what then are we to do? Is there another way we can behave?

Yes! We have the power and ability to change how we react *to* the events that happen to us. We can choose to see others as obstructing our paths and preventing us from achieving our goals, or we can choose to see these others as just like us, trying to accomplish the same sets of tasks we are trying to accomplish (Wallace, 2008). Through cultivating mindful awareness, we can wake up to the reality that we are living in—that we are unconsciously allowing fearful thoughts rooted in the past and the future to dictate our thoughts, emotions, and behaviors rather than being in *control* of these same thoughts, emotions, and behaviors. Rather than mindlessly going through life with stimuli and events happening *to* us and *reacting* in certain ways by default, we can wake up to life and instead act with intention.

Mindfulness is very easy to understand. Simply defined, it is present-moment awareness without judgment (Kabat-Zinn, 1994). Cultivating mindfulness is also easy, but it takes intention and commitment and a desire to disengage from the way you have always operated. Making time to quiet the voice in your head, living in the present moment without ruminating on the past or worrying about the future, and acknowledging when your default way of seeing the world is operating (i.e., a self-biasing lens that is seeking to protect you) can all contribute to living more mindfully (Reina & Goldsmith, 2016). When you take the time and space to identify instances when your body tenses up and you begin operating from fight-or-flight mode (e.g., a family member makes a statement that you find rude or uninformed, or you engage in a heated conversation about politics), the simple awareness and knowledge of what is happening inside your body will help you regain control of your thoughts, emotions, and behaviors, and you will be able to engage your higher-level thinking to consciously decide how to *act* rather than to unconsciously *react*.

When you practice mindfulness, you will feel calmer in the short-term, and you will experience beneficial long-term effects as well. Mindfulness has been linked to increased well-being (Collard, Avny, & Boniwell, 2008); decreased pain, anxiety, and stress (Baer, 2003); improved sleep quality and recovery from work (Hülsheger et al., 2014); and greater job satisfaction (Hülsheger et al., 2013), and this barely scratches the surface of all the positive benefits associated with mindfulness. Additionally, mindful awareness and presence suppresses the obsessive thought processes and the anxiety, stress, and self-reinforcing actions that continually seek to have us exist in a world characterized by the need to prevail, to compete, to overcome, and to fight. Quite literally, mindfulness reduces the fight-or-flight response (see Creswell & Lindsay, 2014). This allows us to consciously control our actions and behaviors because we can take a step back from the stressor without reacting immediately. Pounding our fists on the table or uttering critical words aimed at people rather than ideas no longer happens when we cultivate mindful presence. There is no longer the need to outcompete, reinforce one's ego, prove anything, or be correct no matter what. Self-preservation mode is turned off so that only the reality of the situation is present—that we all exist in a careful balance and that how I treat you as my neighbor absolutely has an effect that comes back to me. When we are mindful, we experience our own humanity in a very special way—in a way that reinforces similarity and common experience rather than highlighting differences and competing goals.

As Marshall Goldsmith says in his book *What Got You Here Won't Get You There*, succeeding in the future requires that you change what you have done up until now (2007). Thriving in the future requires us to fundamentally rethink how we live and interact with others. The way forward is by intentionally cultivating present-moment awareness and connections with others. Indeed, interdependence at work represents an increasingly researched topic in the organizational sciences (see Courtright, Thurgood, Stewart, & Pierotti, 2015, for a meta-analysis).

When we acknowledge that the voice in our head is always trying to take control and fueling the constant need for self-preservation, when we realize our automatic thoughts and actions are really all about us, when we realize that our anger during a political discussion is a fight-or-flight response that triggers physiological responses in our body, such as increased heart rate and blood flow, which then harms our ability to think rationally, and when we realize that all of these processes are continually operating in the background of our consciousness to create a cacophony of "noise," then we can gain control over this noise and combat it by simple awareness. This simple awareness allows us to *consciously* make the choice about how we want to see the world and the people in it and move toward integrative, compassionate solutions rather than distributive, divisive us-versus-them ideologies that fuel the ego and our fight-or-flight responses—only then will the unconscious cacophony give way to a melodious symphony that can fundamentally transform our lives.

If mindfulness is the trump card that can overcome fear appeals and move us toward inclusion rather than division, how can we become more mindful as individuals and use emotional/social contagion to spread this mindfulness to others so that it impacts our politics? As Ohio Congressman Tim Ryan states, "Mindfulness can help all of us, public officials and citizens alike" to effectively address our current challenges by learning to "see them clearly, as an interconnected whole" (Hurlock, 2016). Citizens can take the time to identify their core set of principles and spend time intentionally researching issues and understanding the various sides of issues to go beyond status-quo thinking (Cheresson, 2016).

We can take time before starting a meeting for individual quiet reflection and to set the intention of the meeting in order to create a space where mindful presence can become shared between attendees. We can learn more about mindfulness by attending a retreat or practicing simple breathing exercises to help slow down our racing minds, to fall asleep, or to reduce our cortisol levels.

We can even start to build mindfulness into our politics directly as the United Kingdom is doing (Halliwell, 2014) and Tim Ryan is working to do on Capitol Hill (Ball, 2014). We can harness the power of mindfulness to more effectively deal with the headlines we see daily about violence or political divisiveness or even to better stomach this presidential campaign without getting as emotionally hijacked or going down the path of experiencing knee-jerk reactions (Itkowitz, 2016). We can apply mindfulness techniques to just about any situation where people are frustrated, angry, scared, or facing a lot of unknowns. One such existing program that does this is Now Unlimited in the United Kingdom, which teaches mindfulness techniques to those individuals who are unemployed (2015). In sum, mindfulness can be used as a powerful tool to keep us in the present moment and aware of our underlying feelings and emotions so that we can gain control over them rather than letting them control us. When we succeed in doing this, our personal lives as well as our politics will be less characterized by self-preservation, and we can move toward creating a world in which we can all thrive and flourish together.

Conclusion

Winning at all costs can certainly have short-term gains, but it does not come without a very high long-term cost. The ego knows no boundaries; it only knows how to continually seek out victories to reinforce its own value. Mindlessly living life consumed by past or future concerns relies on our most basic fight-or-flight and ego-driven programming and does not engage our higher-level thinking abilities. It generates fear and hate, which then spread to others via emotional and social contagion. To prevent this, mindfulness is introduced as a tool to remain in the present and retain thoughtful processing when we our constantly bombarded with negativity and information that keeps us on edge. Our ability to thrive as a species depends on our ability to cooperate, not on our ability to divvy up resources and "win" by outcompeting others in a negotiation game, as Mr. Trump advocates. Rather than the idea of self-preservation through survival of the fittest competitor, cooperation, compassion, and sympathy are the primary instincts that make us uniquely human (Boyd & Richerson, 2009; Goetz, Keltner, & Simon-Thomas, 2011; Goguen-Hughes, 2010). Let us be confident that mindfulness holds the trump card in helping us truly embrace and understand that fostering these values is the only way forward.

References

Andreassi, J. L. (2013). *Psychophysiology: Human behavior & physiological response.* Mahwah, NJ: Lawrence Erlbaum Associates.

Baer, R. A. (2003). Mindfulness training as a clinical intervention: A conceptual and empirical review. *Clinical Psychology: Science and Practice, 10,* 125–143.

Ball, M. (2014, September). Congressman Moonbeam: Can Representative Tim Ryan teach Washington to meditate? *The Atlantic.* Retrieved from http://www.theatlantic.com/magazine/archive/2014/09/congressman-moonbeam/375065

Boyd, R., & Richerson, P. J. (2009). Culture and the evolution of human cooperation. *Philosophical Transactions of the Royal Society of London B: Biological Sciences, 364*(1533), 3281–3288.

Bradlee, P. M., & Emmons, R. A. (1992). Locating narcissism within the interpersonal circumplex and the five-factor model. *Personality and Individual Differences, 13,* 821–830.

Brown, K. W., Ryan, R. M., Creswell, J. D., & Niemiec, C. P. (2008). Beyond me: Mindful responses to social threat. In Wayment & Bauer (Eds.), *Transcending Self-interest: Psychological Explorations of the Quiet Ego,* 75–84.

Cannon, W. B. (1932). *The Wisdom of the Body.* New York: Norton.

Cheresson, L. (2016). Politically mindful. Retrieved from http://wanderlust.com/politically-mindful

Christakis, N. A., & Fowler, J. H. (2013). Social contagion theory: Examining dynamic social networks and human behavior. *Statistics in Medicine, 32*(4). doi:10.1002/sim.5408. Retrieved from http://doi.org/10.1002/sim.5408

Collard, P., Avny, N., & Boniwell, I. (2008). Teaching mindfulness based cognitive therapy (MBCT) to students: The effects of MBCT on the levels of mindfulness and subjective well-being. *Counselling Psychology Quarterly, 21,* 323–336.

Courtright, S. H., Thurgood, G. R., Stewart, G. L., & Pierotti, A. J. (2015). Structural interdependence in teams: An integrative framework and meta-analysis. *Journal of Applied Psychology, 100*(6), 1825.

Coviello, L., Sohn, Y., Kramer, A. D. I., Marlow, C., Franceschetti, M., Christakis, N. A., & Fowler, J. H. (2014). Detecting emotional contagion in massive social networks. *PloS one, 9*(3). doi:10.1371/journal.pone.0090315

Creswell, J. D., & Lindsay, E. K. (2014). How does mindfulness training affect health?: A mindfulness stress buffering account. *Current Directions in Psychological Science, 23*(6), 401–407.

Goetz, J. L., Keltner, D., & Simon-Thomas, E. (2010). Compassion: An evolutionary analysis and empirical review. *Psychological Bulletin, 136*(3), 351.

Goguen-Hughes, L. (2010, December 23). Survival of the kindest. *Mindful.* Retrieved from http://www.mindful.org/cooperate

Goldsmith, M. (2008). *What got you here won't get you there.* New York: Hyperion.

Halliwell, E. (2014, May 23). Can mindfulness transform politics? *Mindful.* Retrieved from http://www.mindful.org/can-mindfulness-transform-politics-2

Hatfield, E., Cacioppo, J. T., & Rapson, R. L. (1994). *Emotional contagion.* New York: Cambridge University Press.

Hülsheger, U. R., Alberts, H. J., Feinholdt, A., & Lang, J. W. (2013). Benefits of mindfulness at work: The role of mindfulness in emotion regulation, emotional exhaustion, and job satisfaction. *Journal of Applied Psychology, 98*(2), 310.

Hülsheger, U. R., Lang, J. W., Depenbrock, F., Fehrmann, C., Zijlstra, F. R., & Alberts, H. J. (2014). The power of presence: The role of mindfulness at work for daily levels and change trajectories of psychological detachment and sleep quality. *Journal of Applied Psychology, 99*(6), 1113.

Hurlock, H. (2016, January 29). Can mindfulness out-trump hyper-divisive politics? *Mindful.* Retrieved from http://www.mindful.org/can-government-policy-ever-consider-us-all

Iacoboni, M. (2009). Imitation, empathy, and mirror neurons. *Annual Review of Psychology, 60,* 653–670.

Itkowitz, C. (2016, March 16). Yes, you can practice mindfulness and still stomach this presidential campaign. *The Washington Post.* Retrieved from https://www.washingtonpost.com/news/inspired-life/wp/2016/03/16/this-nasty-presidential-campaign-ruining-your-mindfulness-practice-it-doesnt-have-to

Judge, T. A., LePine, J. A., & Rich, B. L. (2006). Loving yourself abundantly: Relationship of the narcissistic personality to self- and other perceptions of workplace deviance, leadership, and task and contextual performance. *Journal of Applied Psychology, 91,* 762–776.

Kabat-Zinn, J. (1994). *Wherever you go, there you are: Mindfulness meditation in everyday life.* New York: Hyperion.

Klein, S. (2013, April 19). Adrenaline, cortisol, norepinephrine: The three major stress hormones, explained. *The Huffington Post.* Retrieved from http://www.huffingtonpost.com/2013/04/19/adrenaline-cortisol-stress-hormones_n_3112800.html

Leary, M. R., Adams, C. E., & Tate, E. B. (2006). Hypo–egoic self–regulation: Exercising self–control by diminishing the influence of the self. *Journal of Personality, 74*(6), 1803–1832.

Lewicki, R. J., Saunders, D. M., & Barry, B. (2011). *Essential of negotiation* (5th ed.). New York: McGraw-Hill.

McAdams, D. P. (2016, June). The mind of Donald Trump. *The Atlantic.* Retrieved from http://www.theatlantic.com/magazine/archive/2016/06/the-mind-of -donald-trump/480771

McEwen, B. S. (1998). Protective and damaging effects of stress mediators. *New England Journal of Medicine, 338*(3), 171–179.

Miller, J. D., Hoffman, B. J., Gaughan, E. T., Gentile, B., Maples, J., & Campbell, W. K. (2011). Grandiose and vulnerable narcissism: A nomological network analysis. *Journal of Personality, 79*(5), 1013–1042.

Morf, C. C., Weir, C., & Davidov, M. (2000). Narcissism and intrinsic motivation: The role of goal congruence. *Journal of Experimental Social Psychology, 36,* 424–438.

Now Unlimited (2015). Mindfulness for the unemployed. Retrieved from http://www.nowunlimited.co.uk/wp-content/uploads/2015/09/Now Unlimited_MindfulnessForThe-Unemployed_V1.pdf

O'Connor, K. M., & Arnold, J. A. (2001). Distributive spirals: Negotiation impasses and the moderating role of disputant self-efficacy. *Organizational Behavior and Human Decision Processes, 84*(1), 148–176.

Peterson, S. J., Reina, C. S., Waldman, D. A., & Becker, W. J. (2015). Using physiological methods to study emotions in organizations. In N. M. Ashkanasy, W. J. Zerbe, & C. E. J. Härtel (Eds.), *New ways of studying emotions in organizations* (Volume 11, pp. 1–27). London: Emerald Group Publishing Limited.

Phelps, E. A. (2006). Emotion and cognition: Insights from studies of the human amygdala. *Annual Review Psychology, 57,* 27–53.

Raskin, R., & Terry, H. (1988). A principal-components analysis of the narcissistic personality-inventory and further evidence of its construct-validity. *Journal of Personality and Social Psychology, 54,* 890–902.

Reina, C. S., & Goldsmith, J. S. (2016, June 1). Mindful leadership in a world of distractions. *The Huffington Post.* Retrieved from http://www.huffingtonpost .com/jill-s-goldsmith-jd-lac-ncc/mindful-leadership-in-a-w_b _10225152.html

Reina, C. S., Peterson, S. J., & Waldman, D. A. (2015). Neuroscience as a basis for understanding emotions and affect in Organizations. In D. A. Waldman & P. A. Balthazard (Eds.), *Organizational neuroscience* (Volume 7, pp. 213–232). London: Emerald Group Publishing Limited.

Reina, C. S., Zhang, Z., & Peterson, S. J. (2014). CEO grandiose narcissism and firm performance: The role of organizational identification. *The Leadership Quarterly, 25*(5), 958–971.

Rhodewalt, F., & Morf, C. C. (1998). On self-aggrandizement and anger: A temporal analysis of narcissism and affective reactions to success and failure. *Journal of Personality and Social Psychology, 74,* 672–685.

Saper, C. B. (2002). The central autonomic nervous system: conscious visceral perception and autonomic pattern generation. *Annual Review of Neuroscience, 25(1),* 433–469.

Van Dijk, E., & De Cremer, D. (2006). Self-benefiting in the allocation of scarce resources: Leader-follower effects and the moderating effect of social value orientations. *Personality and Social Psychology Bulletin, 32,* 1352–1361.

Wallace, D. F. (2008, September 19). Plain old untrendy troubles and emotions. *The Guardian.* Retrieved from https://www.theguardian.com/books/2008/sep/20/fiction

Afterword

Mari Fitzduff

The United States is not alone in being disconcerted by the extensive followership achieved by Donald Trump. Support for many of his trade and anti-immigration plans are to be found elsewhere in the world. In June 2016, a majority of United Kingdom voters elected to leave the European Union, despite the economic warnings of most bankers, industrialists, and politicians. Those who voted to leave were the poorest, least skilled, least likely to be working, and the less educated. They were also more likely to reject moderate liberal movements such as multiculturalism, feminism, and environmentalism and to perceive current trade policies as outsourcing their traditional jobs to other parts of the world. In addition, they wanted to stop the growth in immigration, which they saw as driving down their wages, clogging up their health services and their schools, and diluting their traditional British cultural norms.

Such economic and social concerns have also been increasing in Europe, where there has been a sizeable rise in right-wing and nationalist parties. In France, Germany, Austria, Denmark, Sweden, Slovakia, Greece, Switzerland, and the Netherlands, as well as in Britain, such parties have made significant gains over the last decade. It seems that while many of the wealthier and more educated sections of the world have been rejoicing in, and gaining from, the benefits of technology and globalization, subsets of their populations feel they are being economically and socially left behind in a context where a better future for themselves and their children no longer seems available to them.

These fears are justified. Globalization has contributed to a significant rise of relative inequality within most countries. Because of the ubiquitous nature of modern communications, such inequalities are also increasingly noticed and felt at a global level and are a significant factor in rising migration. Whether we like it or not, our national borders are becoming increasingly porous. Despite the promises of Donald Trump, there are no walls, no border posts, and no seas so dangerous that they will effectively stop the migration of those who see little hope of any speedy accrual of wealth and security within their own national contexts, many of which are still impoverished and conflict ridden.

So how do we respond to these challenges and the threats they pose for the stability of our societies? As our authors have shown, the rise of Trumpism, and other right-wing movements, has given rise to very serious questions about how easily our neural circuitry can be engaged to elicit populist responses that are disturbing to the foundations of our social and democratic values. We appear as a species to be tolerant—but only to a point. So long as we do not see out-groups as a threat to our welfare, our differences can be relatively well managed. However, once our perceived sense of well-being and security is threatened, our all-too-human tendencies to blame out-groups for our problems can be easily invoked and can increase our willingness to abandon democracy in favor of authoritarianism. This is particularly true if such feelings are elicited and enhanced by leaders and others who would use them for their own ends.

Given that globalization and migration are likely to continue and increase, the findings of this book suggest that we need to take urgent and thoughtful stock of what we are learning about ourselves, our societies, and our human and social natures in light of the allure of Trumpism. We need to understand that without remedial and sustained strategies that address the feelings of resentment, exclusion, and disempowerment on the part of many who feel globalization is passing them by, our national and global systems may be at serious risk. Without such strategies, and wise leaders to lead them, we will, as our authors have noted, become increasingly vulnerable to the seduction of leaders with autocratic and confrontational policies, which have the potential to destroy much of what our world has achieved so far in terms of democracy, global cooperation, and peace.

Index

About the Editor and Contributors

Editor

Mari Fitzduff is the founding director of the international Master's Program in Conflict Resolution and Coexistence at the Heller School at Brandeis University. Previously, she was the first CEO of the Northern Ireland Community Relations Council, which developed and funded most of the peacebuilding organizations in Northern Ireland. She was also chair of conflict studies at the University of Ulster, where she was director of United Nations University—International Conflict Research, which researched peacebuilding programs and practice developments around the world. She has authored or edited five previous books on conflict and peace issues, including *The Psychology of Resolving Global Conflicts* and *Public Policies for Shared Societies*.

Contributors

Mark Chou is an associate professor of politics at the Australian Catholic University. His most recent book is *Democracy against Itself* (Edinburgh University Press). His commentaries on Trump have appeared in the *Washington Post*, *Australian Financial Review*, *Truthout*, and *The Conversation*. He edits the scholarly journal *Democratic Theory* (Berghahn).

Florette Cohen is an associate professor of psychology at the College of Staten Island (of the City University of New York). Her research investigates how subtle reminders of death amplify stereotyping and prejudice and influence individual voting preferences.

Michael C. Grillo, PhD, is an assistant professor of political science at Schreiner University. His research interests include nationalism, ethnic politics, and the psychological and neurocognitive underpinnings of political attitudes and predispositions.

S. Alexander Haslam is a professor of psychology and Australian Laureate Fellow at the University of Queensland. He is a fellow of the Canadian Institute for Advanced Research and of the Association for Psychological Science. His research focuses on the study of group and identity processes in social, organizational, and clinical contexts, and he has published over 200 peer-reviewed papers on these topics.

Gregg Henriques is a professor of graduate psychology at James Madison University, where he directs the Combined-Integrated Doctoral Program in Clinical-School Psychology. Dr. Henriques's primary area of scholarly interest is in the development of a new unified theory of psychology

Karina V. Korostelina is a professor at the School for Conflict Analysis and Resolution at George Mason University and a director of the Program on History, Memory and Conflict. She is the recipient of 39 fellowships and grants, the editor of 6 books, and the author of 9 books and numerous articles.

Mark R. Leary, PhD, is a professor of psychology and neuroscience at Duke University and Director of the Interdisciplinary Behavioral Research Center. Leary's research and writing centers on motivation, social emotions, and the negative effects of excessive self-focused thought. He is past president of the Society for Personality and Social Psychology.

Matthew C. MacWilliams is from the University of Massachusetts Amherst. His articles on Trumpism have appeared in *Politico*, *Vox*, the London School of Economics blog, and *PS: Political Science and Politics* and have been cited in media around the world, including the *New York Times*, *Der Spiegel*, and NPR.

Zachary J. Melton is a graduate student in social psychology at the University of Illinois at Chicago. He studies moral language and the ecology of political hostility.

Matt Motyl is an assistant professor of social psychology and political science at the University of Illinois at Chicago. His research examines moral and political cleavages in society and what can be done to promote more civil dialogue on moral and political matters.

Michael L. Ondaatje is a national head of arts and associate professor of history at Australian Catholic University. He is the author of the prize-winning book *Black Conservative Intellectuals in Modern America* and in 2012 was awarded the Crawford Medal, "Australia's most prestigious award for achievement and promise in the humanities."

Micha Popper is a professor at University of Haifa, Israel. He is the former head of the Israel Defense Forces (IDF) School for Leadership Development and cofounder and director of the Center for Outstanding Leadership in Zikhron Yaakov, Israel. Popper is the author of seven books on leadership and followership and a coauthor of a book on organizational learning.

J. P. Prims is a graduate student at the University of Illinois at Chicago, pursuing a PhD in social psychology.

Tom Pyszczynski is a distinguished professor of psychology at the University of Colorado at Colorado Springs. His research (with Jeff Greenberg and Sheldon Solomon) examining the effects of the uniquely human awareness of death on attitudes and behavior has been supported by the National Science Foundation and the Ernest Becker Foundation.

Stephen Reicher is Wardlaw Professor of Psychology at the University of St Andrews, a fellow of the British Academy, the Royal Society of Edinburgh, and the Academy of Social Sciences. He has been studying issues of social identity and collective behavior for nearly 40 years, including crowd behavior, nationalism, leadership, tyranny, intergroup hatred, and, more recently, obedience and resistance.

Christopher S. Reina is an assistant professor in the Department of Management at Virginia Commonwealth University. His research focuses on the intersection of leadership, mindfulness, and emotions in the workplace, and he consults in the areas of mindful leadership and managing the emotional space within organizations.

Ronald E. Riggio, PhD, is the Henry R. Kravis Professor of Leadership and Organizational Psychology at Claremont McKenna College. He has published nearly two dozen books and over 150 journal articles and book chapters. He writes a leadership blog for *Psychology Today.*

Sheldon Solomon is a professor of psychology at Skidmore College. He is coauthor (with Jeff Greenberg and Tom Pyszczynski) of *In the Wake of 9/11: The Psychology of Terror* and *The Worm at the Core: On the Role of Death in Life.*

Sharlynn Thompson is a graduate student in the Department of Psychology at the University of Colorado at Colorado Springs. Her focus is investigating how secular worldviews (e.g., nationalism, materialism, desire for fame) serve to manage existential terror.